CHRISTOLOGY
BASIC TEXTS IN FOCUS

CHRISTOLOGY
BASIC TEXTS IN FOCUS

Leopold Sabourin, S.J.

ALBA · HOUSE NEW · YORK

SOCIETY OF ST. PAUL, 2187 VICTORY BLVD., STATEN ISLAND, NEW YORK 10314

Library of Congress Cataloging in Publication Data

Sabourin, Leopold.
   Christology: basic texts in focus.

   Includes bibliographies and indexes.
      1. Jesus Christ—History of doctrines. 2. Jesus
Christ—Person and offices. I. Title.
BT198.S11   1984   232   84-12304
ISBN 0-8189-0471-2

Imprimi Potest:
Bernard Carrière, S.J.
Provincial Superior

Nihil Obstat:
James T. O'Connor, S.T.D.
Censor Librorum

Imprimatur:
† Joseph T. O'Keefe, D.D.
Vicar General, Archdiocese of New York
June 11, 1984

Designed, printed and bound in the United States of
America by the Fathers and Brothers of the
Society of St. Paul, 2187 Victory Boulevard,
Staten Island, New York 10314, as part of their
communications apostolate.

---

2 3 4 5 6 7 8 9 (Current Printing: first digit).

CONTENTS

ABBREVIATIONS

BJRL	*Bulletin of the John Rylands Library*
BTB	*Biblical Theology Bulletin*
CBQ	*Catholic Biblical Quarterly*
ET	English Translation
ETL	*Ephemerides Theologiae Lovanienses*
HTR	*Harvard Theological Review*
IrTQ	*Irish Theological Quarterly*
JB	*Jerusalem Bible*
JBL	*Journal of Biblical Literature*
JEvTS	*Journal of the Evangelical Theological Society*
JSNT	*Journal for the Study of the New Testament*
JTC	*Journal for Theology and the Church*
JTS	*Journal of Theological Studies*
JTSA	*Journal of Theology for Southern Africa*
LXX	Septuagint (Greek) translation of the Old Testament
Matthew	refers to L. Sabourin, *The Gospel According to St. Matthew*
NEB	*New English Bible*
NRT	*Nouvelle Revue Théologique*
NTA	*New Testament Abstracts*
NTS	*New Testament Studies*
RSB	*Religious Studies Bulletin*
RSPT	*Revue des Sciences Philosophiques et Théologiques*
RSV	*Revised Standard Version*
ScEcc	*Sciences Ecclésiastiques* (now called *Science et Esprit*)
ScotJT	*Scottish Journal of Theology*
TDNT	*Theological Dictionary of the New Testament* (Kittel)
TOB	*Traduction Oecuménique de la Bible*
TS	*Theological Studies*
TZ	*Theologische Zeitschrift*
ZNW	*Zeitschrift für die neutestamentliche Wissenschaft*
ZTK	*Zeitschrift für Theologie und Kirche*

PREFACE

In 1963 Desclée de Brouwer published in French my book *Les Noms et les Titres de Jésus*, which appeared soon afterwards also in Spanish. In 1967 The Macmillan Company published an American translation, *The Names and Titles of Jesus*, with a Foreword by John L. McKenzie. As far as I know this has been out of print for several years, but some copies of the French edition remain, I believe. It was a good book, although I am certain that *Christology* is a much better one, the reason being mainly that in twenty years I have read and learned a lot, particularly through the composition of my other works, the commentaries on Matthew and on Luke, and of my study on the unity of the two Testaments, entitled *The Bible and Christ* (Alba House 1980). My long years of teaching at the Pontifical Biblical Institute, both in Jerusalem (1964-67), and in Rome (1967-78) have academically well prepared me for the task. My subsequent teaching in lesser posts and the new experience I gained in pastoral work in different areas have told me what the general literate reader needs to hear and what he can understand. In addition my work as book review writer over several years has brought me into direct contact with hundreds of authors and books, and this also has been very profitable. I hope my readers will find all this reflected in these pages, which attempt to answer, in a new way, different questions: What did Christ say about himself, what did the early Church say about him, how was this initial revelation explained and developed in the early Christian centuries, how successful are recent endeavors to give Christology, or the study of Christ, a new profile, more in line, it is claimed, with the progress achieved in relevant areas of human knowledge?

The sub-title, ''Basic Texts in Focus,'' describes well, it would seem, the distinctive approach of the present work: to let the source texts speak for themselves, and in their proper context, not in pell-mell fashion with other texts taken from different writings. The Booknotes often contain material that will appeal more to the specialized reader, but from which everyone, wishing to, can benefit. They include many references that are not always repeated in the general Bibliography. With the Scripture Index and the Subject Index it should be easy for everyone to find rapidly what he or she is looking for. The text of this work shows how much I am indebted to several authors who have published on Christology studies of permanent value. Mine being different in many ways from theirs, and based directly on the sources they also used, will have a place, like these, I trust, among the more successful attempts to provide a comprehensive and yet readable exposition of a complex subject that is basic to Christian faith.

Leopold Sabourin, S.J.
University of Sudbury

CHRISTOLOGY
BASIC TEXTS IN FOCUS

PART ONE
THE NEW TESTAMENT

Introduction to Part One

The earliest Church kerygma proclaims that, in the Christ he raised from the dead, God offers to all eschatological salvation (Ac 3:18-26). Thus does the proclaimer become the proclaimed and Christ's own preaching receives divine confirmation. The question ''Who is Christ?'' would now be answered in a new light. The foundation was laid for the beginning of an explicit Christology.

The NT texts show beyond doubt that Christology developed over a number of years, and it seems possible particularly to distinguish what in this doctrine belonged to the earliest Palestinian stratum from what appeared a few years later and elsewhere on the Hellenistic level. Recent studies, like those of F. Hahn and R.H. Fuller, have contributed a lot to clarify the issues, although of course several of their assertions and even some aspects of their methodology can be disputed. We shall use the results of their work to outline the development of early Christology (Chapter One), after which we will examine a series of texts that testify to the growth of Christology within the New Testament itself.

More often than not studies entitled *Theology of the New Testament* do not try to determine the Christology of each NT book or groups of books, but analyze the different Christological titles as they are attested throughout the New Testament. More specialized studies, like Fuller's and Hahn's, attempt to follow the evolution of the titles and their meaning in the various stages: Early Palestinian (EP), Jewish Hellenistic (JH), and Gentile Hellenistic (GH). This is a laudable procedure, but it leads to repetitious development and can be confusing for the average student. For example, Fuller in his book examines the title "Son of God" in six different places. We intend to present from each NT group of writings texts that are Christologically significant, pausing to examine more fully a title in connection with a particularly meaningful text concerning it. Some of the writings to be examined clearly belong to a particular NT stratum, as for example the Epistle to the Hebrews (JH), while others, like the Synoptic gospels, consist of texts belonging to various strata. JH and GH can further be divided into non-Pauline (Johannine writings and First Peter), pre-Pauline, and Pauline. Whenever possible or useful, the stratum of the texts presented will be indicated, at least in a general way, as in the particular introduction to the different chapters.

Jewish Hellenistic and Gentile Hellenistic Christological Approaches

Pre-Christian Jewish Hellenistic literature finds some expression in the Septuagint, the Qumran scrolls, and the intertestamental Jewish apocalyptic books, but it is mostly represented by the writings from Alexandria, mainly Philo and the Book of Wisdom. Specific texts will offer us the occasion to assign this or that Christological title to a particular stratum, but the situation is usually not that simple. The same title can be used on different levels, sometimes with a slightly different meaning, as we shall indicate. For example, *Christos* is rarely used as a title in JH Christianity, except in the demessianized form of a proper name. When the title "Servant" designates Christ as offering vicarious atonement, as in Mk 10:45/Mt 20:28, EP usage is reflected, under the influence of Is 53.

The LXX translation of YHWH by *Kyrios* opened the way in JH to a certain functional identity between Christ the exalted *Kyrios* and the OT God/*Kyrios*. As will be seen, the use of the title SON OF GOD for Jesus in Palestinian Judaism comes from Ps 2:7, while the continuation of its use among the JH Christians rested on the importance given in JH writings to the just man as son of God (see Ws 2:13; 5:5). In addition, JH authors would easily call "divine" the truly "religious person." But the Palestinian origin of the title "Son of God" to designate Jesus cannot be disputed, as we shall have occasion to state more fully. It will be shown later that a few titles are particularly at home in JH milieu. See Ch. 9 for "Wisdom" and "High Priest" (Hebrews), Ch. 10 for "Logos" (John's writings) and Ch. 8 for "Heavenly Man" (1 Cor 15).

As Fuller notes, in their preaching to the NON-JEWS, the early Christian missionaries "were prepared to select for emphasis those elements in the already Christian tradition which had counterparts in the Gentile world" (p. 86), while they rejected, even combated the pagan features incompatible with the Christian kerygma. In Antioch, which had a strong Jewish community, the Hellenistic Jewish tradition held a dominant position; in cities like Corinth the situation was different. There, a Gentile spirit prevailed, and if the Christians were to have an audience they would have to adopt a language understood by the pagans. As will be indicated in connection with the early Pauline texts, especially 1 Cor 8:5, terms like *kyrios*, "lord," *theos*, "god," and "son of God" were employed in the imperial cult and could serve the Christians to express before the Gentiles their worship of Christ. The same is true with the appellation *sôtêr*, "savior," as will be seen especially where the Pastoral Letters are examined (Ch. 9).

Influence of Oriental Cults and Myths

Both the older Greek mysteries and the Oriental mysteries originally sprung up as fertility or vegetation rites, and as such were based on the myth of nature's death and rebirth, often personified in the descent of deities into the lower world and their ascent from it. "As for the initiate, the documents prefer to speak of their sharing the 'sufferings' (*pathê*) of the god, rather than of death, and of rebirth rather than of resurrection" (Fuller 90). There is no clear expression in the mystery religions of the myth of a "dying and rising God," even though past rationalists have made much of this claim, in order to discredit Christianity. A more acceptable form of contact between the mystery religions and Christianity has been proposed by W. Bousset in *Kyrios Christos*.[1] He wrote, for example, that while in Palestinian Christianity the sacraments proleptically anticipated the future life in the kingdom, they became in Hellenistic Christianity, as in the mystery religions, a sort of participation in the death and resurrection of the cult deity. It would not be difficult to show the weakness of this sacramental hypothesis, but let us rather examine more closely the other area of influence proposed. In Bousset's view *Mar*, "Lord," was referred in Palestine to Jesus as the Son of man, while the Hellenistic Christians saw Jesus/*Kyrios* as a cult deity. Again, it is clear that Jesus was originally called *Kyrios* in connection with Ps 110 (see Mk 12:36 par.), but in Pauline Christianity the designation had greater prominence on account of the prevailing use of the term in Greek circles (more about this in Ch. 8).

M. Lidzbarski published between 1905 and 1925 Mandaean texts, with which R. Reitzenstein produced the theory that the older Iranian gnostic myths, reflected in Mandaeanism of a later date, influenced the formation of an Hellenistic Christology, found particularly in Paul, Hebrews, and the Johannine writings.[2] Replacing the "adoptionist" view of the earliest Palestinian Church,[3] the "new" Christology, patterned on the old Gnostic redeemer myths, represented Christ as a "pre-existent redeemer who becomes incarnate, performs the redemption and reascends to heaven" (Fuller 94). This is a correct although simplified version of a theory which has been built on forced comparisons from texts that are in fact much later than the New Testament. Something can be learned, however, from the studies concerning what can be referred to as a pre-Christian revelation myth, and we shall again refer to this in Ch. 4, about Christ's pre-existence, and in Ch. 8, about the ''heavenly man'' of 1 Cor 15.

CHAPTER ONE

TEXTS REFLECTING EARLY PALESTINIAN CHRISTOLOGY

It seems possible to document the fact that the early Palestinian Christians focused their attention on the "authority" (*exousia*) which Jesus disclosed in his earthly ministry and which he will manifest at the parousia in his appearance as the Son of man. This especially appears in the Aramaic designation of Jesus as *mar*, "lord," and in the recognition that he is the prophet of the end-time and the Son of man to come.

a) Jesus as Servant and Prophet like Moses in the Kerygma

As already suggested, Peter's discourse in Ac 3:13-26 reflects the earliest stage of the Church's kerygma, so that the titles it attributes to Jesus can be seen as representing the earliest Christology. It is striking that there alone, and in 4:27, is Jesus explicitly called the Servant (*pais*). Possibly the designation of Jesus as "the holy one of God" in Mk 1:24 also alludes to the title "Servant," as is suggested by the phrase "your holy Servant" in Ac 4:27. The emphasis here is not on the *suffering* Servant, as later texts suppose (Mk 10:45; 14:24), but on the Servant of God as such. After calling Jesus "Servant" in vs. 13, Peter represents him as "the Holy and Just One," also obviously archaic titles, which recur elsewhere

(7:52; 22:14), especially in quotations (2:27; 13:35). The next designation, ''the Author of Life,'' is found as such only in 3:15, although the name *archêgos*, ''author, prince, leader,'' describes Jesus also in 5:31 and in Heb 2:10; 12:2 (see P.G. Müller's study in the Bibliography).

In Ac 3:22; 7:37 Jesus is identified with the Prophet like Moses mentioned in Dt 18:15, 18. Moses is represented in Dt 34:10 as the greatest of all prophets, and is called God's ''servant'' in Nb 12:7. Like him, Jesus is both Servant and Prophet.[4] In the transfiguration story both Is 42:1 and Dt 18:15 are alluded to, where the voice says: ''This is my beloved Son, with whom I am well pleased; listen to him'' (Mt 17:5). Also the voice at the baptism of Jesus has allusively identified him with the Servant (Mk 1:11 par.), the Servant considered as Prophet, since Ac 10:38 describes the event as a prophetical anointing. This is confirmed by Jesus himself in his inaugural discourse at Nazareth, where he quotes as referring to himself Is 61:1: ''The Spirit of the Lord is upon me, because he has anointed me . . .'' (Lk 4:18). The first sentence recalls Is 42:1: ''I have put my Spirit upon him. . . .'' Although in his temptation Jesus undergoes more precisely the experience of Israel (Lk 4:2; Dt 8:2), the figures of the Servant Moses (Dt 9:9), and of Elijah the Prophet (1 K 19:8) seem also to be evoked with the mention of Jesus' fast lasting forty days and forty nights (Mt 4:2). According to Mt 3:11, John the Baptist called the Messiah *ho erchomenos*, ''he who is coming,'' and this designation recurs later in the mouth of the disciples sent to inquire from Jesus: ''Are you he who is to come . . .?'' (11:3). The one to come was the end-time prophet, and this the Fourth Gospel confirms in reporting the exclamation of the crowd after the miracle of the loaves: ''This is indeed the prophet who is to come into the world'' (6:14).

b) Jesus as the Son of Man

In spite of the contrary claim often made, it is not at all certain that Jesus spoke of the future Son of man as of someone distinct from himself. Since he certainly saw himself as the definitive divine envoy, he easily identified himself with the expected apocalyptic Son of man. He did not, however, explicitly declare this identity before the passion (Mk 14:62). It is possible, on the other hand, to admit that the early Church has a hand in the redaction of several sayings in which Jesus sees his teaching vindicated by the coming Son of man (Lk 12:8-9).

Jesus usually spoke of himself in the third person as the Son of man. This he did also when he was referring to his exalted state as Judge (Mt 19:28). More often he refers to the same figure in connection with his present ministry on earth (Mk 2:10), and particularly with his coming passion (Mk 8:31). In reporting these sayings of Jesus the evangelists express the conviction of the early Church that what Jesus said and did on earth enjoyed the authority of the definitive transcendent figure of the end-time. The Son of man has been rejected by his own generation (Mt 11:16-19), but the Church knows he has already been vindicated (Mk 8:38); the Son of man has been put to death, but he has also risen (Mk 9:31; Ac 2:15). The early Church believed that both Christ's suffering and his resurrection had occurred in fulfillment of Scripture (Mk 9:12; Mt 21:42; 1 Cor 15:3-4). The influence of the Suffering Servant on this concept will be discussed below in the review of particular texts.

c) Texts Connected with Other Early Palestinian Titles

As Fuller explains, ''Son of man'' was not a satisfactory term ''for kerygmatic proclamation, for confession of faith, or for use in Christian instruction and worship'' (p. 155). Other terms were found, which already in Palestinian Christianity do designate Jesus in his earthly ministry, and in his hoped-for return.

According to the Fourth Gospel (1:38) John and Andrew asked

Jesus on their first encounter with him: " 'Rabbi' (which means 'Teacher'), where are you staying?" The same gospel also utilizes several times elsewhere the original form *Rabbi*, which means "my great one," a term in common use for addressing the Jewish teachers of the law. According to Mk 9:5 Peter also called Jesus *Rabbi* at the transfiguration. Only once is *Rabbi* recorded in Matthew, in a question of Judas (26:25). *"Rabbi"* of the Gospel obviously echoes the title which the disciples used in addressing Jesus. It is unclear to this writer why Fuller writes: "Its preservation and circulation in the Church indicates that Jesus continued to be regarded as their Rabbi even after the resurrection" (p. 155). It is true, of course, that Jesus remains Teacher (*didaskalos*) forever (Mt 23:8), but the Palestinian form of the title came rapidly into disuse after Jesus' death, replaced by another title, that of *Mari*, or *Maran(a)*, a Palestinian equivalent of the Greek *kyrios*.

The name *Mari, Maran(a)*, "My Lord, our Lord," deserves special attention also because it occurs in the New Testament, in the form of *Marana tha*, "Our Lord, come!" (1 Cor 16:22; Rv 22:20). In the Eucharistic liturgy (see *Didachê* X, 6) the prayer invoked the Lord for his presence at his Supper, to anticipate in a way his future eschatological coming (1 Cor 11:20, 26). It is hardly doubtful that in several Gospel texts the title *Kyrios* given to Jesus reflects a Semitic form derived from *mar*, "lord."[5] This is particularly true of the remarkable way in which Jesus refers to himself as "the lord" in Mk 11:3 (followed by Mt 21:3 and Lk 19:31). This rather unique case shows that to the disciples he was known already as the lord, particularly on account of his authority as teacher. After the resurrection he would *be invoked* as the Lord, particularly in connection with the future parousia. This shows that the title *Kyrios* can have had a Palestinian origin and does not necessarily derive from the use of the title for gods or Roman emperors in Hellenistic circles. Luke's use of *Kyrios* will be examined in detail later (Ch. 5), as also some texts of Matthew, mainly 7:21-22; 8:25; 24:42 (Ch. 6). It must finally be borne in mind that as soon as Jesus was recognized as divine in some way, it appeared appropriate to call him *Kyrios*, the word for God in the Septuagint.

Certainly Jesus was himself conscious of being the Messiah, although he could not say so openly (see more on this in Ch. 4). It can be shown that the title MESSIAH was used in early Palestinian Christology to refer to Jesus, both as the authoritative teacher during his earthly ministry and as the future Messianic King.[6] The discourse of Peter recorded in Acts 3 represents, it is believed, the earliest formulation of the kerygma, or "proclamation." The following Christological statement it contains takes on, because of this, an exceptional importance: Repent therefore . . . that God may grant you a season of refreshment when "he sends you Jesus, already designated as your Messiah. Jesus must remain in heaven until the time of universal restoration which God spoke of long ago through his holy prophets" (Ac 3:20-21). It should be noted that in this text the term "Messiah," normally used to designate the historical Jesus (Mk 1:1; 8:29), applies here also to the end-time figure designated "Son of man" in Jewish apocalyptic. Already in this literature "Son of man" tended to be associated with Davidic Messianology, particularly in the *Book of Enoch* (see Fuller 36f). Fuller also notes that neither in Ac 3 is there any "Christological assessment of Jesus' continued activity in his exalted state. The interim is purely of a waiting character" (p. 159). Although the Epistle to the Hebrews does speak of an intercessory type of ministry of Jesus in heaven (7:25), in another text it also represents him as having taken his seat in heaven "to wait until his enemies should be made a stool for his feet" (10:13). The view of Ac 2:36 that Jesus became the Messiah at his resurrection appears to stem from a later composition, since in this text Jesus is already recognized as Lord in the Church. Mk 14:62, as we shall see later, also belongs to the early stratum which tended to identify Jesus with the future Son of man.

Messiahship was inseparably associated with the Davidic dynasty since 2 S 7:1-16 and Mi 5:1f (see Mt 2:6). The description

Zc 9:9 gives of the Messianic King would seem at first to explain the scene described in Mk 11:10. A Messianic outburst at this place and time is, however, unlikely, and the acclamation can in fact echo early Palestinian church liturgy. This would explain the apparent reference to the *future* kingdom, that of the end-time: ''Blessed is the kingdom of our father David that is coming'' (see also Lk 1:32). The title SON OF DAVID is therefore also early Palestinian and connected with the *parousia*. No serious reason exists to deny that the tradition of Jesus' birth in Bethlehem contributed to the acceptance of the title as applicable to him.

The earliest use of the title SON OF GOD could very well be found in Rm 1:3-5, since the core of these verses can be isolated as pre-Pauline Palestinian formulation: ''Born of the seed of David; appointed Son of God from the resurrection of the dead.'' In the Palestinian formulae, Fuller explains, Jesus *is not adopted* at the resurrection for a new status or function, ''but *pre-destined* to be the eschatological judge at the parousia'' (p. 166). It can be assumed that the Palestinian Church depended on Ps 2:7 and 2 S 7:14 for its designation of Christ as Son of God. Although Lk 1:32 may belong, as part of the infancy narrative, to later Hellenistic Jewish Christian circles, it can very well have incorporated a very early tradition dependent on the OT Messianic texts referred to above.

CHAPTER TWO

CHRISTOLOGICAL TEXTS FROM "Q"

In many ways the next two chapters will probably appear as the least satisfactory section among the NT writings we have to examine, the main reason for this being that in Q and the Markan tradition are necessarily found sayings from different levels, and it is rarely certain what "sayings of Jesus" precisely means. By "Q" we refer, of course, to texts common to Matthew and Luke, but not found in Mark, while the Markan tradition is in substance the same as the Synoptic tradition, the properly Markan editorial work being excepted. Only the sayings and other texts which appear to represent distinctive perceptions of the early Christian community or reflect Jesus' own consciousness regarding his person and mission[7] will be singled out for consideration.

Introducing "Q"

The form critics of the Gospel postulate the early existence of a source they call "Q", which would account for the texts Matthew and Luke have in common independently of Mark. Although a general consensus is still lacking on the origin and the nature of this source, some aspects concerning it do seem to reflect objective reality. An early Aramaic Q may have existed, but it is the Greek document that Matthew and Luke have incorporated into their gospels. It seems unnecessary to distinguish two forms of the document, one Palestinian, one Jewish Hellenistic, even though the contents of the source may reflect one or the other religious milieu, as will be pointed out.

Indications exist that Luke usually preserves Q slightly better than Matthew, in both content and order. Roughly speaking Q represents about one-fourth of Luke and one-third of Matthew. In his study of *Peter's Pentecost Discourse* (Nashville 1971), R.F. Zehnle sees correspondences between Q and the third chapter of Acts, which to many contains the earliest formulation of the kerygma, as already noted above. Q therefore represents early Gospel tradition, and this seems confirmed by some particular traits of its theology. The fact that the document contained mainly sayings of Jesus sets the composition of Q in the pre-Gospel period, therefore between the years 50 and 60.

In *Jesus in History* (New York 1970), Howard Kee finds seven basic forms of material in Q, and to each can be assigned a certain number of passages, out of the 52 usually recognized as belonging to Q: Narratives (2), Parables (15), Oracles (6), Beatitudes (2), Prophetic Pronouncements (18), Wisdom Words (6), Exhortations (3). According to Edwards (see note 8), "wisdom instruction" dominates in the Q material, that is, exhortation to live righteously in the last days (see Lk 12:42-44/Mt 24:45-47). If parabolic discourse belongs to wisdom, then a large section of Q can be called sapiential. It appears safer, however, to consider the Q sayings source as belonging predominantly to the prophetic tradition. Reflecting on texts like Lk 10:2-12; 12:33f; 14:26; 18:29, par., one can well imagine that "the prophets of the Q community were wandering charismatic prophets who lacked home, close family ties, wealth and security."[8]

For Paul Hoffman (see note 8), the tradition represented by Q of prophetical type, proclaimed the proximity of the Kingdom, recognized in Jesus a prophet of the end-time and identified him with the Son of man, the eschatological Judge. More will be said on the Christology of Q in connection with particular texts. It can still be noted here that the pre-Pauline origin of the Q texts can explain their lack of interest in the saving significance of Jesus' death. This, however, can also depend on the fact that the texts, mostly sayings of Jesus, contain no passion story. It is Mark (10:45; 14:24) who put into narrative form the basic Pauline thought that Jesus died for our sins, to obtain for us divine forgiveness (1 Cor 15:3). Without denying this, the Q document rather situates salvation for believers in the final judgment. Texts like Lk 14:27 can suggest that it viewed Jesus' death in terms of martyrdom. For Edwards Matthew and Luke attempted to accommodate the Q material, and its theology, into their basic Markan point of view (pp. 150f). G.N. Stanton (see note 8) recognizes that a Son of man Christology and an expectation of coming judgment are both prominent in Q, but he questions the claim made by Tödt (see note 10) and others that these components provide the key to the purpose of Q. For Stanton ''Christological titles are of less interest to Q than the grounds of the authority of Jesus'' (p. 35).

Since Luke probably preserved better than Matthew the original order of Q, we will follow the Lucan order in the presentation of the texts of Q, which we have chosen to examine because of their Christological significance.

Baptize with Fire (Lk 3:16; Mt 3:11)

Any Synoptic reader of the gospels will notice that in the report on John the Baptist some verses and words are found in Matthew and Luke only. In Mk 1:8 John says of The Mightier One: ''He will baptize you with the Holy Spirit.'' This is quite clearly a Christianized version of John's message, with a view to the coming Pentecost. Although ''fire'' is also mentioned in Ac 2:3, more likely the addition of ''and with fire'' in Q (Lk 3:16/Mt 3:11) preserves a reference to *the fire of judgment* found in John's original preaching. He probably had said: ''I baptize you with water; The Coming One will baptize you with fire.'' Thus Q tends to define The Coming One as the eschatological Judge, in agreement with the vision of Jewish apocalyptic. As a preceding passage indicates, Mt 3:7-10/Lk 3:7-9, the Q leaders took seriously the apocalyptic expectation of an imminent end (*Naherwartung*) through a sudden and decisive divine intervention.

It can be noted here in passing that as compared to Mark's simple *erchetai*, "comes" (1:7), Matthew's *ho erchomenos*, "He-Who-Is-Coming," expresses a Christological datum which probably belongs to an early tradition. It can be connected with texts like Gn 49:10, "until he comes," Ml 3:1, "behold he comes," and especially Habakkuk's *hoti ho erchomenos hêxei* (2:3 LXX), "because he who is coming will come," a basic Messianic prophecy for the groups to which John the Baptist belonged (see more on the title below, about Lk 7:18-35).

"If you are the Son of God" (Lk 4:3, 9; Mt 4:3, 6)

In contrast to Mark's brief reference to it (1:12f), Luke and Matthew describe Jesus' temptation in the form of three dialogues in three different scenes. As a *narrative* this passage does not too clearly belong to the Q tradition in its content, except as presenting Jesus as model for the disciples in surmounting temptations. Most of Q in fact can be read as a series of instructions to serve as guidelines for discipleship. In my commentary on Matthew (pp 286-305) I have discussed extensively the origin and meaning of the temptation story. It would be hazardous to consider the whole narrative as a product of the Christian community. It is possible, however, that the long version of Q represents a Christian *haggadah* built on a brief report which originated with Jesus.

In the logia (Q) source, the story of the temptations is no homogeneous piece of tradition. The third temptation, in Matthew's order, lacks two features found in the previous passages: Satan's use of a Scriptural quotation and the reference to the title "Son of God." In addition, the first two temptations seem to presuppose the typically Hellenistic concept of "Son of God" (as in Rm 1:4), not Messianically intended, while the world rule of the Messianic King is the theme of the third temptation (Hahn 158). It is quite possible that the first two temptations are meant to dispel a false understanding of the title "Son of God" based on the Hellenistic *theios anêr* concept. Christ the Son of God will not use his divine power to perform spectacular miracles to promote his own image. It is given to him only to perform the works for which God has commissioned him.

Jesus' authority as God's envoy is a key element of the Christology of Q. Not surprisingly, then, the authority of Jesus as Son of God is challenged and vindicated in the temptation story as we have it. Q may have contained also a baptismal narrative, as we shall indicate in Ch. 3. This and the temptation story, observes Stanton, should not be considered merely as "a Christological preface," since "there is plenty of evidence to confirm that for the Q community the actions and proclamation of Jesus marked *the dawn of the new age*, for Jesus was claiming to fulfill the prophetic promises . . . The 'past' of Jesus, as well as his soon-expected parousia, is important in the Q community" (pp. 35-36).

Calling Jesus "Lord, Lord" (Lk 6:46; Mt 7:21f)

In Mt 7:21-23 Jesus warns first that the Kingdom of heaven is for those who do the will of the Father, not for those who only say to Jesus "Lord, Lord." "Lord, Lord" comes again in the other warning of Jesus, to those who believe that prophesying and working miracles can, as such, procure admittance to the Kingdom (compare Mt 25:12). Perhaps originally the sayings stressed the necessity of being prepared for the hour of judgment, but Mt 7:22 uses them against the charismatics and false prophets. A comparison with Mt 24:24 suggests to Fuller that the title *Kyrios* in Mt 7:21-23 is similar in meaning to that of the future Son of man. The sayings can be seen as supplying proof that Jesus was actually addressed as *Maran(a)* in his lifetime (p. 137).

The use of the title *Kyrios* indicates that the disciples recognized that Jesus had the authority to speak definitively as God's representative on earth. To hear the words of Jesus without doing them can only lead to utter ruin (Lk 6:47-49/Mt 7:24-27). The recurrence of the address "Lord" in the Q story of the healing of the centurion's slave (Mt 8:6, 8/Lk 7:6) confirms the use of the title in Jesus' own lifetime. Here, however, the Christological meaning is less evident, since the context is about a master and his subordinates. Besides, the speaker is a pagan, who would not be expected to call Jesus *Rabbi*, the title used by Jews to address their teachers of the Torah. So "Lord" in the present context can be taken in its ordinary secular meaning. It remains of course possible that the evangelists understood "Lord" in a Christological sense. Similar remarks can be made about the title "Lord" found on the lips of the Syrophoenician woman in Mk 7:28.

John and Jesus (Lk 7:18-35; Mt 11:2-19)

The Messianic title *ho erchomenos*, "He-who-is-coming," has already been briefly discussed about Lk 3:16 par. It recurs in this later passage, in which John the Baptist sends the following question to Jesus: "Are you he who is to come, or shall we look for another?" The wording is exactly the same in Mt 11:3 and in Lk, where it is, besides, repeated (7:19-20). Behind the Greek title *ho erchomenos* must lie the Hebrew *habbâ'*, which in Jewish writings refers to the eschatological prophet. "In the Messianic dogma of Judaism, writes J. Schneider, the Messiah is the coming One (*ho erchomenos*) who with his coming inaugurates the time of salvation" (*TDNT* vol. 2, pp. 670).

It is noteworthy that the book of Revelation describes God as "he who is, and who was, and the coming one" (1:4, 8; 4:8), which explicates the revelation of the divine name (Ex 3:14). In Ps 96:13; 98:9 God himself is described as the One-Who-Comes to judge the earth. ''The fact that God *will come* is the only permanent trait in Old Testament eschatology, all the colorings that describe his return are but secondary and impermanent elements.''[9] While in Mt 3:12 ''He-who-is-coming'' refers rather to the eschatological Judge, the same title in Mt 11:3 par. should be more likely referred to the end-time prophet, as in Jn 6:14.

In his answer Jesus calls John's attention to the facts of his ministry, using phrases taken from Scripture, mainly concerning the expectation that in the new age the blind would see, the deaf would hear (Is 29:18), and the lame would walk (35:6f). The raising of the dead figures among the expectations of a (later) apocalyptic passage of Isaiah (26:19) and, of course, in Dn 12:2. The Syriac *Apocalypse of Baruch* (1 Bar), translated from a Hebrew original of probably the 2nd and 3rd cent. B.C., associates the resurrection of the dead with the glorious (second) advent of the Messiah (30:1-2). As for the cleansing of the lepers, it is obviously mentioned having in view what Jesus actually did (Lk 5:12-16). On the other hand, the preaching of the Gospel to the poor fulfills Is 61:1, and this is clear from the quotation of this text in Lk 4:18.

John understood his own mission to consist in preparing Israel for the impending divine judgment, to be enacted by ''The Coming One,'' by ''The Mightier One'' (Mt 3:11f). He found it difficult to harmonize with his own representation the image Jesus' deeds of mercy ascribed to the Messiah. The Messiah, Son of David, was not expected to work miracles or proclaim the good news, as was the end-time prophet. Jesus' answer does, however, suggest that signs connected with his ministry point to the arrival of the Messianic times. In addition, Matthew especially saw Jesus' healing activity as fulfilling a role of the future shepherd of Israel (see my *Matthew* 521). Possibly for this reason Matthew can anticipate his own answer to John's question by writing that John had heard in prison ''about the deeds of the Christ'' (11:2). These are the evangelist's words, because Q never refers explicitly to the *Messiah*.

Having written this, Matthew can conclude with these words from the parable of The Children in the Market Place: "Yet wisdom is justified by her deeds" (11:19). Luke has preserved the original Q version: "Yet wisdom is justified by all her children" (7:35). Although the parable may very well go back to Jesus himself, the conclusion just mentioned is more probably a reflection of the Q writer, who saw Christ's merciful attitude to all as vindicated by the Easter events. No wisdom Christology can be founded on the Q conclusion to the text of the parable. See more on this in Ch. 6 about Matthew's Christology (under 1:16).

Following the Son of Man (Lk 9:58; Mt 8:20)

We will concentrate here on the Christological value of the title "Son of man" used in this Q saying: "The Son of man has nowhere to lay his head." Quite possibly, in this saying, as in others regarding the present (Mk 2:10, 28), "Son of man" simply means "man," like *ben 'ādām* in Ps 8:5; 80:18 or *ben 'enôš* in Ps 144:3. This would correspond to *bar 'enaša'* in Aramaic. There exists no proof, however, that this expression was used as a periphrasis for "I." A shift from the common to the titular use of "Son of man" can probably be recognized in the reports on Jesus' saying about the forgiveness of blasphemy. In Mk 3:28 Jesus says that "all sins will be forgiven the sons of men," not, however, blasphemy against the Holy Spirit, since this supposes obstinate impenitence or refusing to accept what obviously God sanctions. In Mt 12:31 "the sons of men" becomes "men," showing an equivalent meaning in the original. In the Q text which follows (Mt 12:32; Lk 12:10), saying a word against "the Son of man" could refer to the pre-paschal rejection of Jesus, a sin for which the excuse of ignorance about his true status could be pleaded. Mk 3:28 would represent an attempt to make the saying more understandable by removing the obscure reference to the "word against the Son of man." It is unlikely that Mark knew the texts of Q, but he may have known a tradition in which some of them had their origin.

Concerning Mt 8:20/Lk 9:58, it does not seem that even initially "man" stood for "Son of man," or that the saying meant: "Man, homeless in this world, is contrasted with wild beasts." Rather, to the scribe who volunteered to follow him, Jesus wished to explain that "vocation" is the normal gateway to discipleship and that the scribe's offer could be presumptuous, from an unawareness of the difficulties. Jesus equivalently tells him: "Animals have places where to live, but there is a man, the Son of man, who is a homeless wanderer on earth" (see *Vigiliae Christianae* 1964, pp. 219ff). As L. Goppelt notes, Mt 8:20 "did not speak with doleful perception about the homelessness of mankind, but about the Son of man who was a stranger on earth because his home was heaven" (*Theology of the New Testament*, vol. 1, p. 187). In this text therefore, as in a few others concerning the present, the titular use of "Son of man" should be maintained, and this is today increasingly recognized.

On the other hand, several critics find it difficult to admit that Jesus could have referred to himself as the "Son of man" already here on earth, since in its origin the title refers to a transcendent figure coming on the clouds of heaven, as in Dn 7:13 and Mk 14:62. Other serious exegetes think differently. According to I.H. Marshall, Jesus used the title "Son of man" "to give cautious expression to his own unique relationship with God as his Son and agent of salvation": "Son of man" was thus "a perfect vehicle for expressing the divine self-consciousness of Jesus while at the same time preserving the secrecy of his self-revelation from those who had blinded their eyes and closed their ears."[10] A recognized authority in the field, M. Black, had previously written: "No term was more fitted both to conceal, yet at the same time to reveal to those who had ears to hear, the Son of Man's real identity" (see p. 329 of *An Aramaic Approach to the Gospels and Acts* [3rd ed., Oxford 1967]).

In an appendix to Black's work, G. Vermès has demonstrated that, at the time of Jesus or before, the rabbis would use in Aramaic ''son of man'' both to designate generically ''a man'' or ''any man,'' and as a circumlocution for ''I,'' when for some reason they preferred to avoid the use of the pronoun to speak of themselves. This shows therefore that Jesus could very well have used ''Son of man'' to designate himself, even when he was not speaking of his future role as transcendent figure. Texts like Mk 14:21 and Lk 22:48 point to the authenticity of at least some of the Son of man sayings connected with the passion, and the following formulation, with an obvious play on words, must go back to Jesus himself: ''The Son of man will be delivered into the hands of men'' (Mk 9:31 par.). Most critics recognize as authentically from Jesus the sayings in which he vindicates his authority to rule on the Sabbath and to forgive sins (Mk 2:10, 28 par.). Some claim, however, that in these instances ''Son of man'' was not originally a title, but a circumlocution for ''I.'' Others observe correctly that in these sayings ''Son of man'' is used titularly to underline Jesus' unique authority. And there exists no real reason to ascribe this mode of speech to the community rather than to Jesus himself. If all this is true there should be no difficulty in admitting that Jesus did at times refer to himself even in his earthly life as the Son of man. As for the identification of Jesus with the transcendent Son of man, this will be discussed in connection with other texts (see on Lk 12:8 below). The self-description of Jesus as ''Son'' in Lk 10:21f/Mt 11:25-27 will be examined in Ch. 4 in relation to Jesus' own messianic consciousness.

Christology of Superiority: Jonah and Solomon
(Lk 11:29-32; Mt 12:39-41)

As R. Kieffer has shown in detail (see note 11) ''a Christology of Superiority'' is well attested in the earlier gospels: several times Jesus appears in the Synoptics as not only fulfilling in some way, but also as surpassing the figures contained in Scripture. This of course agrees with the general principle that in typology the fulfillment exceeds in quality the promise and the prefigurement.[11]

While in Mark Jesus simply refuses to concede "a sign from heaven" to the Pharisees (8:11-12), in Q an exception is made for "the sign of Jonah," and this further provides the occasion for introducing a comparison also with Solomon (Lk 11:29-32/Mt 12:39-41). The superiority of Jesus over Jonah falls under the general theme of the superiority of Jesus over all the prophets, which is at least implicitly affirmed in the confession of Caesarea Philippi (Mt 16:15 par.) and the transfiguration (17:1-8 par.). While in Luke the sign of Jonah is interpreted as referring to the prophet's preaching—Luke likes to present Jesus as prophet and preacher of the word—the sign becomes in Mt 12:40 a direct illustration of Jesus' future resurrection. How can the preaching of Jonah be a future sign for the present generation? When Jesus appears at the judgment as the Son of man, then will this incredulous generation have to recognize how wrong it was not to have listened to Jesus, a preacher incomparably superior to Jonah. As for the other comparison: whereas the Queen of the South, a pagan, came from a great distance to hear a mortal being, the Jews do not really listen in their own land to a preacher through whom, much more than through Solomon, divine wisdom speaks.

A sign "from heaven," Hahn explains, is not a mighty act wrought by one's own power, but a legitimating miracle granted by God (p. 378). As compared to Mk 8:11 and even to Mt 16:4, the Q passages under review appear as an expansion which can be attributed to the Christian community. The sort of Christology of superiority expressed in these and other texts can have developed as follows. In their liturgical celebrations the Christians would complete the OT readings by comparisons with facts and gestures belonging to Jesus, which naturally led to extolling *Jesus* above the Old Testament figures.

It seems apposite to mention here the verse that follows in

Luke: ``No one after lighting a lamp puts it in a cellar or under a bushel, but on a stand, that those who enter may see the light'' (11:33). The verse appears to concern the same people, warning this ``evil generation'' of unbelievers that it is wholly their fault if the light of Jesus and of the Kingdom does not illumine them. It is also possible to see in ``those who enter'' a reference to the Gentiles coming to Christ.

The Future Son of Man (Lk 12:8; Mt 10:32)

In the view of several NT critics the identification of the Son of man with Jesus came only later: ``Only after the identification of the future Son of man with Jesus had been made could Jesus who worked on earth in full power and authority be described likewise as the 'Son of man,' and this description was finally extended to cover the statements about His suffering and rising again'' (Hahn 28). Four versions of an initial tradition going back to Jesus have to be compared:

Lk 12:8 ``And I tell you, everyone who acknowledges me before men, the Son of man also will acknowledge before the angels of God.''

Mt 10:32 ``So everyone who acknowledges me before men, I also will acknowledge before the angels of God.''

Mk 8:38 ``For whoever is ashamed of me and of my words in this adulterous and sinful generation, of him will the Son of man also be ashamed, when he comes in the glory of his Father with the holy angels.''

Lk 9:26 ``For whoever is ashamed of me and of my words, of him will the Son of man be ashamed when he comes in his glory and the glory of the Father and of the holy angels.''

Of these four texts only that of Mark seems to identify Jesus with the Son of man, because of the mention of ``his Father.'' The first two texts present a Q version, and it is probable that Lk 12:8 is closer to the original. Mt 10:32 excludes that the Son of man can be a figure distinct from Jesus himself. It is impossible in fact to suppose that Jesus saw himself as a mere forerunner or prophet of the Son of man, since he clearly claimed to be the fulfillment of the Messianic hope. It is even less possible to imagine that the Christian community initiated a development in that sense, then dropped it. Jeremias formulates thus the solution which is often proposed in different forms: "The answer can only be that when Jesus speaks in the third person he makes a distinction not between two different figures, but between his present and future state of exaltation. The third person expresses the 'mysterious relationship' which exists between Jesus and the Son of man: he is not yet the Son of man, but he will be exalted to be the Son of man" (*New Testament Theology*, vol. 1, p. 276).

The problem related to the suffering Son of man and to the future coming of the Son of man will be more appropriately discussed in Ch. 3 in connection with Mk 8:31 and 14:62 respectively. Two other texts with Christological significance, involving the Son of man, will be examined at their proper place later on: Lk 22:69 in Ch. 5 (Lucan Christology), and Mt 16:27 in Ch. 6 (Christology of Matthew).

Christological Traits in Q

Summing up, there is no doubt that the Q document testified to an early reflection on Jesus and his mission. John the Baptist felt he himself was the forerunner of The Mightier One through whom God would soon execute a judgment on the wicked. In his temptation Jesus appears as the Son of God, as one endowed with power, which he must use only to accomplish God's will and not to establish himself as "divine man," in the Hellenistic sense. In the Q community Jesus was also known as "the Lord" who could speak definitively as God's envoy on earth. Jesus in Q does not deny he is The Coming One, but he does not describe his mission,

as John did, in apocalyptic terms. He is the dispenser of God's gifts
on earth and he fulfills the figure of the eschatological Prophet (Is
61:1) and at the same time of the Servant prophet (Is 42:1). As
preacher of the Gospel and as bringer of the good news he ushers in
a new age of salvation. He vindicates his authority as Son of man,
to forgive sins and to be the interpreter of God's will on earth, even
in matters concerning the Sabbath. Not surprisingly Jesus ranks
above Solomon and the prophets. He will die as a martyr and his
authority will be vindicated when he will appear as the transcendent Son of man of the apocalyptic expectation.

CHAPTER THREE

CHRIST IN THE MARKAN TRADITION

After extensive reading on the subject and personal reflection I have decided to write ''the Markan tradition'' instead of ''the Synoptic tradition,'' my previous choice. It has become apparent to me that in spite of claims to the contrary it is not often easy to distinguish tradition and redaction in Mark. In the case of Matthew and Luke redaction criticism obtains clear results because their contribution appears from the use they have made of Mark and Q. In the case of Mark's gospel we have no such basis, and as yet, Perrin admits, ''we have had no such breakthrough in connection with the theology of Mark.''[12] There exists, however, a certain Christology of Mark, and some of its traits will be pointed out in this chapter. It is not possible to assert in a general way that Mark is older than Q or Q older than Mark. ''Although it is not likely that Mark knew Q, we cannot exclude the possibility that he was acquainted with this collection but deliberately made no use of it, or that the sayings of Jesus which he reports are derived in part from this source'' (E. Schweizer, *The Good News According to Mark*, p. 12). Although we will examine separately the Christology of both Luke and Matthew, the present chapter will offer different occasions to point out some of their redactional interventions in the area of Christology.

Several methods have been proposed for the task of distinguishing tradition and redaction in Mark's gospel. Vocabulary and style serve the purpose at times, but it must not be forgotten that the Synoptic tradition or the triple tradition is known through Mark almost exclusively. Attempts have been made to isolate definite units of pre-Markan tradition, like miracle stories and Son of man sayings, but the results are more often than not disputable, for the reasons already mentioned. Other critics have sought to determine the "literary model" which Mark has used for his writing. Has he simply added a long introduction to a passion narrative, or composed a sort of aretalogy (a Greek literary genre; biographical accounts of brave or wise men enrolled among the gods), with miracles as the backbone, or is Mark to be understood mainly in apocalyptic terms? In my view all three models contribute in Mark to the making of a unique composition: "the gospel of Jesus Christ, the Son of God." As for the purpose of his "didactic narrative," there seems to be a sort of consensus on this: Mark wishes in particular to correct a false Christology, one that led also to an incorrect notion of discipleship (see especially 8:27-38).

Much of the earliest gospel, Mark's, reflects a common tradition preserved in separate units. Form criticism attempts to isolate these units and trace their history before they were collected. Mark was the first writer, it seems, who collected these units together in one composition, which he called *euaggelion*, "good news" or "gospel." In more than one sense Mark can be called "a kerygmatic story."[13] In this framework the contents receive additional significance and Mark's message appears particularly in the arrangement he gave to the different materials he had received. It is the work of redaction criticism precisely to discover the distinctive orientation of the editorial activity of the Gospel writers.

The Gospel is for Mark more than a message from God concerning Jesus Christ. It proclaims God's action among men. The manifestation of Christ, Son of God, will take place in two phases: in the first (1:1-8:30) Jesus shows his power in miracles often directed against the forces of evil, and his opponents claim he is an instrument of Satan himself. Gradually the disciples recognize in him the Messiah, but are told to keep that revelation secret, just like the demons who know who he is. In the second phase the true mystery of Jesus' saving mission is revealed: the Son of man must suffer, die, and then be risen. The final conflict with Jesus' adversaries will take place in Jerusalem, and there also the centurion will finally declare openly who Jesus is: the Son of God. Mark wrote his book for non-Jews living outside Palestine. Possibly Jesus' sayings on carrying one's cross behind him (Mk 8:34-38) represent for Mark an instruction to the persecuted Christians of his church, particularly during the last years of Nero's reign (54-68).

The Gospel of Jesus Christ, the Son of God (Mk 1:1)

"The beginning of the gospel of Jesus Christ" can be understood in two ways: either as the beginning of Jesus' own proclaiming of the coming Kingdom (1:15), or as the beginning of the joyful news *about* Jesus Christ, who is himself the bringer of salvation. For J. Schmid this second meaning is preferable, because when Mark wrote his gospel it had long been accepted that Jesus Christ was himself the central object of the Gospel and of the apostolic preaching (*The Gospel According to Mark*, p. 17). The inscription accordingly refers to the facts which constitute the message of the Gospel preaching. This *begins* with the proclamation of John the Baptist about Jesus Christ, "The Mightier One." Of the four evangelists only Mark uses the expression "the Gospel of God" (1:14), which probably reveals an influence of Paul. But whereas in Paul the Gospel refers to what is proclaimed orally (1 Cor 9:14), and heard (Col 1:23), the early Church understood that *euaggelion* could apply also to the written message, and this seems to be reflected in the title of Mark's writing (1:1).

The appellation "Jesus Christ," which occurs only here in Mark, is a personal name, as it is usually in Paul. Initially, however, and this was certainly still felt in the Synoptic tradition, *Christos* referred to "the Anointed One," to the royal Messiah. In writing "Jesus Christ" Mark makes it clear that Messiahship has taken a new meaning: there has been a shift from Messianology to Christology. Only once in Mark a human being recognizes Jesus as the Messiah, and he is immediately told not to reveal this (8:29-30). Jesus himself will give a qualified approval to the title "Christ" only during the trial (14:61-62).

"Son of God" is absent from several NT manuscripts, but it was probably part of the original text. In any case, it agrees with the Christology of Mark and of the Synoptic tradition as a whole. The evangelists gave the title its fullness of meaning, implying Jesus' divine nature. It does not follow from this that the full meaning is to be attributed to "Son of God" every time it occurs in the gospels, for example in the mouth of Peter (Mt 16:16). It took time to reconcile belief in Jesus' divinity with the strict monotheistic faith of Israel. In spite of Psalm 2, the title "Son of God" did not normally designate the Messiah in the Judaism of Jesus' time (Schmid 20). In Christian usage "Son of God" can serve as a corrective to the ambiguous designation "Messiah" (see Mt 16:16).

The Father's Beloved Son (Mk 1:11)

The voice from heaven is an essential component of the Baptism of Jesus. Mark describes the baptism from the standpoint of Jesus' subjective experience, whereas Matthew presents it as an objective event: "behold, the heavens were opened," and "lo, a voice from heaven is saying, 'This is my beloved Son, with whom I am well pleased.' " Luke also has objectivized the event: although he has the voice use the 2nd person, as in Mark, unlike Mark he does not say that (only) Jesus *saw* the heavens open and the Holy Spirit descend, but he notes mainly that these events took place while Jesus was praying. Because the voice speaks there in the 3rd person, it is clearer in Matthew that the proclamation is a composite quotation of Ps 2:7, "*You are my son*, today I have begotten you," and of Is 42:1, "Behold my servant, whom I uphold, my chosen, *in whom I delight.*" That Jesus is called *agapētos*, "beloved," in the Mt/Mk accounts of the baptism and transfiguration almost certainly reveals an influence of Gn 22:2, 12, 16. It is well known that the figure of Isaac plays a major role in the Targums of the time of Jesus (see *Religious Studies Bulletin* 1981, pp. 37-45). What the voice says at the baptism of Jesus can be described as a midrashic composition in which a Christian reflection expresses the meaning of a decisive historical event.

The following question seems appropriate for our purpose: was the original reference to the Son of God or to the Servant of God? The influence of Ps 2:7 on the transmission of the words from heaven appears particularly in manuscripts of Lk 3:22 which refer explicitly to the psalm. Possibly, when the early Church recognized that Ps 2:7 was fulfilled in Jesus (Heb 1:5; Ac 13:33), it began to read "Son of God" instead of "Servant of God" in the message from heaven at his baptism. This could be easily done since the Greek word *pais* means both "son" and "servant." For J. Jeremias "my Son" in Mk 1:11 represents the Christological development in a Hellenistic milieu of an original "my Servant" (*New Testament Theology* 54). Of course, "with thee I am well pleased" is an explicit quotation from Is 42:1. It should also be noticed that the mention of the Spirit in Mk 1:10, 12 seems to confirm the interpretation proposed, since Is 42:1 continues: "I have put my Spirit upon him, he will bring forth justice to the nations" (see Mt 12:18). As also Ac 10:38 suggests, Jesus received at his baptism the charismatic Spirit which would assist him throughout his whole Messianic mission.

Two texts from the Jewish apocalyptic writing called *Testaments of the Twelve Patriarchs* seem directly relevant for the baptism of Jesus: "The heavens shall be opened, and from the temple of glory shall come upon him sanctification, with the Father's voice as from Abraham to Isaac. And the glory of the Most High shall be uttered over him, and the spirit of understanding and sanctification shall rest upon him . . . [cf. Is 11:2]''(*Testament of Levi* 18:6f); ''And no sin shall be found in him. And the heavens shall be opened unto him, to pour out the spirit, the blessing of the Holy Father'' (*Testament of Judah* 24:2). In the first text the Messianic Priest, in the second the Messianic King are referred to. Whether these texts are authentically Jewish or partly of Christian inspiration, they illustrate a trend of thought very similar to that expressed in the baptism scene. For W. Grundmann, ''the story of Jesus' baptism reveals the eschatological fulfiller as the Messianic High Priest'' (*Marcus* 33), or the voice from heaven calls Jesus to the office (*Amt*) of the Messianic High Priest, in which ''the Son stands before men in the place of the Father'' (*Lukas* 108). It is interesting to note in this connection that Heb 5:5 refers to both Ps 2:7 and to Ps 110:4 to establish the calling of Christ to a unique priesthood. However, a reference to Jesus' priesthood at his baptism should be seen as conjectural, while a prophetic investiture remains the most likely meaning of the rite for Jesus. He himself quoted Is 61:1 at the inaugural address in Nazareth (Lk 4:18). It is recognized that the poem of Is 61:1-11 has connections with the Servant songs, particularly with Is 42:1 and 50:4-11. But another text should not be excluded from consideration, the promise of the Spirit to the future Messianic King (Is 11:2). This aspect J.D. Kingsbury particularly emphasizes in his studies on the Christology of Mark (see note 13). ''For Mark,'' he writes, ''the Holy Spirit stands for the power and presence of God. To depict Jesus Christ as receiving the Holy Spirit at his baptism is, in Mark's perspective, to see him as being equipped by God with divine power and to see God as being fully active in him'' (''The Spirit . . . ,'' p. 201). It is noteworthy that also in Lk 1:35 the Holy Spirit seems to correspond to ''the power of the Most High.''

''The Holy One of God'' (Mk 1:24)

As symbolized in the cure of the blind man (Mk 8:22-26), only gradually did the disciples learn to know who Jesus was, and never completely before the resurrection, but the demons from the beginning of the public ministry declare Jesus' special status: ''I know who you are, the Holy One of God'' (1:24). The closer a creature comes to God, the holier it is. ''The Holy One of God'' appropriately describes one designated also as God's anointed, as the Son of God. It does not seem that in Judaism the Messiah was called the Holy One of God, but, as we have seen in Ch. 1, the early Church did call Jesus ''the Holy and Righteous One'' (Ac 3:14), or God's ''Holy Servant'' (4:27, 30). The Fourth Gospel has preserved the following confession of Peter: ''We have believed, and have come to know, that you are the Holy One of God'' (6:69). This looks like another version of Caesarea Philippi, especially as found in Luke, where Peter defines Jesus as ''the Christ of God'' (9:20).

At the end of a Sabbath, Mark notes further on, Jesus ''healed many who were sick with various diseases, and cast out many demons; and he would not permit the demons to speak, because they knew him'' (1:34). The rule of the ''messianic secret'' applies even to the otherworldly creatures. The confrontation opposing Jesus and the demons, agents of Satan on earth, is public, and it testifies to Jesus' superhuman power (1:27). But to reveal its secret meaning now could endanger the gradual unfolding of the mission received. We do not have to suppose that the demons had a full knowledge of Jesus' true being. They sensed, however, that he was different from the other exorcists, that he possessed a supernatural power which could only come from his special relationship to the divinity. It can be noted, besides, that natural psychiatric explanations of demonic possession, proposed by some, cannot account for the superior knowledge of Jesus which the demoniacs display.

Jesus as Bridegroom (Mk 2:19-20)

The Synoptic gospels present Jesus as the bridegroom in an

allegory describing the effect of his departure on the subjects of the Kingdom—sorrow will follow upon joy. The expression "will be taken away" (Mk 2:20 par.) corresponds to the term used in the Greek Bible to signify the temporal end of the suffering Servant (Is 53:8), but this may be a coincidence. In the Old Testament God himself is Israel's bridegroom, or her husband, as Is 54:1, 5 testifies. Psalm 45, originally a secular song of praise in honor of a young king and his consort, a princess of Tyre, may have been admitted into the Psalter as referring typically to the Royal Messiah. Several Christian interpreters consider Ps 45 as directly Messianic, that is, written by the inspired writer himself as celebrating the sacred nuptials of the Messianic King with Israel or with the Church. We have no indications, however, that the Judaism of Jesus' time would depict the Messiah as the bridegroom of Israel. It is unlikely that Jesus represented himself as the Messianic Bridegroom. The Epistle to the Hebrews does, on the other hand, apply Ps 45:7 to Christ, to describe his enthronement in heaven (Heb 1:8). This may suggest that the early Church was behind the bridegroom sayings found in Mark and elsewhere.

The Fourth Gospel quite explicitly presents John the Baptist as the friend of the bridegroom, who is Christ, in a text (3:29) which seems in many ways related to the Synoptic passage. According to Mt 3:11 John declared himself unworthy to carry Jesus' *sandals*. Several ancient Latin writers perceived in the Baptist's declaration a specific juridical meaning, which can be thus outlined. As Dt 25:9-10 indicates, the sandal played a role in sanctioning agreements, and consequently in dispossessing someone of his rights. In Jn 1:24-27 the Baptist would state he has no authority to deprive Jesus of his right to be the bridegroom, for *he is* the Messiah. For a full treatment of this rather complex interpretation, see *Biblica* 1978, pp. 1-37.

It is interesting to note that Mt 9:15 reads "can the wedding guests mourn?" instead of Mark's "can the wedding guests fast?" It must also be observed that Christ clearly appears as the bridegroom in the Parable of the Maidens (Mt 25:1-13). Surprisingly the bride does not figure in the story. Paul, for his part, saw the Corinthian community in terms of a chaste bride-to-be presented to Christ (2 Cor 11:2). In the later Ephesians the community is the whole Church, and a true marriage replaces the simple betrothal (5:25-27). Finally, in the book of Revelation "the marriage of the Lamb" symbolizes the establishing of the heavenly kingdom (19:7), while the spouse of the Lamb is the Messianic Jerusalem or the Church (21:9; 22:17). In Matthew's version of the parable Jesus says: "It is the same with the Kingdom of Heaven as with a king who gave a marriage feast for his son" (22:2). It is not difficult to believe that by its very structure and essential contents this parable was allegorical from the beginning: Christ is the divine spouse sent to establish on a new basis the union with God's people after the failure of the old covenant.

"You Are the Son of God" (Mk 3:11)

We have seen how a demon had cried out: "I know who you are, the Holy One of God" (Mk 1:24). Later, in a sort of "summary" of Jesus' activity Mark reports how "the unclean spirits" fell down before Jesus and cried out to him: "You are the Son of God" (3:11). The change of title can be due to the fact that this is an editorial text of Mark, for whom Jesus is "the Son of God" (1:1; 15:39). In attributing to the demons the knowledge of Jesus' sonship Mark suggests that "Holy One of God" and "Son of God" were for them equivalent titles, denoting a close relationship between Jesus and the divinity. The Christian believers, including Mark, understand more precisely that applied to Jesus the title "Son of God" does not simply express a special moral relationship of Christ with God, but reflects what actually took place in his being at the Incarnation (Lk 1:35).

Side by side with the Son of man Christology, the early Palestinian Church developed, in Hahn's view, a conception which regarded Jesus as the new Moses, in line with the ideology of the OT charismatic men of God (p. 291). The Gerasene demoniac reacted to Jesus' presence in much the same way as the demoniac of Capernaum. Compare the two texts:

Mk 1:24 "And he cried out, 'What have you to do with us, Jesus of Nazareth? Have you come to destroy us? I know who you are, the Holy One of God.' "
Mk 5:7 "And crying out with a loud voice, he said, 'What have you to do with me, Jesus, Son of the Most High God? I adjure you by God, do not torment me.' "

These two reports evidently follow the same model. In the second text the divine predicate "Most High" points to the Judaism of the Diaspora. "In our passage it signifies that we are in the sphere of early Hellenistic Jewish Christianity" (Hahn *ibid.*). It can be noted that "Most High God" occurs in the OT particularly where non-Israelites are concerned (Gn 14:18-20; Is 14:14; Dn 3:26), and the Gerasene demoniac dwelt in a half-pagan territory. In Ac 16:17 the title recurs in the mouth of a kind of demoniac, of a person having a spirit of divination.

"The Stronger One" (Mk 3:27)

The Beelzebul controversy (Mk 3:23-30 par.) bears all the marks of an authentic episode. There is no doubt that Jesus did function as an exorcist. He was so successful in this that his adversaries attempted to discredit him with the claim that he obtained his power from Beelzebul, the prince of demons. In his answer Jesus makes the following statement, "No one can enter a strong man's house and plunder his goods, unless he first binds the strong man; then indeed he may plunder his house" (Mk 3:27). By implication Jesus appears in Mark as The Stronger One who vanquishes Satan, the strong one, and ruins his power. Lk 11:22

specifies that the stronger (*ischuroteros*) will defeat the strong one. John the Baptist had spoken of the one coming as one mightier (*ischuroteros*) than himself (Mk 1:7 par.).

Only in Q does Jesus say positively by whose power he casts out demons, by the Spirit of God (Mt 12:28) or the finger of God (Lk 8:20). In Mark he leaves the listener find the answer by himself. The Judaism of Jesus' time also expected that in the final era of salvation Satan would be shackled (*Assumption of Moses* 1,0:1; *Testament of Levi* 18:12). The influence of Is 49:24 on the Synoptic tradition concerning the despoiling of the strong can be retained, as well as that of Is 53:12: "Therefore I will divide a portion with the great, and he shall divide the spoil with the strong, because he poured out his soul to death, and was numbered with the transgressors."

"Who then is This One?" (Mk 4:41)

It is in the story of the stilling of the storm that Jesus is called for the first time *didaskalos*, "Teacher," at least in Mark (4:38). We have already discussed briefly this title in Ch. 1, mainly in connection with *Rabbi*, its equivalent in Hebrew. In all, *didaskalos* occurs twelve times in Mark, and *Rabbi* four times. Without doubt *Rabbi* was the regular title used to address Jesus, and it was employed for the teachers of the law as well.

We have singled out for presentation this episode of the stilling of the storm (Mk 4:35-41) because it contains an implied Christology. The question of the disciples, "Who is This One?" will be found equivalently later in the mouth of "many": "Where did this man get all this? What is the wisdom given to him? What mighty works are wrought by his hands!" (6:2). Jesus had shown his authority to teach, to expel demons, to cure, and soon he would raise a person from the dead (5:35-42). These signs indicate a certain mastery over the physical world, but the calming of the storm, like the miraculous feeding, and the walking on the water constitute more properly nature miracles, which natural "spiritual energy" can in no way explain. This the disciples understood, and filled with awe after the calming of the storm they could only exclaim: "Who then is This One, that even wind and sea obey him?"

Some of the nature miracles have been worked for the immediate need of the people around Jesus, but independently of this they have their own motivation. They convey in their own way the revelation of the advent of God's Kingdom. Jesus had come, especially for Mark, to overthrow Satan's power. On the other hand, it is not difficult to document the claim that the NT authors represent Satan as having a certain dominion over the whole world (See, for ex., Lk 4:6; 2 Cor 4:4; Jn 12:31; 1 Jn 5:19). This dominion is challenged by Jesus particularly in some nature miracles he performed. Significantly Jesus commands the winds and the sea as if they were personal powers, presumably because behind destructive forces a demoniacal power is understood to be at work. Jesus "rebukes" the wind (Mk 4:39), as he "rebukes" the unclean spirits (1:25). This is not to say that the Gospel narratives belong to the same literary category as the mythic dramas opposing the primitive demons of chaos and the divinities who organized the cosmos. The Gospel narratives can be seen to demythologize the cosmic struggle by giving to it a concrete and verifiable setting. The presumption is that Jesus did historically accomplish these nature miracles and thus showed his dominion over creation, fulfilling *in truth* what the psalmist said of every man: "You have given him rule over the works of your hands, putting all things under his feet" (Ps 8:7). In Heb 2:8f this passage is used to show that the whole of creation is under the lordship of Jesus, to whom also Paul applies the words "putting all things under his feet" (1 Cor 15:28; Ep 1:22). The following words describe accurately the impact of the stilling of the storm: "In the self-revelation of Jesus to his disciples, this scene marks an important step forward. In a way that a mere 'exhibition-miracle' could not do, it reveals Jesus as Lord over the world and nature'' (Schmid 109). We shall see in Ch. 6 that Matthew has drawn an ecclesial teaching from the same miracles (see under 14:33).

''Who do men say that I am?'' (Mk 8:27)

This question clearly indicates that the scene of Caesarea Philippi raises a Christological issue. The story has an historical background, but it also reflects the situation in the early Church, particularly as Mark saw it. The Caesarea episode opens a new section in Mark (8:27 to 10:52), in which the private instruction of the disciples plays a predominant role. In the following pages we will look particularly into the Christological teaching found in the first section, 8:27-9:13, on which J. Lambrecht has focused his study on ''The Christology of Mark'' (*Biblical Theology Bulletin* 1973, pp. 256-73).

To Jesus' question, ''Who do men say that I am?'' different answers are offered. The view that he was John the Baptist *redivivus* had been proposed or shared by Herod (Mk 6:14, 16). ''Others say, Elijah'' rested on the belief, founded in Ml 3:23-24, that ''Elijah comes first to restore all things,'' which in Mk 9:12-13 applies to John the Baptist. In the episode involving Herod already mentioned Jesus was also reportedly considered by some to be ''a prophet like one of the prophets of old'' (Mk 6:15). Only Matthew suggests the name of Jeremiah (16:14). Clearly setting apart the disciples from the people in general, Jesus then asks: ''But who do *you* say that I am?'' Usual spokesman for the twelve Peter, according to Mark, answered simply: ''You are the Christ'' (8:29), while in Luke he says ''the Christ of God'' (9:20), a phrase which occurs more than once in the OT to designate the Davidic king (see 2 S 1:14f), in its related form, ''the Lord's anointed'' (Lk 2:26). Matthew reports a more elaborate answer: ''You are the Christ, the Son of the Living God'' (16:16). Peter's simple answer is followed in Mark by the first prediction of the passion and the rebuke of Peter (8:31-33), and this also is Christologically meaningful. ''It would seem that the title 'Christ' had become for Mark and his contemporaries a title that was too easily confessed, that expressed too little and was somewhat vague. The title therefore had to be explained and given a deeper meaning. Mark wanted to give a specific content to it. He achieved this in 8:27-9:13 with the help of the other titles 'Son of man' and 'Son of God' '' (Lambrecht 272).

"The Son of Man Must Suffer" (Mk 8:31)

The concept ''Son of man'' has been examined first in connection with Early Palestinian texts (Ch. 1), which indicate that the Church knew that Jesus, the Son of man on earth, had been vindicated of his rejection. The title came up again in Ch. 2, about a Q text referring to the Son of man's lack of abode on earth (Lk 9:58 = Mt 8:20). With Lk 12:8 the question was raised about the identification of Jesus with the future Son of man. In the present text, the first prediction of the passion, we meet for the first time in the Markan tradition the mention of the Son of man in association with suffering. Before this problem is examined something has to be said about the predictions of the passion found in Mk 8:31; 9:31; 10:33f.

There is no difficulty in recognizing that the third prediction, so circumstantial, was composed by Mark himself, expanding 9:31 with a few additions from the actual course of events. It is noteworthy that the necessity of suffering (''must'') for the Son of man finds expression only in 8:31, the first prediction. This could indicate it is less primitive than the second prediction: ''The Son of man will be delivered into the hands of men, and they will kill him; and when he is killed, after three days he will rise'' (9:31). Remarkably, Lk 9:44b has retained only the first sentence, which has every chance of going back to Jesus, with its play on words (see my commentary on Luke). Also ''after three days'' points to an early tradition, when the formula had not yet been adapted to the fact that Jesus rose ''the third day'' (Mt 16:21; Lk 9:22; 1 Cor

15:4). While Mk 9:31 can be traced back to an early Palestinian source, the expressions "suffer many things," "be rejected," "be treated with contempt" (Mk 8:31; 9:12b) point rather to later Hellenistic formulations (Hahn 42).

A majority of authors, I presume, take for granted that the association of the figure of the Son of man with suffering is basically Christian. Since Jesus used "Son of man" as self-designation in his earthly life, he naturally spoke also of the Son of man who was going to his passion. Other authors underline the fact that in the concept of a suffering Son of man two figures are identified in the one person of Jesus: the apocalyptic Son of man of Dn 7 and the suffering Servant of Is 53. C.F.D. Moule, Morna Hooker, and R.N. Longenecker maintain that Dn 7 contains the concept of a suffering Son of man.[14] In Dn 7, they claim, "Son of man" stands for a loyal, martyr group brought to glory and vindicated through suffering. M. Casey disagrees with this interpretation (see note 14), stating: "There is no trace of a suffering Son of man in Dn 7: on the contrary, the man-like figure was deliberately chosen as a symbol of Israel in triumph" (p. 205). Hooker's stand on this subject seems to be linked with her consistent attempt to downgrade the influence of the Isaian suffering Servant texts on the New Testament. See her book *Jesus and the Servant* (London 1959), whose thesis also Longenecker considers unproved and unacceptable (p. 106).

The Rebuke of Peter (Mk 8:32-33)

The twelve were naturally shocked by this unexpected and blunt announcement of Jesus' forthcoming fate. Their spokesman, Peter again, began to rebuke Jesus (Mk), in words which only Matthew reports: "God forbid, Lord! This shall never happen to you" (16:22). In both Mark and Matthew Jesus' rebuke of Peter swiftly follows: "Get behind me Satan! For you are not on the side of God, but of man." It is generally thought that "the Satan logion'' cannot be a construction of the early Church or of Mark. This is not certain for several reasons: Jesus' temptation, as reported in Q, may have suggested the tone of the rebuke; Peter did actually deny his Master; and Mark or his source could be addressing the rebuke to those who were not prepared to carry their cross behind Jesus in a time of persecution. These wavering Christians could call Jesus ''the Christ,'' but did they know what they were saying? Could they seriously listen to Jesus' words: ''If anyone would come after me, let him deny himself and take up his cross and follow me'' (8:34)? If not, they would have to face the terrible consequences: the Son of man would be ashamed of them upon his coming in the glory of his Father with the holy angels (8:38). In other words, Mark is warning the Christians that the man Jesus who suffered and died and rose again will also be the judge of the living and the dead. For the sincere Christians this represents a hope, for the others a warning.

''Listen to Him'' (Mk 9:7)

I have no intention of offering here an interpretation of the transfiguration story (see *Matthew* 699-706). My purpose is rather to show how the story contains traits which are consistent with Mark's Christology, as he presents it at this stage of his gospel. Significantly the transfiguration occurs shortly after Caesarea, with which it is obviously also conceptually connected. As Lambrecht (p. 27) and others understand it, Mark sees the transfiguration as already fulfilling the promise made not long before: ''Truly, I say to you, there are some standing here who will not taste death before they see the kingdom of God come with power'' (9:1). The presence of Jesus transfigured in glory anticipates the glorious coming of the Kingdom. The one who has suffered is also the exalted one.

In Matthew Jesus' baptism was already a proclamation of Jesus' divine sonship, since in the first gospel the voice of heaven speaks already there in the third person (3:17). But in Mark Jesus' baptism was a personal epiphany; the proclamation comes at the transfiguration, with the voice from heaven saying: "He is my beloved Son; listen to him" (9:7). With this declaration Mark's gospel reaches a central climax, about halfway between the initial inscription (1:1) and the centurion's testimony: "Truly this man was the Son of God" (15:39). But this Jesus who suffered and will judge the world, is also the Lord worshipped in the Church. To be Christian is to be his disciple, and to follow his example. "Listen to him" reminds us of these truths. This injunction can be pre-Markan and reflect, as we have seen (Ch. 1), the early Palestinian representation of Jesus as Servant and Prophet like Moses, but in the second gospel it emphasizes the duty of discipleship, especially after the basic instruction of 8:34-38. The disciples are then charged "to tell no one what they had seen, until the Son of man should have risen from the dead" (9:9). Taking into account the instruction that preceded the transfiguration, this means that "Jesus can only manifest his identity as the Christ and the Son of God within the context of his passion" (Lambrecht 273).

The Ransom Saying (Mk 10:45)

As already noted above, the second main section in Mark, 8:27-10:52, is largely devoted to Jesus' private instruction of the disciples. "As they were going up to Jerusalem," a request of two disciples offered Jesus an opportune occasion to tell the twelve they should have no other ambition than to put themselves at the service of others. Still thinking, it seems, even after the passion predictions, that Jesus would soon establish the Kingdom, James and John proposed the request that they should be given a position of authority and rank alongside Jesus in the Messianic Kingdom (Mk 10:37). Jesus concludes his instruction with the following words: "For the Son of man also came not to be served but to serve and to give his life as a ransom for many" (10:45). As Schmid writes,

"Nowhere else in the whole N.T. is the basic opposition between worldly domination and Christian service brought out with such clarity and striking effect" (p. 200).

The ransom saying is certainly remarkable also for the fact that in it Jesus spells out so clearly the redemptive character of his forthcoming death. It is obvious that "to give his life as a ransom for many" reflects the wording of Is 53:10, in this reading of the Hebrew text: *'emet śam 'āshām napshô*, "truly he gave his life as a sin-offering." The ransom saying as a whole apparently combines this statement with some words of Ps 49:8-9a, where the terms *pādâh*, "redeem," *kepher*, "ransom," *nefesh*, "life," occur in Hebrew, and in Greek several terms formed from the root *lutron*, which appears also in Mk 10:45/Mt 20:28 "*lutron anti pollôn.*" In Jesus' saying we learn that the ransom will be paid with the life of the Son of man offered in sacrifice, but "the way in which this ransom sets men free is beyond our comprehension" (A. Plummer, *An Exegetical Commentary on the Gospel According to S. Matthew*, London 1910, p. 280). Jesus will formulate again the sacrificial meaning of his death at the last supper (Mk 14:24/Mt 26:28), using the expression "for many," which quite certainly should be referred to the term *rabbîm* (Gr. *polloi*) represented five times in the fourth Servant Song (Is 52:14; 53:11f). "Many" in these different texts is not restrictive but designates *all* the beneficiaries of redemption: "many" is used in contrast to the "one" sacrificial victim. In 1 Tm 2:6 *pantôn*, "all," substitutes *pollôn*.

The idea of service was extremely important to set the Church to be founded on the right path, and Jesus represented his own death as laid down in the service of humanity. Within the framework of the last supper Luke has preserved an instruction of Jesus which for both wording and context has affinities with the ransom saying. Having reminded the disciples that they should wish to serve others, not dominate them, he proposes himself in example: "For which is the greater, one who sits at table, or one who serves? Is it not the one who sits at table? But I am among you as one who serves'' (Lk 22:27). Of course Jesus illustrated his *diakonia* to others when he washed the feet of the disciples (Jn 13:1-15), in a gesture meant, at least originally, to express Jesus' voluntary submission to the humiliation of the passion. The sacramental references would have been added later, in reaction to certain gnostic claims. Luke's text probably goes back to a tradition which is literarily independent of both Mark and John, while it is dependent on the Servant ideology, on Is 53 in particular. It can be held with Feuillet and others that the Markan text is more archaic and Palestinian in its terms. For J. Roloff texts like Mk 10:45, Lk 22:27, and also Lk 12:37b, Jn 13:1-20 do seem to reflect Jesus' own interpretation of his coming death. More recently, in *Dansk Teologisk Tidsskrift* (1979, pp. 217-54), D. Lorenzen has maintained that both Mk 10:45 and 14:21-25 belong to a very early tradition and ''can with great probability be considered true representatives of Jesus' words, and give strong evidence that Jesus took on himself the role of Suffering Servant.''[15]

Of particular interest in the ransom saying, as in other texts (for ex. Lk 7:34 = Mt 11:19), is the use of *êlthon*, ''came,'' which suggests pre-existence. But this will come in for treatment more appropriately in Ch. 4, about Christ's self-understanding and pre-existence.

''Son of David'' (Mk 10:47)

While in Matthew ''Son of David'' occurs as a title of Jesus at the very beginning (1:1), it is found for the first time in Mark at 10:47. As Jesus was leaving Jericho on his way to Jerusalem, a blind beggar ''began to cry out and say: 'Jesus, Son of David, have mercy on me!' '' The Synoptic gospels report the healing of one blind man at Bethsaida (only Mk 8:22-26), of two blind men at an unidentified place (only Mt 9:27-31), of one or two blind men near Jericho: Mk 10:46-52; Lk 18:35-43; Mt 20:29-34. Both in 9:27-31 and 20:29-34 Matthew writes of two blind men, not one, and in both cases they use the title ''Son of David.'' We will have more to say in Ch. 6 on Matthew's special interest in the title ''Son of David'' (see under 1:1). It can be noted in particular that in the Messianic entry only in Matthew do the crowds acclaim Jesus as ''Son of David'' (21:9), while in Mark they only come close to this: ''Blessed is the kingdom of our father David that is coming'' (11:10).

In fact, only the blind man Bartimaeus calls Jesus ''Son of David'' in Mark's gospel. The title *ho Christos* has a broader extension than ''Son of David.'' Jesus as the Christ is Son of David, but he is more than this, since *ho Christos*, as ''The Anointed One,'' is equivalent to ''Messiah,'' and this term received in the course of time more than one accepted meaning. Even the connection of messiahship with the Davidic line has not been uniform. The Messianic expectation, first based on the prophecy of Nathan to David (2 S 7:2-13), was also connected by the writer-prophets with the Davidic lineage (Is 11:1-5; Jr 23:5), although quite early a new line of David came to be envisaged instead of the old historical one (cf. Is 7:14 and Mi 5:2). The Messianic ruler will be endowed with the divine spirit and will judge with equity (Is 11:1-5). With the fall of the monarchy the hope for a new Davidic king receded considerably, although Haggai attempted to revive it in the person of Zerubbabel, while Zechariah set beside him the priestly figure of Joshua, preluding to the later speculation on a priestly Messiah. The Maccabeans dreamt of restoring the monarchy in the light, it seems of Dt 17:14-20, but their main aim may have been ''the restoration of the institution of God's people'' (Hahn 140). In pre-Christian Jewish literature ''Son of David'' is attested as a Messianic title only in Ps Sol 17:21, but it designates regularly the expected national liberator in later rabbinical literature (compare Mk 11:10). It is noteworthy that the healing of the blind figures among the signs of the Messianic kingdom in ''Q'' (Lk 7:22 par.), obviously referring to Is 35:5. There seems to exist also a literary connection between Mk 10:46-52 and Is 42:18.

It is appropriate to mention here the episode in which Jesus, teaching in the temple, raised a debated issue with a question: "How can the scribes say that the Christ is the Son of David?" David himself in Ps 110:1 "calls him Lord; so how is he his son?" (Mk 12:35-37). As Schmid explains, the question should not be understood as Scriptural proof that the Messiah would *not* be a Son of David. "What Jesus says is this: If David himself sets the Messiah alongside of God, then the fact that the Messiah is a son of David cannot be uniquely significant or constitute his true identity as Messiah. He is more than a Son of David" (p. 228). The Davidic descent of the Messiah may have been a sort of embarrassment for the early Church, because of the nationalistic overtone this belief had in Judaism, but the fact remained, rooted in prophecies (see Mt 2:6) and in the accepted genealogy of Jesus himself. How the Church corrected the concept appears in Rm 1:3f (see Ch. 7): "In contrast to the Jewish expectation, Jesus was not enthroned at Easter in an earthly, political kingship, but in the heavenly, and therefore everlasting, Kingdom of God" (Schweizer 257).

"Nor the Son" (Mk 13:32)

At his baptism a voice from heaven described Jesus as "my beloved Son" (see above on Mk 1:11). "Son" used absolutely to designate Jesus occurs, besides, in the Markan tradition only by allusion in the parable of the Wicked Tenants, where a clear distinction is made between the servants and the "beloved son" (12:6), thus called probably under the influence of the baptism scene (1:11). In Matthew "the son" is singled out even more clearly (21:38). The invocation of God as *abba* in Mk 14:36 also attests Jesus' unique sonship, as it does in "Q" in the hymn of jubilation (Mt 11:27 par.). See more on these texts and others on the same theme in Ch. 4.

In both Matthew and Mark the statement on the Son's ignorance of the date of the *parousia* serves as transition to the exhortation to vigilance: these events no doubt will take place, but at a moment we cannot determine, so be on the alert always! If "this generation" of Mk 13:30 is taken to mean the contemporaries of Jesus, then *the ignorance of the time* of the *parousia* is only relative: noboby except the Father knows *the exact date*. More probably "this generation" refers to mankind under a certain aspect, mankind as unbelieving. In that case a period of indefinite length can separate the time of the earthly Jesus from the *parousia* of the Son of man. It must be admitted that the confession of ignorance of the date of the *parousia* appears strange after the emphatic utterance on the words that do not pass away. But the connection of these verses in our text may not be original. The difficulty of the statement was felt early: Luke omits it and some manuscripts of Mt 24:36 omit "not even the Son." A few authors see the statement of ignorance on the part of the Son as contradicting Mt 11:27 par. on the knowledge the Son has of the Father. This "Q" text does, however, also state that this knowledge is communicated only to those whom the Son chooses to reveal it. It may be that the date of the *parousia* does not belong to the knowledge he can reveal (see Ac 1:7).

If the designation "the Son" does not go back to Jesus himself, it must have originated from his known habit of addressing God as "Father." In fact, unlike "Son of God," "the Son" stands clearly in contrast to "the Father," as Mt 11:27 par. indicate. It means also subordination to the Father, at least in a certain sense: "When all things are subjected to him, then the Son himself will also be subjected to him who put all things under him, that God may be everything to everyone" (1 Cor 15:28). A commentator writes of this quite remarkable text: "The formula is thus designed to safeguard against a wild exaltation Christology which forgets the still awaited consummation and which timelessly makes Him who is enthroned at God's right hand a second God."[16]

Truly the Son of God (Mk 15:39)

Other texts could have been examined before this one, for example the important testimony of Jesus on himself in Mk 14:62. We leave this, however, for the following chapter, where it will come up appropriately for special treatment. A few other passion and resurrection texts from Mark relevant for Christology will be at least mentioned in Chs. 5 and 6, as parallels to Matthaean or Lucan texts.

The confession of the Roman centurion at the death of Jesus certainly comes as the Christological climax of Mark's gospel, in 15:39: "And when the centurion, who stood facing him, saw that he thus breathed his last, he said, 'Truly this man was the Son of God.' " It is not possible to be certain that the centurion actually pronounced these words. If he did, they might have been: "Truly this man was a son of God." Although the Greek text used allows this interpretation, Mark certainly understood "the Son of God," as in Mt 14:33; 27:40, 43; Lk 1:35; Jn 10:36. The possibility remains that the cry of the centurion belongs to dramatized dogma, the Roman soldier being for Mark a prototype of the future pagans who will accept the Christian faith. For W.E. Bundy, the voice of the centurion completes the dramatic presentation of Mark's dogma of the Son of God, like the scenes of Jesus' baptism and transfiguration, with a difference: the voice of confession now comes from the earthly scene and is man's response to the divine initiative (*Jesus and the First Three Gospels* 547).

According to Lk 23:47 the Roman officer "praised God," as if he were a prototype of Christian believers who glorify God for the wonderful salvation he has brought to his people (see 7:16). Also in Luke the centurion says: "Certainly this man was innocent!" This is historically more credible and could be more primitive than the "higher Christology" declaration in Mark. It also suits Luke's context well, since he insists on Jesus' innocence throughout his account of the trial (see 23:4, 14, 22). Luke may also have omitted the title "Son of God" at this place to avoid suggesting that Christ was a "demi-god" in the heathen sense. It can be added that in the third gospel no human confession of Jesus as Son of God is found. Perhaps Luke found the title too mysterious to be placed on the lips of ordinary human beings (George 224).

Conclusion

As was suggested earlier, Mark certainly intended to correct a false Christology, one that could lead to an erroneous notion of discipleship. For him, and for the common tradition he represents, there is no genuine following of Jesus except on the way of the cross (8:34). The concept of the glorious Son of man is not abandoned (13:36; 14:62), but the figure of a suffering Son of man is given particular prominence (8:31; 9:31; 10:33, 45). The secret of Jesus' divine sonship finally surfaces in Mark's story of the passion. In the parable of the Wicked Tenants this had been anticipated. Clearly "a beloved son" in 12:6 indicates that Jesus is meant, and the added quotation of Ps 118:22-23 shows unmistakably that the parable illustrates the fate of Jesus—rejected by man and vindicated by God: "The very stone which the builders rejected has become the head of the corner" (Mk 12:10). Accordingly, writes Kingsbury, "the cross is the place within Mark's story where the secret of Jesus' divine sonship comes to full disclosure" (*Jesus Christ* 37). In contrast to a Christology that would see Jesus primarily as a miracle-worker, "Mark emphasizes the point that one can truly see Him as the Son of God only if one understands that He shows Himself to be such in the passion, death and exaltation of the Son of Man" (*TDNT* 8, p. 379). Mark does report stories of mighty acts attributed to Jesus, but he forbids their proclamation before the passion and resurrection (messianic secret), for only in the light of these decisive events could the miracles be seen as signs of divine sonship and not as manifestations of a sort of magic power.

CHAPTER FOUR

THE PRE-EXISTENCE OF CHRIST AND HIS SELF-UNDERSTANDING

Rather than attempt a comprehensive treatment of these two difficult and far-reaching problems this chapter will present a sort of outline of the NT affirmation about them, together with appropriate reference to the exegetical and theological debate concerning the central issues. Although pre-existence and self-understanding in this context can be interrelated—a pre-existent Christ is more likely to have known who he was from the beginning—this will not be emphasized or even discussed at any length here. We will consider those problems as two different issues, and the NT texts regarding them rarely overlap. Secondly, I would like to note that I leave to Ch. 7 a more explicit presentation of the origin and doctrine of the early Christological hymns, some of which will be used here.

a) Christ Pre-existent

The Christian believers who accept without reservation that Christ should be identified as the second person of the Holy Trinity, face no particular problem in accepting his pre-existence as the Son of God, with the theological doctrine thus formulated: "Because the eternal Logos, begotten by the Father from all eternity, has become Man, the *Person* (traditionally conceived thus) who becomes man as Jesus Christ did not originate with the temporal beginning of Christ's human nature (body and soul), but was always in existence beforehand."[17] There exists NT evidence to support this, but it is not as compelling as some texts seem to suggest. Particularly difficult and debated is the proposition that pre-existence can be attributed to Jesus as man or as Son of man.

"First-Born of All Creation"

This title is taken of course from Col 1:15, from one of the Christological, probably pre-Pauline hymns (see 1:15-20) which will come up later for a more detailed study (see Ch. 7). In it the Son is first declared to be "the image of the invisible God," which can refer to man created in God's image (Gn 1:26), but in this context refers rather to Wisdom, which already in the Old Testament is seen as God's image (Ws 7:26), as active at creation, and even as having *pre-existed* to every creature (Pr 8:22-31). In this text, however, Wisdom seems to represent an aspect or activity of God rather than a pre-existent divine being distinct from God (see *Oxford Annotated Bible*).

"First-Born of all creation" reflects the special meaning attached to the "first-born" in Israel (see Ex 13:11-16), but also alludes again to Wisdom: "The Lord created me at the beginning of his work" (Pr 8:22), or "before all things else wisdom was created" (Si 1:4). Appropriating the Jewish speculation about Wisdom, early Christian writers applied it to Christ, on an even higher level. In the Christian hymn Christ's uniqueness is referred to, much more than his priority in time. The Christian confession expresses the universal validity of the Christ-event (Lohse 50; title in n. 28), and Paul echoes this where he states that there is "one Lord, Jesus Christ, through whom are all things and through whom we exist" (1 Cor 8:6). This verse itself could be a quotation from an earlier source, and "very possibly the earliest statement of belief in

the pre-existence of Christ'' (Dunn 179). I cannot be sure, however, that Dunn is correct, when he later writes that for Paul
''Christ is being identified here not with a pre-existent being but
with the creative power and action of God'' (p. 182). As I have
indicated elsewhere (RSB 1983, p. 113), Dunn tends to minimize
in several key texts their affirmation of Christ's pre-existence. He
can thus claim that the Johannine writings for the first time contain
''the understanding of Jesus' sonship in terms of the personal
pre-existence of a divine being who was sent into the world and
whose ascension was simply the continuation of an intimate relationship with the Father which neither incarnation nor crucifixion
interrupted or disturbed'' (p. 59).

The pre-existence of Christ seems presupposed also in other
texts which associate him with the original creation of the world.
Thus the statement in Heb 1:2 that God created the world through
the Son matches that of Jn 1:3 which says that through the Word all
things were made. It is well known that the Christology of the
exordium of Hebrews has close affinities with that of the prologue
of John. At the origin of John's assertion can be seen the affirmation of the beginning of Genesis that God created everything
through his word. This was developed further with the help of the
Wisdom passages referred to above, and the formulation shows the
influence of Philo's speculation on the Logos. Schnackenburg
summarizes thus the end result: ''The Logos-hymn, like Heb
1:10ff., transfers God's creative activity to the *pre-existing* Christ,
but the use of the concept of Logos safeguards the truth that God is
the Creator, who called all things into being through his 'Word' ''
(*The Gospel According to St. John*, vol. 1, p. 238).

Pre-existent Son of God

Possibly, Hebrews is ''the first of the NT writings to have
embraced the specific thought of a pre-existent divine sonship''
(Dunn 55). However, for Dunn the concept of pre-existence in

Hebrews seems to have emerged "more as a corollary to the author's Platonic idealism than as a firm christological perception. It would certainly go beyond our evidence to conclude that the author has attained to the understanding of God's Son as having had a real personal pre-existence" (55f). Real pre-existence seems, however, presupposed by the statement that God brought his first-born into the world (1:6), "for whom and by whom all things exist" (2:10), and that Christ entered into the world at a point of time (10:5).

For John the pre-existence of Christ is an indisputable fact. It is affirmed in the Prologue and also in the testimony of John the Baptist: "After me comes a man who ranks before me, for he was before me" (1:30). In the Fourth Gospel Jesus clearly affirms his own pre-existence: "Truly, truly, I say to you, before Abraham was, I am" (8:58). The important *egô eimi* ("I am") formula will be discussed in Ch. 10. A statement like Jn 8:58 does not come as a surprise in John, for whom Christ's pre-existence, both as Logos and as Son, is a possessed revealed truth. In contrast to John the Baptist, who could only say "he was before me" (Jn 1:15, 30), "Jesus speaks in the present, which places him in God's existence beyond time, in his eternal present" (Schnackenburg, vol. 2, p. 223).

The Logos is no longer mentioned outside the Prologue, for the main reason, we can suppose, that in his gospel proper John describes the teaching and actions of the Logos incarnate, Jesus Christ. In John Jesus refers to his pre-existence also in the figure of the Son of man, who will return to the place he was before (6:62). Although several points on this subject are disputed, it would seem that pre-Christian Jewish apocalyptic knew of a pre-existent Son of man. Some authors see a connection between the Son of man and the Primordial Man of ancient oriental myth (see on this the end of the Introduction). Judaism, however, as Mowinckel observes, "was completely unaware that the Son of man was really the Primordial man. What it had to say about the Primordial Man was connected with the biblical figure of Adam as he is presented in the rabbinic legend of Adam'' (p. 346). Biblical pre-existence should not be confused with a certain kind of Gnostic pre-existence. They belong to two different worlds of thought, as Schnackenburg has explained (vol. 1, pp. 500-3). In Gnosticism, pre-existence has little temporal connotation; it is referred to mainly to designate the particular nature of the Gnostic man, as in the *Gospel of Thomas*, ''Jesus said: Blessed is he who was before he became'' (log. 19), or the *Gospel of Philip*, ''The Lord said, Blessed is he who is before he came into being. For he who is, both was and shall be'' (log. 57).

Whereas John fills the time between the incarnation and the death of Jesus, with a description of his activity on earth, the early hymn to Christ of Ph 2:6-11 retains only the movement from pre-existence to glory through incarnation and obedient death (more generally on the hymn see Ch. 7). ''Though he was in the form of God'' quite clearly refers to pre-existence. The present participle *huparchón* can mean simply ''being,'' but its more precise sense is ''being from the beginning,'' from all eternity, if it is referred to God. *NEB* does not translate literally, but could render correctly the meaning of the main part of vs. 6: ''For the divine nature was his from the first; yet he did not think to snatch at equality with God, but made himself nothing, assuming the nature of a slave.'' Some commentators do not, however, take for granted that pre-existence is referred to in Ph 2:6 (see Dunn 114). If no pre-existence is involved, then the text can point to an Adam Christology: whereas Adam, made in the image of God, lost his share in God's glory through his disobedience, Christ did not unduly prize his equality with God, but outwardly discarded it to appear as a slave, and accept death in obedience to the Father. More probably, however, Christ's *kenosis*, according to Ph 2:6-8, took place in two stages: the first was the incarnation, the second his death as the suffering Servant of God.

The Son Who was Sent

Jesus is described as the Son sent into the world particularly in the Fourth Gospel, where the idea is mentioned 24 times with the verb *pempein* (see 4:34; 5:24), and at least 15 times with the verb *apostellein*, as in 8:42 and 10:36. The following is also typically Johannine: "In this the love of God was made manifest among us, that God sent his only Son into the world, so that we might live through him" (1 Jn 4:9). To this can be compared Jn 3:17: "For God sent the Son into the world, not to condemn the world, but that the world might be saved through him."

The sending of the Son clearly involves pre-existence in John, but the case is not so clear in other NT writings. In Ph 2:6-11 Christ seems to come into the world on his own decision (see also Heb 10:7). In Gal 4:4, as in John, it is God who sends forth his Son, to redeem those who were under the law. It is possible, of course, to argue that pre-existence is not affirmed in Gal 4:4, but perhaps Dunn overstates the case when he writes: "It is evident from this that *exapostellein* when used of God does not tell us anything about the origin or point of departure of the one sent; it underlines the heavenly origin of his *commissioning* but not of the one commissioned. So far as its use in Gal 4:4 is concerned therefore all we can say is that Paul's readers would most probably think simply of one sent by divine commission" (p. 39). It does not do to equate the sending of the Son in Gal 4:4 with the allusion to the same in Jesus' own words of the Markan tradition (Mk 9:37; 12:6), where commissioning can simply be meant. For in Gal 4:4 as in Rm 8:3 a new meaningful element is involved. "But the motif of the sending of the Son of God receives an entirely new accent the moment it is associated with the idea of the incarnation, for thereby it is related to the conception of pre-existence" (Hahn 304).

Comparison with Gal 4:4, Jn 3:16f, 1 Jn 4:9, Käsemann believes, suggests that Rm 8:3 can be "a liturgical statement which describes the incarnation of the pre-existent Son of God as the salvation of the world'' (*Romans* 216): ''God sent his own Son in the likeness of sinful flesh and as an expiatory sacrifice, condemning sin in the flesh'' (Rm 8:3). Käsemann correctly understands *kai peri hamartias* in terms of ''expiatory sacrifice,'' confirming in fact the position on this I took several years ago (see Lyonnet 249f). ''In the likeness of sinful flesh'' refers particularly to humanity as condemned to die because of sin (see Rm 5:12-14), therefore as mortal, and this is strikingly similar to the statement of Ph 2:7, where we are told that Christ ''emptied himself, taking the form of a servant, being born in the likeness of men.'' In both verses are combined pre-existence, incarnation, sacrifice.

With a view to 1 Cor 8:6, and other texts, it seems possible to assert that Paul took for granted the notion of the pre-existence of Christ, basing himself ''on a Jewish exegetical tradition which had no knowledge of a redeemer-myth, but had a strongly developed doctrine on the Wisdom of God'' (Schweizer 69; see title in Booknote 17). The ''spiritual rock'' which followed the Israelites in the desert (1 Cor 10:4) is obviously for Paul a symbol of the pre-existent Christ already present among the Israelites. Philo had already referred the rock to Wisdom, for example in his *Allegory of the Law* (II, 86).

The Elthon-Sayings

In several Gospel sayings Jesus uses the past verb *êlthon*, ''I came,'' to express the origin of his saving mission in the world. Where authentic, these sayings could reflect Jesus' consciousness of his own pre-existence. In his book on the subject (see Booknote 17), E. Arens would consider Lk 12:49 as authentic, at least as echoing the voice itself of Christ, if not his very words: ''I came to cast fire upon the earth; and would that it were already kindled.'' In this connection W. Bundy writes: ''Verse 49 has the transcendental and superhistorical implications involved in all the 'I came' utterances'' (*Jesus and the First Three Gospels*, p. 364). Also Mt 11:19 would be authentic, since the Church could hardly have formulated such an uncomplimentary statement on Jesus: "The Son of man *came* eating and drinking, and they say, 'Behold, a glutton and a drunkard' " (see Arens 243, 345). Pre-existence in the case of Jesus is not necessarily excluded by the fact that in vs. 18 *êlthen*, "came," occurs also for John the Baptist. The verb is secondarily applied to John, primarily to Jesus, probably with a broader meaning than simply pointing to the commission he received for his public ministry. For Arens Mk 2:17b and Mt 10:34b are doubtfully authentic, while other *êlthon*-sayings are to be considered inauthentic. These remarks are valuable indications, even if particular cases can be disputed.

In his analysis of the Gospel "I"-Sayings, Bultmann claims that the *êlthon*-sayings are "under suspicion of being Church products because this terminology seems to be the means of its looking back to the historical appearance of Jesus as a whole" (*History* 155). There is an echo of this in Käsemann's claim that the sayings "look back over and sum up the finished work of Jesus . . . and cannot therefore originate with the earthly Jesus but make the voice of the exalted Lord heard through a prophetic mouth."[18] J. Schneider's more moderate view must be closer to the truth: "Some of the *êlthon*-sayings were perhaps given their final form by the community, but we should not be so sceptical as to say that they have no connection with Jesus. . . . They derive from the Messianic self-awareness of Jesus and are to be explained thereby" (*TDNT* 2, p. 668). In themselves the *êlthon*-sayings do not necessarily refer to pre-existence, but they can be interpreted in that sense in the light of other indications that do quite clearly point to the reality of pre-existence.

A Pre-existent Jesus?

At the beginning of this section I have referred to the traditional view, for which Christ pre-existed as the divine person who has assumed in time a human nature in Jesus. In a recent article P.

Benoit has proposed that other views on the subject should not be excluded. He writes, for example, summing up his own opinion: ''We have understood that before thrusting himself into our human time, Jesus already existed wholly, man and God, in a time which is sovereignly real, distinct from ours without being for all that the pure eternity of God.''[19]

Before discussing Benoit's opinion, let us call our readers' attention to some texts which he brings forth, in addition to those I have already referred to. Among the *êlthon*-sayings the following can also be singled out. In them Jesus says he ''came out'' to proclaim the Gospel (Mk 1:38), to call sinners to repentance (2:17), and the Son of man ''came'' to give his life as a ransom for many (10:45). The pre-existence of Jesus is directly implied where he says: ''Moses wrote of me'' (Jn 5:46), or when the evangelist explains that Isaiah ''saw his glory and spoke of him'' (12:41). One particularly interesting text is 2 Cor 8:9: ''For you know the grace of our Lord Jesus Christ, that though he was rich, yet for your sake he became poor, so that by his poverty you might become rich.'' This verse, which could depend on a pre-Pauline source, seems to allude directly to the incarnation, and also perhaps to the cross, like Ph 2:7, with which it has obvious affinities. Finally, one could adduce texts that present Christ's coming as a ''manifestation,'' like the first words of an early Christian hymn preserved in 1 Tm 3:16: ''He was revealed in the flesh.'' For M. Dibelius and H. Conzelmann, *the pre-existence concept* ''does not necessarily belong to the *epiphany schema* as an essential element, but is by nature easily combined with it'' (*The Pastoral Epistles*, p. 63). To a similar context belong Tt 2:11; 3:4, and also 1 P 1:20: ''Predestined before the foundation of the world, he was made manifest in this last period of time for your sake'' (*NEB*).

In *Euntes Docete* 1974 A. Contri has presented quite an impressive documentation on the issue of Christ's pre-existence, including some biblical and patristic evidence, as well as present-day opinions. Contri defends Benoit's position, and doing this he also describes objections raised against it (pp. 301-3). It is asked, for example: How can the pre-existing Christ be both creator and creature? If Jesus pre-existed in the sense proposed by Benoit, how can he be said to be a *man like us* (Ph 2:7; Heb 2:17; 4:15)? These two objections can be in fact raised also against the traditional understanding of the mystery of Christ. More to the point perhaps is the difficulty of positing two natures in Christ *before the hypostatic union took place through the assumption by the Word of the human nature*. In favor of Benoit can be adduced the fact that in the Old Testament, Wisdom appears to be both created and in some way creating (see Ch. 4 below). The type of time proposed by Benoit appears pure speculation, but we know very little about conditions of life outside the created world. Benoit seems to assign to Christ a pre-existent life which is the privilege of the *risen*. It does not seem impossible, however, to think of a unique mode of being for a person unique from so many other angles. The discussion could continue. Finally, I am inclined to state that Benoit's proposal is unnecessary, and seems, besides, to raise more problems than it solves. It deserves, however, to be taken seriously and to be the object of further study.

b) Jesus' Self-understanding

A lot is being written on the Christology of the New Testament, on the way in which the early Church understood Christ. This early Church Christology is of course often expressed also in *sayings attributed to Jesus himself*, be it in "Q" or in the Synoptic or Markan tradition. In the Fourth Gospel the discourses of Jesus reflect in great part John's understanding of the Son of God worshipped in the Church, although some sections of the Johannine discourses can go back to Jesus himself in his earthly life. It does not seem well founded to claim, as some authors do, that it is not possible to go back beyond the mediation of the early Church in

Christology, that the relevant sayings of Jesus simply only show that primitive Christology retrojected Jesus' Messiahship into the consciousness of the historical Christ. In this section we will attempt to show that some texts do tell us something of Jesus' own self-understanding. The appropriateness of this type of research does not have to be demonstrated. In Pannenberg's words, "Christology cannot avoid the question of Jesus' self-consciousness, however difficult it may be exegetically and historically."[20]

Four Sayings in Mark

A well-known biblist, Joseph Coppens, has devoted more than ten years of the latter part of his life to the investigation of Messiahship, especially as applied to Christ. In a book published posthumously (1981),[21] he has carefully formulated six criteria (see *CBQ* 1983, p. 309), which, he believed, allowed him to single out as *ipsissima verba Jesu*, as authentic words of the historical Jesus, four sayings preserved in Mark: 8:29; 9:12; 13:26; 14:62 (see p. 143). The examination of these texts will come first in our present investigation.

Mk 8:29 relates to the Caesarea Philippi episode, which clearly raises a Christological issue. It can hardly be doubted that Jesus did actually put this question to the disciples: "Who do men say that I am?" If so, he certainly understood himself as endowed with a special vocation, as placed before God and his fellowmen in a special relation to them. He does not deny being "the Christ," in reaction to Peter's words, he only forbids the disciples to declare it publicly. As Lambrecht and others have shown, the Caesarea confession as a whole does reflect Christological issues debated in the early Church. In particular, the title "Christ" appeared ambiguous to Mark, and had to be given a deeper and more precise meaning. For this reason the confession marks a turning-point in Jesus' ministry: from now on he will more clearly define his mission in the light of the Servant prophecies, as Mk 10:45 openly testifies. What interests us here is that Jesus in the middle of his public mission on earth revealed his awareness of the fact that his person and his deeds invited speculation on his true identity hiding behind the name "Son of man" which he used to designate himself.

After the transfiguration came the disciples' question: "Why do the scribes say that first Elijah must come?" Jesus answered: "Elijah does come first to restore all things; and how is it written of the Son of man, that he should suffer many things and be treated with contempt?" W. Manson wrote of this saying (Mk 9:12): "It has the rugged and irreducible form of an original oracle" (p. 129). This prophecy, like parts of 8:31; 9:31; 10:45, does not refer to concrete details from the passion narrative and as such does not qualify as a *vaticinium ex eventu*. The saying as a whole, and the reference to contempt in particular (see Is 53:3), point to the suffering figure of the Servant, as R.H. Fuller also admits (p. 56). On God's side, writes Michaelis, the fate of Jesus is that "he should suffer many things," on man's side that he "be treated with contempt" (p. 914). The same combination of the two ideas appears also in Lk 17:25 and goes back to a very early date, probably to Jesus himself. However, because of its Greek form the saying should be said to have a dominical origin, rather than be a dominical saying, which, on the other hand, applies well to what we find in Mk 9:31, par.: "The Son of man will be delivered into the hands of men," a more Semitic formulation of the prophecy. Both verbs *exoudenesthai*, "be despised" (Mk 9:12), and *apodokimasthênai*, "be rejected" (Lk 17:25), can also be referred to Ps 118:22 (Boismard 255). In any case, these authentic sayings point to Jesus' deep understanding of his mission in terms of the Suffering Servant of God.

After a Son of man saying with no particular reference, and one connected with Jesus' passion, we have two sayings relating to the Son of man in glory, obviously reflecting the language of Dn 7:13.

The first of these occurs in Mark's little apocalypse: "And then they will see the Son of man coming in clouds with great power and glory" (Mk 13:26). "They" here is an indefinite plural, which does not refer to any group of persons in particular (in French read "on verra"). It is not the place here to demonstrate that when Jesus speaks of the Son of man, he is not referring to a third person, but to himself, even in Lk 12:8 (see Mt 10:32; Mk 8:38).

It is not the purpose of Mark 13 to describe chronologically a series of events that will take place in the future. It is rather to give a new meaning to the end of history expected in apocalyptic. There is hope in suffering, for nothing happens unless ordained by God. In the end what really matters is that God will reveal his power in the appearance of the Son of man. In this "collection of various bits of tradition combined by the editor" in Mk 13 (Schweizer 276), the early Church says what underlies her strength at the hour of trial: the firm expectation of the return of Christ as the glorious Son of man. In spite of Coppens' assurance we must reckon with the possibility that Mk 13:26 does not go back to Jesus himself. It would seem, writes C. Colpe, that Mk 13:24-27 "do not go back to the oldest tradition but have been added by the Jewish Christian community" (p. 450). The first part of Mt 24:30 cannot, on the other hand, because of its obscurity, be assigned to the Church: "Then the sign of the Son of man will appear in the sky, and then all the tribes of the earth will mourn, and they will see the Son of man coming on the clouds of heaven with power and great glory." It has its origin in an authentic saying of Jesus, which clearly points to his consciousness of being God's envoy, whose mission would find its final achievement in the world to come.

The last of the four texts, supposedly authentic, comes from Jesus' trial before the Sanhedrin. To the high priest's question, "Are you the Christ, the Son of the Blessed?" Jesus answered: "I am; and you will see the Son of man sitting at the right hand of Power, and coming with the clouds of heaven" (Mk 14:62). Although Jesus does not deny being the Messiah, he gives to the title a new interpretation: "Jesus thus professes messiahship and divine sonship in that he speaks of his eschatological office and of his appointment to the dignity and power of the one who, appearing in splendor, brings salvation" (Hahn 285).

It is instructive to compare Mk 14:62 with the simpler version of Luke: "From now on the Son of man shall be seated at the right hand of the power" (Lk 22:69). In this form the saying has a better claim to authenticity, since it is much less dependent on Dn 7:13. "We simply have a judgment scene in heaven in which the Son of man sits beside the supreme Judge" (Colpe 435). It can be claimed, however, with Casey (p. 184), and other commentators, that it is Luke who has deleted "coming with the clouds of heaven," in order to refer the saying to the present exaltation of the risen Christ. But Luke does refer to the parousia in other texts (Lk 12:40; 18:8; 21:27; Ac 1:9). In its Lucan form the statement can be referred also to Ps 110:1, where the enemies of him who sits at God's right hand are subdued under his feet. Again, in whatever form, the saying reflects Jesus' own awareness of having been called to fulfill the prophecies concerning a transcendent figure who would mediate divine salvation.

Son of the Father

Only in one NT text is Jesus explicitly called "the Son of the Father," in 2 Jn 3, although in a large number of passages, particularly in the Fourth Gospel, Jesus himself calls God his Father (see Jn 17).

Any study on Jesus' self-understanding has to take into account his baptism by John (see Ch. 3, "The Father's Beloved Son"). Bultmann himself admits the historical character of Jesus' baptism (see Mk 1:9-11 and Mt 3:16-17), although for him the gospel report takes the form of a biographical legend (p. 247). Before him, Dibelius had noted that at least originally the passage was "the story of a divine adoption," although Mark "by no means understands that Jesus only became at this point what he had not hitherto been'' (p. 231). The literary analyses of the origin and composition of the reports on Jesus' baptism agree on the substance of the message: at the beginning of his public life Jesus received, if not the knowledge, certainly the confirmation of his prophetic calling (see Ac 10:38). In Ezk 1:1 and Rv 4:1, the opening of heaven is part of the apocalyptic imagery; it signifies that the seer has access to the secrets of the divine mysteries. At Jesus' baptism the opening or the rending of heaven means that the communication between heaven and earth is re-established, that the Spirit of God can truly descend upon the earth and settle there in perpetuity, first on Jesus (see Jn 1:33), who is the representative *par excellence* of the true people of God.

The Hymn of Jubilation and Other Texts

Jesus quite rarely reveals in the Synoptic gospels his inner sentiments. One exception is the so-called ''hymn of jubilation,'' reported in both Matthew (11:25-27) and Luke (10:21-22). In this ''Q'' text Jesus expresses his thanksgiving to God, whom he calls ''Father,'' as in Luke's version of the Lord's Prayer (11:2), and in the prayer of Gethsemane, with the original *abba* preserved (Mk 14:36). By invoking God under this title Jesus manifests his own consciousness of enjoying a personal and absolutely unique relationship with God, of being closely united with him as with his Father. If ''no one knows the Father except the Son,'' Jesus' teaching is revelation, the ultimate and definite revelation (see Marchel 167). For A.M. Hunter, the fact that God is Jesus' Father in the proper sense ''is the final secret of the work and ministry of Jesus'' (p. 43).

The consciousness Jesus had that with him the kingdom of heaven was revealed, in fact made present, appears in several texts. He told his disciples, according to Mark: ''To you has been given the secret of the kingdom of God, but to those outside everything is in parables'' (4:11). This becomes in Matthew, with the probable influence of Dn 2:28-29: ''To you it has been given *to know the secrets* of the kingdom of heaven, but to them it has not been given'' (13:11). Always in Matthew, Jesus adds afterwards: ''Blessed are your eyes, for they see, and your ears, for they hear'' (13:16). Another important text belongs to the Beelzebul controversy, which is generally recognized to be founded on an historical episode: ''But if it is by the Spirit of God that I cast out demons, then the kingdom of God has come upon you'' (Mt 12:28). In another ''Q'' text Jesus had given the disciples of John two signs which implicitly testified that he was ''he who is to come'': the miraculous cures he performed and the fact that the Gospel was being preached to the poor (Lk 7:18-23 par.). Jesus also claimed absolute authority in his teaching, and set himself above Solomon, the temple, the Sabbath, Scripture itself, and the angels (see lists of texts in Schmid 162-5, about ''the self-consciousness of Jesus according to the Synoptic gospels''). Most of the texts referred to by Kieffer in his study ''A Christology of Superiority in the Synoptic Gospels'' are sayings of Jesus that have a claim to authenticity. On the authenticity and relevance of the *egô eimi*, ''I am,'' sayings, see Galot 55-75.

Regarding again the hymn of jubilation, older form critics tended to deny, for a variety of reasons, the authenticity of Mt 11:27 par., judging that Jesus could not have described himself absolutely as the Son, and that the logion should be ascribed to a Johannine source, that is, to later theological reflection. It is true that the knowledge of the Father by the Son is a well attested Johannine theme (Jn 14:7; 15:15; 17:25), but this is not a sufficient reason to exclude that the development it represents could have originated in a genuine revelation of Jesus himself. In fact, in another Synoptic text, which is generally recognized as reporting an authentic saying of Jesus, we find the Son mentioned absolutely in connection with ''the Father'': ''But of that day no one knows, not even the angels in heaven, nor the Son, but only the Father''

(Mk 13:32). To this significant evidence other texts could be added, including the baptismal formula of Mt 28:19. As a matter of fact a connection can hardly be denied between Mt 11:27-30 and 28:18-20. In the first text the entire revelation is given to the Son, in the second the entire *exousia*, the spiritual "power."

Conclusion

The New Testament expresses Christ's pre-existence in a number of ways: he is the First-Born of all creation; his unique divine Sonship sets him before and above all created beings; as the Logos he appears co-eternal with the Father in John's prologue; as the One Sent he is represented as having existed before the incarnation. The same conclusion can be drawn from Jesus' own *êlthon*, "I came," sayings. The manner of this pre-existence remains mysterious. It appears difficult to accept the view that Jesus pre-existed both as a human being and as a divine person.

With regard to Jesus' own self-understanding, several texts show that he saw his mission as fulfilling that of the Servant of God, his destiny as best expressed in the Danielic Son of man figure, and his personal relationship with God, as of a Son to his Father. He claimed to have divine authority both to forgive sins, to reveal God's will, and to perform by his own power miracles and exorcisms, which were signs of the advent of God's kingdom. Minimal without doubt, but true, is the following assertion: "Jesus must thus have been conscious of a unique position among his contemporaries, which he may have expressed by accepting the title of Messiah or, alternatively, by applying to himself the image of the heavenly Son of Man—two categories each connoting a human being called to be God's special servant and agent on earth" (Hick 173, see Booknote 21).

CHAPTER FIVE

CHRISTOLOGY IN THE LUCAN WRITINGS

Luke generally remains dependent on the common tradition for his interpretation of Christ. However, he does independently underline some Christological traits. These we will examine in connection with some specifically Lucan texts taken from the third gospel and Acts. For a more comprehensive survey of Luke's Christology and soteriology see the Introduction to my commentary on the third gospel.

He Will Be Called "Son of God" (Lk 1:35)

In vs. 32 "the Son of the Most High" refers rather to Messianic sonship (2 S 7:14; Ps 2:7) and is applied to Jesus as the descendant of David. In 1:35 "Son of God" should probably be understood in a transcendent sense, as it comes after a statement on the power of God at work: "The Holy Spirit will come upon you, and the power of the Most High will overshadow you; therefore the child to be born will be called holy, the Son of God." This *RSV* translation seems better founded than the other one, also possible: "Hence, the holy offspring (or child) to be born will be called Son of God." The term *hagion*, "holy," denotes an exclusive appurtenance to God and could figure among the earliest designations of the divinity of Jesus (see also Ac 3:14; 4:27, 30). Unlike Matthew (14:33;

16:16; 27:54) and Mark (15:39), Luke does not attribute to any man the confession of the title "Son of God," but apart from the angelic message it is found in statements of demons (4:41; 8:28) and of Jesus himself (equivalently 10:22). Apparently, for Luke the title "Son of God" was too mysterious for the confession of earthly beings, and perhaps too ambiguous for a Greek readership. In Mk 15:39 the centurion calls Jesus "Son of God," in Luke he declares: "Certainly this man was innocent" (23:47).

Differently from Matthew, Luke places the genealogy after Jesus' baptism and extends it to Adam himself, who is called "son of God" (3:38). Jesus is not the Son of God because he was son of Adam—this is true of all men—but Adam's divine origin did in a mysterious way foreshadow the figure of Jesus. See more on this in Ch. 8, about Rm 5:14 and 1 Cor 15:45-49. In 1:35 Luke made it clear that Jesus had his divine sonship by birth through the operation of the Holy Spirit, embodiment of God's powerful presence in Mary. It would be a mistake, however, to imagine that Christ could be both God and man only if he was conceived miraculously. The verb *episkiazein*, "overshadow," used in the annunciation to Mary also occurs in the transfiguration story, in connection with God's special presence (Lk 9:34 par.). Lyonnet has argued quite convincingly that if Mary's womb was to become God's tabernacle, as the angel's words seem to imply, then her child would be Son of God in a transcendent sense.[22]

Lk 1:35 can also be compared with the primitive confession preserved in Rm 1:3f, which refers to the Gospel of God "concerning his Son, who was descended from David according to the flesh and designated Son of God in power according to the Spirit of holiness by his resurrection from the dead, Jesus Christ our Lord." What Lk 1:35 says of the incarnation is seen here connected with Christ's resurrection. For Paul, as for the New Testament in general, Jesus was indeed Son of God by birth, but with the resurrection this privilege, kept relatively hidden during the *kenosis* period, blazed forth with Jesus' glorification (cf. Ph 2:6-

11), and now he appeared as the Son of God "in power" through "the Spirit of holiness."

"A Savior, Who Is Christ Lord" (Lk 2:11)

In his redaction of the angelic message to the shepherds Luke has put together three Christological titles which reflect the faith of the early Church. The combination *Christos Kyrios*, "Christ Lord," without articles, occurs nowhere else in the New Testament. But perhaps the original reading was *Christos Kyriou*, "the anointed of the Lord," as in 2:26. If retained as the better attested reading, *Christos Kyrios* can be translated "Christ (and) Lord," the second title having been added to elucidate the first for non-Jewish readers. There may be more than a coincidence in the fact that we find the same three titles in Ph 3:20: from heaven "we await a Savior, the Lord Jesus Christ."

On Luke's tendency to use "Lord" to designate Jesus already in his public ministry, see below on Lk 19:31. The Lucan understanding of "Christ" will be examined in connection with Ac 2:36. The title *sôtêr*, "Savior," occurs only here in Luke, is found neither in Mark nor Matthew (but see Mt 1:21), and appears only once in the Fourth Gospel (4:42). But John did write to the communities of Asia: "And we have seen and testify that the Father has sent his Son as the Savior of the World" (1 Jn 4:14).

Three texts of the Greek OT assign the title of "saviors" to the liberators of Israel known as "Judges" (Jg 3:9, 15; Ne 9:27). Although Scripture does not call Moses "savior," the role assigned to him by God is certainly that of a savior. If the function of "Savior" is rarely attributed to the Messiah (see Zc 9:9 LXX), it is doubtless due to the OT custom of reserving the title and role of "Savior" to *God Himself*, a custom followed by the majority of books, especially Isaiah (see 12:2; 45:21f) and the Psalms (see 60:1f LXX).

In the religious literature of Hellenism gods or supermen receive the title *sôtêr*, when they deliver mankind from temporal evils such as sickness or public catastrophes. Mystery religions also grant this title to the divinity that wins immortality, while the deified sovereign is most often called "Savior" and also frequently *Kyrios*, "Lord." However, the Christian use of the title "Savior" owes its origin to three chief factors: Old Testament usage, the name of Jesus, the advent of Messianic salvation.

The fact that Christ is called *Savior* especially in *the more recent* NT works has been explained in different ways. Would it indicate opposition to Jewish hopes for the coming of a political "savior" (see Jn 6:15)? In the spiritual sphere, Qumran testifies, Jesus' contemporaries awaited the advent of *a master of doctrine* and persisted in considering God as the only possible Savior. Perhaps, too, pagan religious use of the title delayed its Christian usage. One thing is certain: because the name *Jesus* means "Savior" in Hebrew and Aramaic (see Mt 1:21), this *title* was to know only a limited diffusion in Palestine. It is equally clear that the title *Sôtêr* was applied to Jesus only in a postpaschal climate when belief in his divinity was openly expressed. So we should not be surprised that the two titles, *Sôtêr* and *Kyrios*, are often associated, as in the nativity account, and especially in the Second Epistle of Peter (1:11; 2:20; 3:2). This literary juxtaposition also appears in the single Pauline text which applies the title "Savior" to Christ before the Pastoral Epistles, that is, in Ph 3:20 which speaks of eschatological salvation, to be wrought at Christ's parousia.

The New Testament, Luke in particular, transferred the title of "Savior" from God to Jesus. In the *Magnificat* Mary exclaims: "My spirit exults in God my Savior" (Lk 1:47), while the angel tells the shepherds that a Savior/Lord is born to them (2:11). The transfer affirms "that God has determined to make available in Jesus the deliverance, or salvation, that otherwise only he can accomplish" (Kingsbury, *Jesus Christ* 99). The following question does provide the basic reason for which true spiritual salvation can only come from God: "Who can forgive sins but God alone?" (Mk 2:7).

"I Must Be In My Father's House" (Lk 2:49)

The first words of Jesus recorded in the Gospel are found in the answer to Mary's question in the temple: "He said to them, 'How is it that you sought me? Did you not know that I must be in my Father's house?' " Taken literally the Greek *en tois tou patros mou*, "in the (things) of my Father," seems at first sight better rendered in *The Jerusalem Bible*: "Did you not know that I must be busy with my Father's affairs?"[23] But the neuter plural, to be supposed here, of the definite article is certainly attested with a special meaning in the Septuagint of Jb 18:19, "Strangers will dwell in his place (*en tois autou*)," and of Esther 7:9, "A gallows has been set up in the premises of Aman (*en tois Aman*)," while "an important parallel" (Brown 476) is found in Josephus' *Against Apion* (I, 118): "in the place (temple) of Zeus (*en tois tou Dios*)." In English the word "house" has to be supplied, but the situation itself suggests it, as well as the texts where God calls the temple "my house" (Lk 19:46) or Jesus speaks of "my Father's house" (Jn 2:16), of "the house of God" (Lk 6:4). External support for the translation "in my Father's house" comes from several ancient versions (Syriac, Armenian, Persian), from the Greek Church Fathers, and many Latin Fathers, following Augustine. However, the Vulgate had a different influence with "*in his quae Patris mei sunt*," "in the things which are my Father's."

Lk 2:49 is the only text in which Jesus is reported to have called God his Father in the presence of Joseph himself, although of course he does make the same claim also elsewhere (10:22; 22:29; Jn 20:17). In addition, we find here in Lk 2:49 the first occurrence of *dei*, "must," in the mouth of Jesus, a "necessity," then, which Luke particularly emphasizes: Jesus in Luke sees his whole life, activity, and particularly his passion as unfolding in the light of

God's will comprehended in a *dei*. In Lk 2:49-50 the misunderstanding of Jesus' parents does not concern his divine sonship, in some way already revealed to them, but the manner in which that sonship finds expression: the Father's "must" which calls Jesus away from family obligations. In Brown's view (p. 492), "the answer of Jesus in Jn 2:4 and Lk 2:49 anticipates the kind of statement found in the heart of the ministry in Mk 3:31-35 when his mother and brothers came seeking him: 'Whoever does the will of God is my brother and sister and mother.'"

"No Prophet is Acceptable in His Own Country" (Lk 4:24)

In the episode of Jesus' rejection in Nazareth, proper to Luke (4:16-30), perhaps an explicit Christological statement is lacking, but Jesus appears there clearly as endowed with a prophetical mission, even more explicitly than at his baptism (see on Mk 1:11 in Ch. 3). Luke attached great importance to this episode, which he considered programmatic and as inaugurating effectively the new period of salvation history in the middle of time. The story serves as a prefiguration of the rejection of the Gospel by the Jews and its acceptance by the Gentiles. The account seems to be a literary conflation with a double teaching. "The fulfillment-story stresses the success of his teaching under the guidance of the Spirit, but the rejection story symbolizes the opposition that his ministry will evoke among his own" (Fitzmyer, *Luke* 529).

"Today this scripture has been fulfilled in your hearing" (Lk 4:21) reflects quite explicitly Lucan themes, connected with some aspects of the theology of Deuteronomy. This is true, of course, of the "today" in salvation history (see also Lk 2:1; 19:9; 23:43, and Dt 8:11). The "today" theme is coherent with Luke's tendency to actualize eschatology, to see salvation fulfilled in Christ's ministry. "In your hearing" renders the Greek "in your ears," which Lagrange suggests, would mean "under your eyes." But "hearing" is important for Luke, because he insists so much, like

Deuteronomy, on the theology of the spoken word, as also Paul did (see Rm 10:14-18).

By quoting from Is 61:1f Jesus presents his own preaching ministry as prophetical. Isaiah 61 relates the vocation of a prophet who has received from God a message of consolation for Israel. The poem recalls the Servant Songs, especially Is 50:4-11. The occurrence in vs. 1 of the verb *euaggelisasthai*, "evangelize," made the passage very appropriate in the mouth of Christ inaugurating the preaching of the Gospel. Although Luke avoids using in his gospel the noun *euaggelion*, he often uses the verb "evangelize," in both the gospel and Acts (on the concept "evangelize the poor" see *Religious Studies Bulletin* 1981, pp. 101-9). Of particular interest is the expression "to evangelize the kingdom of God" (Lk 4:43; 8:1). In contrast to what we find in Matthew, the Kingdom is not in Luke the epitome of the good news; what counts for Luke is to evangelize, to proclaim, hence the importance of "the word" (1:2). "Fulfillment" is also important, but not of time, as in Mk 1:15, but of Scripture, today, with the presence of Jesus himself (Lk 4:21).

The words spoken by Jesus in Nazareth were not meant to please: in substance they appear as a comment on the axiom mentioned in vs. 24, "No prophet is acceptable in his own country." The origin of this axiom cannot be determined, but it served Jesus himself and then the Church to explain the apparent failure of the Savior's mission among his own people (see also Mk 6:4 par.). The existence of the proverb as a detached saying is confirmed by Jn 4:44 and by other documents, like the 3rd cent. *Oxyrhynchus* papyri, and the *Gospel of Thomas*: "No prophet is acceptable in his native city (or village), no physician works cures on those who know him" (log. 31). In the Fourth Gospel "his own country" is Jerusalem, where the Father of Jesus resides (see Jn 2:16; Lk 2:49). "His own received him not" (Jn 1:11) would refer mainly to the Jerusalemites. J. Willemse who sustains this (*NTS* 11, 1964f, 349-64) also discusses the Synoptic parallels. By using

the proverb Jesus seems to identify himself as ''prophet'' (see also
Mt 21:11), although he does so much more clearly in Lk 13:33: ''It
cannot be that a prophet should perish away from Jerusalem.''
Some interest has been found in the fact that a Qumran fragment on
Melchizedek speaks of one ''anointed with the Spirit'' (see Fitzmyer 530). It is probable that *The Damascus Rule* contains the
expression ''the anointed of the Holy Spirit'' (CD II, 12), although
different translations of the line are proposed.

Lk 4:25-27, without Synoptic parallel, could be a Lucan addition to the material found in his source. Consistent with his insistence on the role of the preached word in the new economy of
salvation, Luke gives prominence in his gospel to the figures of
Elijah and Elisha. In the Nazareth episode the first reference is to
the *three year* drought mentioned in 1 K 17:1; 18:1. It is generally
thought that the addition of six months in Lk 4:25 and Jm 5:17 can
be ultimately traced back to Dn 7:25; 12:7 through the Jewish
apocalyptic tradition, for which the eschatological woes would last
three and a half years (Rv 11:2-3; 13:5). The stories of the other
references are found in 1 K 17:7-24 and 2 K 5:1-27. The examples
proposed, to illustrate the work of an Israelite prophet in favor of
foreigners, appears so striking that their selection must go back to
Jesus himself. Luke would be responsible only of their insertion in
the present context. The prophets had been sent to Israel, but they
were better received outside Israel or by non-Jews than in their own
country. The same will happen with the Christian missionaries (Lk
11:49).

Again Jesus as Prophet (Lk 9:51; 11:29-32)

The first verse of Luke's middle journey section (9:51-19:27)
has a Christological content worth noticing: ''When the days drew
near for him to be received up, he set his face to go to Jerusalem''
(9:51). The Greek text behind ''for him to be received up'' really
speaks of Jesus' ''assumption,'' his *analêmpsis*. Although this

term, a NT *hapax* (used once only), can refer to death, its use by Luke quite certainly belongs with other passages where Jesus appears as a new Elijah (see above). 2 K 2:10f reports how Elijah ''was taken up'' in a fiery chariot, and the same verb *analambanein* is used to denote Jesus' ascension (Ac 1:2, 11, 22). This figurative way of referring to Jesus' departure from this world (see Jn 13:1) can also be connected with the description of his death as an *exodus* (see Lk 9:31).

''He (steadfastly) set his face to go'' reflects the OT form of expression *śim panîm* (Jr 21:10; Ezk 6:2) and may contain an allusion to the Servant's setting his face like a flint in total confidence in God (Is 50:7). Lk 9:51 declares Jesus' firm intention to pursue without deviation the mission given to him by the Father to redeem the world through his death to be undergone in Jerusalem. In Plummer's words ''the thoroughly Hebrew cast of the opening sentence seems to show that the source here used was either an Aramaic original which Luke translated, or a translation from the Aramaic which he modified'' (p. 262).

Luke tends to underline Jesus' mission as that of a prophet, and this appears also in the way he reports a ''Q'' text, already examined in Ch. 2 under another angle. While in Luke THE SIGN OF JONAH (11:29-32) is interpreted as referring to *the prophet's teaching*, it becomes in Mt 12:40 a direct illustration of Jesus' future resurrection. Luke has often noted how the crowds were attracted by Jesus' teaching. See also 4:42; 5:1; 6:17; 8:4; 9:37; 12:1; 14:25; 18:36; 19:48. He does not say, as Matthew does (13:36), that at a certain point in his ministry Jesus ceased to speak to the crowds.

If it is true that Luke presents Jesus particularly as preacher of the word, not surprisingly he understood the sign of Jonah as referring to his activity as preacher. Lk 11:31-32 make it clear enough how Jesus' preaching can be a *future* sign for this generation. ''Will arise'' in both verses implicitly refers to the general resurrection. Whereas the Queen of the South, a pagan, came from the end of the confines of the earth to hear a mortal being, the Jews do not really listen in their own land to a preacher through whom, much more than through Solomon, divine wisdom speaks. When Jesus will appear at the judgment as the Son of man, then will the incredulous generation have to recognize how wrong it was not to have listened to Jesus, a preacher incomparably superior to Jonah. In this sense Jonah can be seen as a *future* sign or warning for this evil generation.

Departure from Galilee (Lk 13:33)

Mt 23:37-39 places "the lament over Jerusalem" after the entry into the holy city, while Luke reports it when Jesus is still in Perea, in Herod's domain (13:34f). In Luke the lament is connected with the death of Jesus, in Matthew it concerns directly the Jewish persecution of the Christian missionaries (compare here Lk 11:49 with Mt 23:34). Significantly, the lament is immediately preceded in Luke by the answer of Jesus to the report about Herod: "Nevertheless I must go on my way today and tomorrow and the day following; *for it cannot be that a prophet perish away from Jerusalem*" (13:33). This is one more instance of Luke's tendency to describe Jesus as a prophet going to his martyrdom.[24] Not surprisingly the Emmaus disciples perceived that Jesus was "*a prophet* mighty in deed and word before God and all the people" (24:19).

The texts we have seen suffice to show Luke's special interest in Jesus as Prophet. We do not discuss here the presentation of Jesus as "the eschatological prophet," since this has been referred to in the first section of Ch. 1.

"The Lord Has Need of It" (Lk 19:31)

I have explained briefly in Ch. 1, under c), the NT use of the name *Mari, Maran(a)*, "my Lord, our Lord," as an early Christian address to Christ. In Ch. 2 we have seen (under Lk 6:46) that the recurrence of the address "Lord" in Q stories confirms the use of the title *Kyrios* in Jesus' own lifetime. Lk 19:31 suggests now a discussion of the use of *Kyrios* as a designation of Jesus in the *narratives* of Luke. Lk 19:31 is a particular case inasmuch as the expression derives here from Mark 11:3, the only place where *ho Kyrios* designates Jesus in the narratives of the second gospel, even though the title is used as address in 7:28. The situation is different in Luke who from 7:13 onwards constantly refers to Jesus as the Lord in his own narratives (see also 10:1; 11:39; 12:42; 17:5f). In these and in other occurrences, which refer to the earthly Jesus, there is no connotation of divinity, Hahn believes, but *ho kyrios* "emphasizes fullness of power which moves human beings to self-surrender and implies the recognition of Jesus" (p. 85). This usage is founded on the Palestinian form of address, *mari*, which adapted to Greek became *ho kyrios*. Paul himself has used the name in this sense, where he is referring to the earthly Jesus (1 Cor 7:10; 9:5, 14).

Adopting other viewpoints, A. George sees in both Luke and Acts the title *Kyrios* applied to Christ in a variety of contexts: as King-Messiah (Lk 19:31; Ac 2:36), as Savior (Lk 2:10f; Ac 15:11), as Lord of the Church (Lk 10:1; Ac 9:1), as the risen Lord (Lk 24:3; Ac 1:21f). George (pp. 237-55) shows also that Christ's kingship had little in common with that of this world, since Christ's "lordship" belongs to another order: it draws its meaning from that of the Old Testament *Kyrios*, the Greek name designating God himself. This does not mean, of course, that Luke identifies Jesus with God, but the repeated use of *Kyrios* prepared the way for such a transcendent meaning.

It can be said, to conclude, that Luke calls Jesus *Kyrios* only where the title serves to explain who he is in fact. He avoids using *Kyrios* in a purely historical sense to designate Jesus (see *Mélanges Bibliques Rigaux*, pp. 117-46).

"Blessed is the King" (Lk 19:38)

Another text in the same episode of the Messianic entry into Jerusalem calls for a comment. For "Blessed is he who comes in the name of the Lord! Blessed is the kingdom of our father David that is coming! Hosanna in the highest!" (Mk 11:9b-10), Luke (if he is following Mark) substitutes "Blessed is *the King* who comes in the name of the Lord! Peace in heaven and glory in the highest!" This peace acclamation has close affinities with the angels' hymn at the birth of Jesus (2:13-14). There the acclamation proceeded from heaven earthwards; here in Lk 19:38b it proceeds from below heavenwards. It is, on the other hand, remarkable that in both John (12:13) and Luke (19:38a) the acclamation goes explicitly to the Messiah-King, while the blessing is addressed in Mark to "the kingdom of our father David" (11:10), and to "the Son of David" in Matthew (21:9). "King" occurs, however, in Zc 9:9, quoted by Matthew (21:5).

The royal emphasis is not accidental in Luke, who had allusively announced such a development in the parable of the Pounds (see Lk 19:12). It is true, on the other hand, that Ps 118:25-26, quoted in Lk 19:38, seems to have referred originally to the king of Israel. George (p. 275) finds in Lk 19:29-38 several royal traits that can be referred to Solomon's enthronement (1 K 1:33-40). It is a matter of debate whether the acclamation at the entry fulfills a previous prophecy of Jesus himself (see 13:35). Probably Luke did not wish to have here an acclamation to "the kingdom" (Mk) because Jesus in Lk 19:11 had denied that the kingdom was about to appear. The description of the Messiah as "prince of peace" in Is 9:6 may have suggested to Luke or to his source the motif of "peace" in the acclamation to the king approaching the holy city. As was explained in my article "The Eschatology of Luke" (*BTB* 1982, pp. 73-76), Jesus appears as King in the Messianic entry because this episode represents for Luke the first of the final stages that will lead the Messiah to his exaltation to the right hand of God as Lord and King already now over the worshipping Church (see more on this about Ac 2:36, below).

Three Titles in Lk 22:67-70

In 22:67-70, connected with Jesus' "trial" before the Sanhedrin, Luke introduces, with regard to Mark, changes that have Christological significance. As compared to Mk/Mt, Luke's version distinguishes quite clearly, as already in 1:31-35 the title MESSIAH from the title SON OF GOD. For Mark, "Are you the Christ, the Son of the Blessed?" (14:61), Luke has simply, "If you are the Christ, tell us" (22:66), but later a separate question is asked, "Are you the Son of God, then?" It remains true, on the other hand, that Luke, from a Christian viewpoint, can equate the two titles, as he does in 4:41 and Ac 9:20-22. From this equivalence, already present in the annunciation story (Lk 1:32-35), and alluded to at the baptism (3:22), it can be deduced that Luke understands "Son of God" as applying to the Messiah, "to the Messiah in all the newness of his mystery" (George 222).

Luke introduced another important change in what can be referred to as the Markan or Synoptic tradition. He omits in vs. 69 Mk/Mt's reference to the Son of man's "coming with the clouds of heaven" (see Mk 14:62). Writing later, when an imminent *parousia* was contradicted by the facts, Luke could not tell his readers that Jesus had announced precisely such an event to the Sanhedrin. It must be noted, however, that Matthew and Mark do not say that the Jewish leaders will *see* the event during their lifetime! Lk 22:69 evokes Ps 110:1, already applied to Christ (see 20:41-44), to announce the Messianic enthronement of Jesus, following his resurrection (see Ac 2:32-36). For the national Messianism of the Jews, Jesus in Luke substitutes the transcendent Messianism, that of the SON OF MAN seated at the right hand of the Power of God. It is in this transcendent sense that "Son of God" is then understood, a meaning, it must be admitted, more

Christian than Jewish (George 227). The prominence given in Luke to the title "Son of God" as the basis for Jesus' condemnation echoes Jn 10:33, 36: "The Jews answered him, 'We stone you for no good work but for *blasphemy*; because you, being a man, *make yourself God.*' . . . Jesus answered: 'Do you say of him whom the Father consecrated and sent into the world, "You are blaspheming," because I said, "I am the Son of God"?' "

Although in 22:69 the paschal exaltation of Christ is assumed instead of the Son of man's *parousia* (Mk 14:62), Luke knows also of a coming on a cloud (see 21:27), and of a "return" modeled on the ascension (Ac 1:11). The singular "cloud" used by Luke in these texts, and in Ac 1:9, points to presence (see Lk 9:34 par.) rather than vehicle (Dn 7:13; Mk 13:26). Let me add here, with George (p. 40), that Luke's tendency to "de-eschatologize" the kerygma does not stem from the delay of the Parousia only, which constituted a serious but common problem for the whole primitive Church. Luke's motives for separating as clearly as he did the time of the Church from the time of Jesus were above all the following *new factors*: the gift of the Holy Spirit, the apostolic preaching, the persecution of the disciples, the mission to the Gentiles.

"Made Lord and Christ" (Ac 2:36)

Having referred to Ps 110:1, Peter on Pentecost day told the assembled Jews: "Let all the house of Israel therefore know assuredly that *God has made him both Lord and Christ*, this Jesus whom you crucified" (Ac 2:36). Although attributed to Peter the statement reflects also, as it seems, Luke's own Christological conception, with an emphasis on Christ's exaltation as Lord, as the Son of man seated *already now* at the right hand of the power of God (see again Lk 22:69). It is more difficult to understand why Luke would say that Jesus *became* "Christ" at his resurrection. There is a traditional explanation, which is certainly not false: through his resurrection Jesus came into possession of that state in which *he enjoys* the divine prerogatives to which he was entitled by birthright from the beginning (see Lk 1:32-35). According to I.H. Marshall, Peter's argument in Ac 2:32-36 obviously does not mean that Jesus *became* Messiah by being raised from the dead, "but rather that since the Messiah must rise from the dead, and since Jesus rose from the dead it follows that Jesus was already the Messiah during his earthly life" (p. 77). A similar reasoning is found in Paul's proclamation to the Jews of Antioch in Pisidia, "It was to our ancestors that God made the promise but it is to us, their children, that he has fulfilled it, by raising Jesus from the dead. As scripture says in the first psalm: *You are my son: today I have become your father*" (Ac 13:33). For this see also the following commentary in the *Jerusalem Bible*: "By his resurrection Christ was enthroned as Messiah, and from then on *his human nature* enjoyed all the privileges of the Son of God." In Romans Paul will say that "Christ was designated Son of God in power according to the Spirit of holiness by his resurrection from the dead" (1:4).

Ac 3:20 can also be given a meaning close to that of 2:36. There Peter tells the Jews that if they repent God may send to them Jesus "who has been constituted Christ" for them. "He may send Christ Jesus who has been foreappointed for you" would be closer to the Greek text. For R.H. Fuller "the earliest Palestinian Christology" held that at the parousia Jesus would return as "the Christ appointed for you" (p. 159), that he is "pre-destined to be the eschatological judge at the parousia" (p. 166). In fact, in both 10:42 and in 17:31 Acts attributes to Jesus the office of end-time Judge. Through his resurrection Jesus was established as Judge of the living and the dead. In Acts these texts are meant as an incentive to repentance. Ac 3:19-21 does seem to envisage an intermediate period, allowed as a time of repentance, between the resurrection of Christ and his return.

It has been said before, that Peter's discourse in Ac 3:13-26 reflects the earliest stage of the Church's kerygma. This is particularly true of some archaic titles found there, to which I have already referred in Ch. 1. This does not mean that the whole discourse of Peter belongs to the same early level. Possibly, Luke in his editorial role has incorporated into it later Christological perceptions. He shows a special interest in defining Jesus as the Messiah. To the texts already mentioned can be added his report about the apostles: ''And everyday in the temple and at home they did not cease teaching and preaching Jesus as the Christ'' (Ac 5:42). Later on, he writes that in Corinth ''Paul was occupied with preaching, testifying to the Jews that Jesus is the Christ'' (18:5). It is interesting that in Ac 9:20, 22 the titles ''Son of God'' and ''the Christ'' appear in parallel, as in Lk 22:67, 70, where, however, ''Son of God'' seems to be closer than ''Christ'' to a divine title. For D.L. Jones, Luke's use of *Christos* has distinctive aspects (see *CBQ* 1970, pp. 69-76).

To conclude this very incomplete presentation of the Christology of Acts, one more text will be considered, where soteriology overlaps with Christology.

''The Church of God'' (Ac 20:28)

According to one version, Paul tells the elders of the Church: ''Take heed to yourselves and to all the flock, in which the Holy Spirit has made you guardians, to look after the Church of the Lord, which he bought with his own blood'' (Ac 20:28). Thus read, the verse gives an obvious sense, the Lord being Jesus Christ who, as Paul says elsewhere, ''loved the Church and gave himself up for her'' (Ep 5:25). There is, however, a variant reading in the manuscripts, ''the Church of God,'' which as the more difficult reading is probably the original one, for this and other reasons pointed out by B.M. Metzger in *A Textual Commentary on the Greek New Testament*, pp. 480f. For example, ''Church of God'' occurs eleven times in the Epistles, but ''Church of the Lord'' nowhere (else) in the New Testament, although *ekklêsia Kyriou*, ''assembly of the Lord'' is found seven times in the Septuagint.

Could Paul have said that the Church was acquired by God's

"own blood"? It is unlikely he called Christ "God" in this text, in spite of Rm 9:5. Quite possibly, instead of "by his own blood," one should read "by the blood of his Own (Son)." Thus in Rm 8:3 Paul says that God sent "his *own* Son" as an expiation for sin. Other commentators plausibly suggest to read "by his own blood," understanding "his own blood" to represent God's Son in his sacrifice. It seems in any case that Ac 20:28 can figure among the texts showing that Luke too, attributed redemptive value to the death of Christ, although for some reason he has omitted to report the ransom saying (Mk 10:45). By substituting at the Last Supper *huper humôn*, "for you," for Mark's *huper pollôn*, "for many," Luke has suppressed the allusion to the Fourth Servant Song, but not the salvific efficacy of Jesus' death: "This cup which is poured out for you is the new covenant in my blood" (Lk 22:20; not all manuscripts, however, carry this second word of institution, probably because of vs. 17).

Conclusion

The Christology of Luke does not differ radically from that of the Synoptic tradition. He tends to associate the high titles of Christ with his resurrection, but these he also reads back into his narrative of the annunciation (Lk 1:32-35). The same can be said of the title "Savior" (2:11), which appears rather late in other NT writings. Luke certainly also tends to downplay the role of John the Baptist, the last of the OT prophets (the probable interpretation of 16:16), while Jesus assumes in full the role of prophet in the Messianic times. Jesus dies as a martyr after professing to be the Son of God in a transcendent sense (22:70). Luke does not reject the traditional eschatology, but for him Jesus already rules here and now as Lord over the Church, as the Son of God in a sense that transcends infinitely the OT claims for David's divine sonship.

CHAPTER SIX

DISTINCTIVE CHRISTOLOGICAL TRAITS IN MATTHEW

Having devoted quite a long chapter to the Christology of Matthew in my commentary on the first gospel (vol. 1, pp. 125-56), I feel it will be sufficient here to bring out some particularly revealing traits which may contribute to the overall picture I am attempting to draw of NT Christology. As in the other chapters I will connect my remarks with especially representative texts. Not surprisingly three out of six will be taken from Matthew's infancy narrative, where the evangelist has most clearly left the marks of his own views.

The Son of David, the Son of Abraham (1:1)

The first verse of the New Testament is the beginning of Matthew: ''The book of the origins of Jesus Christ, the son of David, the son of Abraham.'' More probably this title applies mainly to the first section of Mt (1:1-4:6). ''Christ'' in ''Jesus Christ'' figures as a proper name, although elsewhere the original ''Messianic'' meaning of *Christos* is preserved (see about 1:16).

The title SON OF DAVID has already been examined in Ch. 3, in connection with Mk 10:47 (see also Ch. 8, about Rm 1:3f and Booknote 33). As its first verse suggests, the first gospel does contain a distinctive Davidic Christology. The title ''Son of

David'' has, it is true, also a Messianic sense in two texts which Matthew has in common with Mark and Luke: Mt 20:30f; 22:42, 45. It happens, on the other hand, that Matthew inserts the title in Marcan sequences which do not have it; thus Mt 15:22 and 21:9. The title occurs in the mouth of several persons: the angel (1:20), two blind men (9:27; 20:30), ''all the people'' (12:23), the Canaanite woman (15:22), the children in the temple (21:15). As for the religious leaders they oppose the proclamation of the title (cf. 12:24; 21:15f). The purpose of the main pericope on this subject, Mt 22:41-46, is not to deny the Davidic ancestry of Jesus but to go beyond the Pharisaic concept of ''Davidic Messiah'': the ''Son of David,'' for Matthew, is also ''the Lord of David,'' since he is also ''Son of God'' in a transcendent sense (cf. 16:16; 26:63). Matthew has sharpened the issue of who the Christ is by introducing a separate question: ''Whose son is he?'' (22:42). Jesus is Son of David according to the flesh, but still more Son of God, and as such David's Lord. But among the listeners the Pharisees—in Mark they are the Scribes—''No one was able to answer a word'' (vs. 46), for only by a special revelation is Jesus' sonship revealed. If the Pharisees suspected what the answer was, they wouldn't express it, for fear of confessing who Jesus truly was.

While Luke places a certain emphasis on the figure of Abraham, in line with Pauline theology, Matthew has only three other references to the patriarch (3:9; 8:11; 22:32), which are also found in Luke and are linked with eschatological themes (beginning and end of salvation history). It is often said that Matthew with his ''SON OF ABRAHAM'' wanted to show Christ as rooted within his own people. This is not entirely true, since we know that Matthew does not accept the traditional Jewish interpretation of ''people of God.'' Matthew believes, like Paul (cf. Gal 3), that Abrahamic descent does not of itself characterize the ''people of God'' (cf. Mt 3:9), that *the* offspring of Abraham and David is Jesus (see Gal 3:16). So the title of the gospel should read: ''It is Jesus Christ *who is* the son of David, the son of Abraham.''

"Who Is Called Christ" (1:16)

We will not here discuss the textual problems regarding Mt 1:16, which says literally: "And Jacob begat Joseph, the husband of Mary, of whom was born Jesus, the one called Christ." In this vs. 16 the same verb *gennaô* is used first in the active (usually for males in the NT), "to beget," then in the passive, "to be born (from)." When used in the active for mothers (Lk 1:57; Jn 16:21) the verb does not mean (as for males) "to procreate" (to become father in the legal sense), but "to give birth" (usually *tekein*), the second phase in the process of generation.

"Jesus, the one called Christ" is a distinctively Matthean formula, also ascribed to Pilate in 27:17, 22. For W. Grundmann, the point of the statement in Mt 1:16 "is that Jesus is the Messiah as the son of David and offshoot of Abraham, that he belongs to Israel, and that by virtue of his royal descent He is the kingly Messiah who comes at the end of the world period which extends *heôs tou Christou*, up to the Christ, 1:17" (*TDNT* vol. 9, p. 531). "Christ" in 1:16 should therefore be taken as a title, "the Christ, the Messiah," not as a proper name. The Messianic meaning of "Christ" appears also in the story of the Magi, when they ask: "Where is he who has been born king of the Jews?" (2:2). Unlike the usurper Herod, Jesus is by birthright king of Israel, like the expected Messiah. Perhaps to remove the connection of "Christ" with a purely national hope Matthew adds to Peter's confession. Instead of "you are the Christ" (Mk 8:29), we find in the first gospel: "You are the Christ, the Son of the living God." In addition, two notations proper to Matthew in the infancy narrative qualify Jesus' Messianic status: he has come to "save his people from their sins" (1:21); his birth will begin to fulfill the hope attached to the promised Emmanuel, "God with us" (1:23). Compare with 28:20.

Matthew's special interest in presenting Jesus as the Messiah appears also in his wording of the Q text on the deputation of the

Baptist: "Now when John heard in prison about *the deeds of Christ*, he sent word by his disciples . . ." (11:2). Here Matthew expresses his own knowledge, that Jesus is the Christ, in spite of the Baptist's doubts. With *ta erga tou Christou*, "the deeds of the Christ," he anticipates the answer that Jesus will suggest by referring to what is happening in his ministry.

The section on John and Jesus concludes thus in Luke: "Yet wisdom is justified by all her children." This is probably what Jesus would have said, rather than what is reported in Mt 11:19: "Yet wisdom is justified by her deeds." Here Matthew remembers what he wrote in vs. 2. Jesus' credibility, he means, is founded not on what people think, but on the works he does as the bearer of wisdom, as the envoy of God himself. It would be, in my view, a mistake to use this text, or others, like 23:34-36, to look for a Wisdom Christology in Matthew. It can even be said that Matthew deliberately seems to avoid identifying Jesus with Wisdom. For him Jesus is more than Wisdom, he is the Son of God.

"Out of Egypt I have called my Son" (2:15)

Most of Mt 2 is better explained as a midrashic reflection on Scripture, than as a report based on historical events. In particular, with this literary genre the evangelist created the context allowing him to quote a text from Hosea connected with sonship. Joseph with "the child and his mother" departed to Egypt, and remained there until the death of Herod the Great. This was to fulfill what the Lord had spoken by the prophet, "Out of Egypt I have called my son." This is one of the ten or eleven "formula quotations," or better "fulfillment quotations," used by Matthew to show the Christwards movement of salvation history (on these quotations see my *Matthew*, vol. 1, pp. 41-47, and on Matthew's midrashic compositions, pp. 226-37).

"From Egypt I have called my son" apparently translates directly the Hebrew of Hosea 11:1, while we read in the Greek OT,

"From Egypt I summoned his children." Israel is called God's (first-born) son also elsewhere, mainly in connection with the exodus (Ex 4:22f) and with the hope for a return of "Ephraim" from the Assyrian exile (Jr 31:9, 20; also the context of the quotation in Mt 2:18). Being formulated in the past, Hosea's oracle is not strictly a prophecy, although it has more truth when said of Christ, Son of God in the full sense. Matthew evidently saw an analogy between Israel and Jesus: both sojourned in Egypt before entering the land to which God led them to accomplish their destiny. Besides suggesting this parallel, which conforms to Matthew's views, the oracle contained a geographical name, "Egypt," which would fit in the itinerary leading from Bethlehem to Nazareth and at the same time explain the transfer.

It can be argued, with Kingsbury and others, that the title "Son of God" plays in Mt 1:1-4:16 (the double prologue) a major role in defining who Christ is. The first clear affirmation is found in 2:15, the second is the voice from heaven at Jesus' baptism. It is not by chance that the voice in Matthew speaks *in the third person*, "This is my beloved Son" (3:17): it is the Father's proclamation of the divine Sonship which had been prepared in different ways in the preceding chapters. There is more to say on the Son of God in Matthew in connection with 14:33.

"Truly You Are the Son of God" (14:33)

The story about Jesus' walking on the water, which is reported also in Mark (6:45-52) and in John (6:15-21), has this ending only in Matthew: "And those in the boat worshipped him, saying, 'Truly you are the Son of God' " (14:33). "Those in the boat" obviously stand in Matthew for the worshipping Church, since it can easily be proved that "the twelve disciples" in the first gospel do represent, as prototypes, the Christian community that fulfills God's will in following Jesus (see my introductory chapter on "discipleship" in *Matthew*, vol. 1, pp. 109-124). Connected with this is the particular emphasis given to the title *didaskalos*, "teacher, master," in the first gospel. Only in Matthew do we hear Jesus tell the disciples: "But you are not to be called *rabbi*, for you have one teacher (*didaskalos*), and you are all learners" (23:8). In vs. 10, omitted by some authorities, we find combined two titles underlined by Matthew: "master" (here *kathêgêtês*), and *ho Christos*, "the Christ." Corresponding to this, Matthew accentuates the duty of the disciples to obey, not only God, but Jesus as well. When Jesus asks them to fetch the riding ass, and to prepare the Passover, they do exactly what they were told (Mt 21:6; 26:19), while in Luke they find everything as he had told them (19:32; 22:13), underlining Jesus' gift of clairvoyance, as suits a prophet. Finally, in the paschal proclamation the disciples are instructed to teach the nations "to observe all that I have commanded you" (28:20).

What has been said helps us to understand that the Twelve can be shown to "worship" Jesus at this early stage as *the Son of God*. This title, already well represented in the infancy narrative, as we have seen, finds several ways of expression in Matthew. Jesus speaks to his disciples on the mountain (Mt 5:1f) as the Son of God, for it is not Moses but Yahweh who spoke on Sinai, the prototype of all holy mountains. Jesus' thanksgiving to the Father (11:25-27), which is often labeled Johannine for obvious reasons, appears far less out of place in the light of what has been said: namely that Jesus reveals himself to the disciples as the Son of God. Matthew finds ways to underline the title "Son of God" also during the passion. If the first gospel has "Son of God" in 26:63, instead of "Son of the Blessed" (Mk 14:61), it may be under the influence of the Christological confessions in use in Matthew's church. A similar explanation can be proposed for two mentions of "Son of God" found only in the Matthean narrative of the passion (27:40, 43). But when his enemies say of Jesus, "Let God deliver him now, if he desires him; for he said, 'I am the Son of God,' " they may express what in Matthew's view was a fact: Jesus had repeatedly presented himself as the Son of God. The Trinitarian formula in the final proclamation represents the last stage of the Matthean development of the Son of God Christology (28:19).

The Son of Man with His Angels (16:27)

There is no doubt that Matthew has accentuated the glory of the future Son of man, as in the opening words of the judgment scene, proper to him: "When the Son of man comes in his glory, and all the angels with him, then he will sit on his glorious throne" (25:31). Instead of the glory of "his Father" (16:27), Matthew now speaks of the glory of the Son of man himself, a transfer of attribute. "All the angels with him" does not specify nor negate that they are "his angels" (13:41; 24:31), but the formulation reflects Zc 14:5: "The Lord your God will come, and all the holy ones with him" (see also Dt 33:2 LXX). The phrase, "he will sit on his glorious throne," also used in Mt 19:28, reflects an apocalyptic scenario, similar to that which we find in Dn 7:9, *Enoch* 61:8; 62:2; 69:27, and Rv 20:4. (See the fully documented article "Apocalyptic Traits in Matthew's Gospel," *Religious Studies Bulletin* 1983, pp. 19-36.)

In 16:27 Matthew writes: "For the Son of man is to come *with his angels* in the glory of his Father, and then he will repay every man for what he has done" (compare 1 Cor 3:8). The cortège of angels is meant to glorify the heavenly figure, but in Mk 8:38/Lk 9:26, they are simply "the holy angels"; only in Matthew are they the angels of the Son of man, while Paul writes that at the second coming the Lord Jesus will come "with all his saints," perhaps influenced by Dn 4:10 LXX.

Does the following verse confront the Christian interpreter with an unfulfilled prophecy of Jesus? Apparently referring to the parousia Jesus is reported to have said: "Truly, I say to you, there are some standing here who will not taste death before they see the Son of man coming in his kingship." Matthew seems to have altered purposely the second half of the saying which reads in Mark, "before they see the kingdom of God come with power" (9:1). Matthew has intentionally substituted "the Son of man" for "the kingdom of God," not only because he thought they were more or less equivalent concepts, but also to connect more closely the saying of vs. 27 with that of vs. 28, which may have initially existed in another or without context. More important still, he took this occasion to reaffirm his concept of a first coming of Jesus as the risen Son of man "in his kingship," that is as Lord of the Church, who will entrust the disciples with their second, universal, mission (see 10:23). The disciples are told not only that the Son of man will come at the end as the rewarding judge, but that he will come visibly as exalted Lord in his kingdom very soon and will *be seen* by some of his present followers. The transfiguration, which takes place soon after Jesus' prediction, will anticipate in a way the glorious appearance of the exalted Christ to his disciples (28:19). Even more generally, the death/resurrection of Jesus was an eschatological event, manifested in apocalyptic signs, which Matthew has accentuated more than the other evangelists (see *RSB* 1983, 19-36).

Only Matthew, in 13:41; 16:28; 20:21, speaks clearly of the kingdom of the Son of man. It would be a mistake to identify it simply with the kingdom of God, and it appears to me possible to see in this kingdom of the Son of man a replica of the Messianic kingdom referred to in *Jubilees*, *2 Baruch*, and *4 Esdras*, obviously in dependence on Daniel 7. According to R.H. Charles, the eschatology of the *Book of Jubilees* is that of *Enoch* 91-104: the judgment will take place at the end of the Messianic kingdom and will be followed by the bliss of the just (*The Apocrypha and Pseudepigrapha of the Old Testament*, vol. 2, p. 49). In Rv 20:1-10 the reign of 1000 years begins with the *parousia*.

Judging, as a Shepherd (25:32)

As the author of Genesis represents the putting in place of the material world *as a separation* (1:4-18), so does Matthew describe the last judgment as a *separation* of the good from the wicked. The Judge will accomplish this ''as a shepherd separates the sheep from the goats'' (25:32). Some commentators read this simply as a good comparison: ''In Palestine mixed flocks are customary; in the evening the shepherds separate the sheep from the goats, since the goats need to be kept warm at night, for cold harms them, while the sheep prefer open air at night'' (J. Jeremias, *The Parables of Jesus*, p. 206). More can be read in the comparison, when it is admitted that also elsewhere Matthew likes to present Jesus as the Shepherd of God's people (see F. Martin, ''The Image of Shepherd in the Gospel of Saint Matthew,'' *Science et Esprit* 27, 1975, pp. 261-301).

For Matthew *the healing Christ* is the merciful Savior, who like the Servant took upon himself our infirmities and bore our diseases (8:17; Is 53:4). As healer he also fulfills the Shepherd ideology. The summary statement, ''healing every disease and every infirmity among the people'' (Mt 4:23), can be related, it seems, to Ezekiel 34, where we read that God himself will become the Shepherd of Israel, leading the flock to good pasturage, and taking a special care of the weak and wounded sheep (vs. 16), until, in the Messianic times, a faithful Shepherd is raised up, the new David, who will be prince among the people. This reference is confirmed in the other summary, which says that seeing the crowds Jesus had compassion for them, ''because they were harassed and helpless, *like sheep without a shepherd*'' (9:35f).

The healing ministry of Jesus is particularly stressed by Matthew when he writes that Jesus ''*healed* their sick'' (14:14), or ''he *healed* large crowds'' (19:2), where Mark represents him as *teaching* those who followed him (6:34; 10:1). In the context of the Messianic entry into Jerusalem Matthew adds to the Synoptic report: ''And the blind and the lame came to him in the temple, and he *healed* them'' (21:14). Once again Matthew underlines the call to salvation of those in greater need (cf. 9:12; 11:5). According to an old saying "the blind and the lame" were not admitted to the house of the Lord (2 S 5:8). But they follow the *new David* into the temple, where he heals them.

To conclude, Jesus' miraculous healings are closely connected with his Messianic call. They manifest the Savior's solicitude for the destitute, and accomplish OT prophecy converging on the Servant's mission and the expected role of the Messianic Shepherd.

Matthew's interest in representing Jesus as the Shepherd of Israel, of the true Israel, appears already in the Magi episode, where through Mi 5:1 Jesus is described as "a leader who will shepherd my people Israel" (Mt 2:6). In line with this Jesus himself declares: "I was sent only to the lost sheep of the house of Israel" (15:24). The disciples had already been instructed "to go rather to the lost sheep of the house of Israel" (10:6), but when the Jews had refused to recognize Jesus as the Messiah the disciples were commissioned to make disciples from all the nations (28:19).

Conclusion

Matthew has underlined the Messianic mission of Jesus with the emphasis he gives to the titles *Christos* and "Son of David." At the same time he has stressed the title "Son of God," in order to give the proper value to the meaning of "Messiah."

J.D. Kingsbury has attempted to demonstrate, with limited success in my view, that for Matthew the title SON OF MAN is "public" in nature and is meant to complement the title SON OF GOD, which is "confessional" in nature (*CBQ* 1975, pp. 193-202). However, the summary he wrote later on Matthew's Christology seems illuminating. "Matthew's view, then, is that if Jesus is known by his disciples during his ministry and by his church following Easter as the Messiah, the Son of God, he interacts with the world, first Israel and then the Gentiles, as the Son of man. At the consummation of the age, however, Jesus will appear visibly as the Judge and Ruler of the universe. At that time, the whole world will see what until then only the eyes of faith had ever been given by God to perceive: that in Jesus, God is present with his end-time rule. Consequently, at the parousia both the church and the world will behold Jesus in all the majesty of God as the Son of man. Yet, even as he appears in splendor as the Son of man, Jesus remains the Son of God, the King through whom God exercises his rule'' (*Jesus Christ* 73).

Matthew has made ''kings'' the commanding figures in several parables: 17:25; 18:23; 25:34-40, possibly to make the application to God or to Christ easier. In the scene of the last judgment the Son of man is also called ''king'' (vs. 34 and 40). This probably reflects Matthew's tendency to attribute to the Son of man the prerogatives of God himself, the eschatological Judge. This application was made easier by the identification of the Son of man with the Son of the Father, clearly implied in 16:27: ''For the Son of man is to come with his angels *in the glory of his Father*.'' For Bundy Mt 16:27 ''is a piece of pure Jewish eschatology, closely related to what follows in vs. 28 and its Old Testament prototype (Dn 7: 13-14), and it has a far better chance of being an authentic word of Jesus than the parallels in Mark and Luke'' (*Jesus and the First Three Gospels*, p. 303). Under ''pure Jewish eschatology'' one can understand also ''pure Jewish apocalyptic.''

CHAPTER SEVEN

THE EARLY CHRISTOLOGICAL HYMNS

Apart from Christ's own self-understanding (see Ch. 4) the kerygma contained in Peter's discourse of the third chapter of Acts is a primary source for the earliest expression of reflection leading to Christology, a perception of the meaning of Christ. Next in line, it is believed, come the early Christological hymns, which we know mainly because they have been inserted in different writings of the New Testament. It is not possible to state with certainty which of these hymns is the earliest, although it seems that Col 1:15-20 and Jn 1:1-14, with their ascription to Christ of a leading role in creation, would be somewhat later. A few authors consider Heb 1:1-4 as an early Christological hymn, but these verses should more probably be ascribed to the author himself of the Epistle. As we shall see later, other verses of First Peter can be listed as early Christological fragments, but this chapter will mainly examine in succession: Ph 2:6-11; 1 P 3:18-22; 1 Tm 3:16; Col 1:15-20; Jn 1:1-14.

From Kenosis to Lordship (Ph 2:6-11)

As far back as 1967, when R.P. Martin published his book *Carmen Christi*, there already existed a vast amount of secondary literature on this famous hymn, and the number of studies has since continued to grow.[25] Several of these studies have truly contributed to a better understanding of the hymn, and will be taken into account, even where no true consensus has yet been reached. Although the hymn is termed "Christological," it says less who Christ is than what he has done. In other words, it combines soteriology and Christology, and for this reason also the analysis to be offered here will concentrate on a few central aspects.

It is almost unanimously admitted that the hymn is pre-Pauline, that it was already in use in the liturgy before Philippians was written, therefore around the year 50. The rhythmical form of the piece, some of the unusual terms it uses, and the disturbance it brings into the contextual exhortatory flow of the letter, all point to an insertion. There are indications, however, that Paul has added "even death on a cross" to the existing text. It is quite common opinion that the hymn is of Hellenistic Christian origin (see the Introduction to Part One), while Grelot has argued that it may have arisen in a milieu where Aramaic and Greek were concurrently used. According to D. Georgi, the hymn utilizes the framework of the *sophia* ("wisdom") myth, but re-interprets it in the light of the early Hellenistic Jewish Christian claim that places Jesus on a par with YHWH as Lord of the world (see Martin 318). For others, like R. Brown, the hymn would combine the Gnostic motif of the descent of the pre-existent One with the Biblical concept of humiliation and exaltation.

In his *Christology*, Dunn argues that too many translations of Ph 2:6-7 presuppose, without real proof, that pre-existence is involved. He does not, and reads the text as follows: "Who being in the form of God did not count equality with God something to be grasped, but emptied himself, taking the form of a slave, becoming in the likeness of men" (pp. 114f). He claims that the Adam Christology, implied in the text, leaves no place for the involvement of pre-existence. In my view, this is a dubious contention, and my translation of the hymn, according to the sense, already indicates the direction which the interpretation will follow (the rendering of vs. 9-11 is borrowed from the *RSV*):

5 *Have this mind among yourselves, which you have in Christ Jesus,*

6 *who, though he did enjoy a divine status,*
did not hold fast to his equality with God,

7 *but emptied himself, becoming like a servant,*
being born in the likeness of men.

8 *Acknowledged as a human being,*
he humbled himself even more,
and became obedient unto death
(even death on a cross).

9 *Therefore God has highly exalted him*
and bestowed on him the name
which is above every other name,

10 *that at the name of Jesus every knee should bow,*
in heaven and on earth and under the earth,

11 *and every tongue confess that Jesus Christ is Lord,*
to the glory of God the Father.

It does not seem possible to admit that at any time the mainstream early Christian Church believed that Christ, born as a mere human being, was made God as a reward for the unconditional surrender of his life to the Father's will. It is known, on the other hand, that quite early the Church rejected the Ebionite form of *adoptionism*, which denied Christ's pre-existent divinity and claimed he was adopted by God as Son at his baptism in the Jordan (see Booknote 61).

The text itself of the hymn clearly suggests, it seems to me, that Christ went through his first abasement in the incarnation itself, probably in the following sense: entering this world Christ did not wish to be treated in his humanity like a divine being, but like a servant. More precisely, as T.A. Thomas explains, "the form of God," of which Christ divested himself, would not be his divine nature, but the outward, visible manifestation of it, the reflection of God's glory, as Heb 1:3 calls it, and which became palpable at the transfiguration. As Hoover further notes, Christ would not use that glory to his own advantage, seizing upon it with avidity (*harpagmos*). In this, Christ was the exact contrast of Adam who, created in God's image (Gn 1:27), treasured this privilege to the point of wishing to be like God himself, the temptation which the serpent proposed (3:5). Christ's second abasement, his utter obedience, stands again in contrast to Adam's disobedience, which brought about the fall (Rm 5:19). Christ, who entered this world in a spirit of obedience (Heb 10:7), soon recognized the vocation of the suffering Servant (Is 53) as his own, and accepted to redeem the world through death, death on a cross (Ph 2:8).

While the disobedient Adam was expelled from paradise (Gn 3:23f), Christ returned to heaven in a glorified humanity, and was exalted to the right hand of God (Ep 1:20), even given *the name* which is above all names (Ph 2:9), that of *Kyrios*, the name of God himself in the Septuagint (Ac 2:21, but see Booknote 5). "That every knee should bow," borrowed from Is 45:23, confirms this interpretation, and the cosmic sovereignty granted to Christ finds expression also elsewhere (Ph 3:21), together with the basic universal confession of his Lordship (Rm 10:9; 1 Cor 12:3). "To the glory of God the Father" suggests the correct understanding of what precedes: Christ is not a second God beside the Father; he is the divine Son, who shares deity with the one true God of the traditional faith. In Conzelmann's words, "originally, in his preexistence," Christ "had been God's son, now he is appointed 'Lord' " (*An Outline* 80).

In Ch. 4 it was noted that Ph 2:6-11 retains only the movement from pre-existence to glory through incarnation and obedient death. It says nothing of Christ's public ministry, and in this sense is not a gospel presentation of him. Nor is there any allusion to the second coming, although this was a major belief in the early Church. These omissions can be explained from the nature of the hymn, an epiphany schema which retains only the bare essentials of the primitive confession (see also Heb 12:2). As vs. 5 says, the hymn is inserted as a basis for the exhortation to follow Christ's example. In a way ''the community is drawn into the cosmic event'' (Conzelmann 80), but it is also brought to proclaim Christ as the Lord and thus fulfill its role as Christian witness in the world below.

Preacher to the Spirits (1 P 3:18-22)

Different commentators recognize a number of insertions in the First Epistle of Peter. Leaving 1 P 1:18-21 and 2:21-25 for consideration elsewhere (see Booknote 44), we will examine here the more difficult passage, which represents Christ as ''Preacher to the spirits.''

In 1 P 3:18-22 the example of Christ is proposed to strengthen the Christians who in the Roman provinces of Asia Minor (see 1:1) were undergoing persecution. Put in rhythmical form the lines that concern us appear as follows (mostly *RSV* rendering): [26]

18 *For Christ also died for sins once for all,*
    the righteous for the unrighteous,
    that he might bring you to God,
    being put to death in the flesh
    but made alive in the spirit;
19 *in which he went and preached to the spirits in prison,*
20 *who formerly did not obey,*
    when God's patience waited in the days of Noah. . . .
22 *who is at the right hand of God*
    having gone into heaven
    with angels, authorities, and powers subject to him.

Several commentators prefer the reading *epathen*, ''suffered,'' in v. 18, instead of *apethanen*, ''died,'' arguing that the first occurs often in the epistle, while *apethanen* only here. But this argument has little value, if we are dealing with an inserted hymn which reflects the primitive confession, as contained, for example, in 1 Cor 15:3. ''That he might bring you to God'' almost certainly carries the sacrificial meaning attached to *prosagein* in some OT contexts, regarding offerings brought to the altar (Ex 29:10) and the consecration of priests (Ex 29:4). First Peter elsewhere refers to the priestly character of the Christian community (2:5). In this perspective Christ can be called a *prosagôgeus*, ''one-who-brings-to-God,'' the one Mediator between God and men (1 Tm 2:5).

According to the more common, and perhaps more traditional interpretation, defended also by C. Spicq (pp. 136-9), 1 P 3:19 says that while his body was in the tomb, Christ in his spirit, that is, in his soul, descended into Hades, and there proclaimed to the captive spirits (the souls of the dead; see Is 24:22), the advent of redemption, giving them the hope of an early release from their captivity. A few NT texts seem to favor this interpretation, as Rv 1:18, ''I have the keys of Death and Hades,'' or Rm 10:7, ''to bring Christ up from the dead,'' but they are far from compelling. Early apocryphal writings also understood the text in this sense, like the *Gospel of Nicodemus*, the *Gospel of Peter*, and the *Odes of Solomon*, but these reflect simply local or individual beliefs, not a serious study of the text. Also for G. Friedrich the *pneumata* who receive the proclamation are ''souls of the dead'' (*TDNT* 3, p. 707).

Already in 1911, C. Gschwind proposed that the preaching of Christ be understood as having followed his resurrection, and taken place during his ascension. He referred to 1 Tm 3:16, ''seen by angels,'' and to Ep 1:20, but particularly to 1 P 3:22 in this respect. In his article on *pneuma*, ''spirit,'' E. Schweizer rejects the interpretation sometimes proposed, that Christ ''in the Spirit'' had preached in the time of Noah to those who are now in prison and further explains that at least the *original* conception behind the hymn was that Christ's preaching to the spirits took place during the ''ascent'' journey of the risen Lord back to his Father (*TDNT* 6, p. 447). ''In the present context'' the *pneumata*, ''spirits,'' would refer to "the departed" (*ibid.*) Later on in the same volume other authors claim that "went" more probably refers to "the descent of Christ" into Hades (p. 577). This view may be influenced by 1 P 4:6: "For this is why the gospel was preached even to the dead, that though judged in the flesh like men, they might live in the spirit like God."

In his doctoral thesis on the subject, W.J. Dalton has argued at length for the interpretation first proposed by Gschwind. "Made alive in the spirit," he explains, refers to the *bodily* resurrection of Jesus, and "he went" refers to his ascension. On his way to his celestial abode, the risen Lord proclaimed his victory to the hostile spirits inhabiting the lower heavens, and kept there in a sort of captivity, according to the Jewish apocalyptic tradition. For this P. Benoit's recent article on "Pauline Angelology and Demonology" (see Booknote 27) provides a general background which can be illuminating also for 1 P 3:19. He writes, in particular, "willing or unwilling the Powers will be finally lined up under the feet of Christ, their leader; see Col 1:20" (p. 18).

Taken up in Glory (1 Tm 3:16)

Leaving to Ch. 9 the task of presenting at least briefly the Pastoral Epistles, it will suffice to note here that the early liturgical fragment we will comment upon is inserted at the end of an instruction on bishops and deacons. As Dibelius/Conzelmann explain,[27] the last three verses of ch. 3 in the First Epistle to Timothy constitute a transitional passage leading to Paul's testament described in ch. 4 showing that the Church is prepared for the post-apostolic period. "The basis for this testament is a liturgical piece, which thus appears as apostolic tradition" (p. 60). For the Pastorals tradition often expresses itself in the liturgy. The beginning of v. 16 includes the phrase *mystêrion tês eusebeias*, which can be translated either "mystery of piety" or "mystery of (our) religion," consisting here in the revelation of Christ himself in his mysteries, as outlined in the poetic quotation that follows. The phrase corresponds to "mystery of faith" used in 3:9. The hymnal fragment consists of six parallel phrases. It can be described as an early liturgical confession in praise of the exalted Christ and probably used originally in the churches of the Jewish Christian community (see Stenger).

Some manuscripts have an initial neutral pronoun, which would refer to *mystêrion*, but the masculine pronoun *hos*, referring to Christ, probably named in a preceding unreported line, is the more likely reading, which is adopted here:

> *who was manifested in (the) flesh*
> *was justified in (the) spirit*
> *was seen by angels*
> *was proclaimed among nations*
> *was believed in (the) world*
> *was taken up in glory.*

As *ephanerôthê*, "was manifested," in the first line suggests, the incarnation appears in the fragment as Christ's "epiphany." It is obvious that the components of the hymn follow a thematic or poetic pattern, not the chronology of the mysteries, since "was taken up in glory" is not immediately preceded by "was justified in the spirit," a clear reference to the resurrection, but comes last in the series. Rather, we have different contrasts, the first between flesh and spirit, then two others, angels/nations, world/(heavenly) glory, which set in antithesis the earthly world and the heavenly. Although the parallelism of members and some of the terms point to a Jewish Christian origin of the poem, it is possible to detect in it the Hellenistic notion of spheres dividing the lower and the upper worlds. Also by its contents 1 Tm 3:16 is quite original, even unique, even though it can be partly compared to other passages, like Rm 8:3f and Col 1:22.

Rm 1:4 suggests that "justified in the spirit" refers to the resurrection. As Dibelius/Conzelmann explain, "vindicated" or "justified," in this context, does not refer to forgiveness of sins, but rather to entrance into the divine realm, the realm of "righteousness" (p. 62). The statement refers therefore to the exaltation of Jesus, and this is also represented by the line immediately following: "was seen by angels." Several NT texts connect Jesus' exaltation with his triumph over the spirits (see on 1 P 3:19 above). The contrast between humiliation and exaltation is not accentuated here, as it is in Ph 2:6-11, but the cosmic dimension of Christ's mystery is underlined, as it is also in Col 1:15-20. The last line reminds the worshipper that the whole purpose of the poem is precisely to sing the glory of the exalted Christ.

Head of the Cosmos (Col 1:15-20)

The universal cosmic role of Christ receives praising expression in Col 1:15-20; Heb 1:1-4; Jn 1:3, 10; 1 Cor 8:6; and Ep 1:10. The original inspiration for this theme is traced by some to Hellenistic, even Gnostic redeemer-myths, but more likely the original hymn was a *response* to these Hellenists who saw themselves subject to the evil forces dwelling in the upper regions of the universe. The answer was: no reason to fear or feel threatened; it is Christ who rules over the universe. For the Gnostics Christ was indeed the embodiment of the cosmos, but unlike them both Paul and the hymn insist that redemption took place through the historical saving act of the cross (see Conzelmann 315). The composition itself of the hymn shows the influence of Jewish wisdom speculation, as it was pointed out in Ch. 4, in the section titled "First-Born of all Creation," which dealt with the affirmation of Christ's pre-existence in Col 1:15.

Several attempts have been made to reconstruct the original hymn, eliminating later additions. Lohse rightly believes "there is no valid reason for reckoning with further interpretive additions" than the two glosses in vs. 18a and 20 (in parentheses below), which clearly reveal the theology of the author of the epistle.[28] Lohse can be followed also in the way he presents the structure of the hymn as we have it. The phrase *hos estin*, ''he (who) is'' of v. 15 and *autos estin*, ''he is,'' of v. 18 indicate, as it seems, beginnings of a new strophe, while the following lines are expansions of the two capital statements: ''He is the image of the invisible God,'' ''He is the beginning.''

15　*He is the image of the invisible God,*
　　　　the first-born before all creation,
16　　*for in him all things were created*
　　　　in the heavens and on the earth,
　　　　the visible and the invisible,
　　　　whether thrones or dominions,
　　　　principalities or powers;
　　　　all things are created through him
　　　　and for him.
17　　*And he is before all things,*
　　　　and in him all things are established.
18　　*And he is the head of the body, (the church),*
　　He is the beginning,
　　　　the first-born from the dead,
　　　　in order that he might be the first
　　　　in all things,
19　　*for in him all the fullness was pleased to dwell*
20　　*and through him to reconcile all things toward him,*
　　　　making peace (through the blood of his cross)
　　　　　through him
　　　　　whether on earth or in the heavens.

A few commentators believe that vs. 12-14 are also part of the hymn, while for Lohse these verses served only as an introduction to the solemn song of the community, which followed (p. 33). T. F. Glasson suggests that the text behind the Latin version of Si

24:9, *"primogenita ante omnem creaturam,"* could have influenced "first-born before all creation," its exact translation in Col 1:15b. The hymn transfers to Christ what was said of Wisdom. Something similar can be said about the Latin version of Si 24:6: *"et in omni populo et in omni gente primatum habui,"* adapted to Christ in Col 1:18c, "in order that he might be the first in all things." *Prôtotokos*, "first-born," in v. 15, does not simply denote the priority in time of the pre-existent Lord. The first strophe (vs. 15-18a) acclaims the unique supremacy of Christ over all creatures as the Mediator of their creation (see *TDNT* 6, pp. 878f). In v. 17 it is possible to understand "and he is *above* all things." In the last statement of the first strophe, in v. 18a, it is probable that originally the *sôma*, "body," referred to the cosmos. "Then the author of Colossians reinterprets the body of Christ in Pauline style as the community or Church" (*TDNT* 8, p. 1075). For Lohse (p. 54) the statement about the head of the body is to be explained from the Hellenistic conception concerning the cosmic body and not from the Old Testament.

With the second strophe, from v. 18b, "He is the beginning," onwards, the role of Christ as Redeemer is celebrated. In Judaism both Wisdom and Logos were connected with the beginning (see Pr 8:22f). In Rv. 3:14 Christ is called "the beginning of God's creation," and in 1:5 he is described as "the first-born of the dead." Through him the eschatological event leading to the general resurrection has been initiated. Also the hymn of Colossians calls Jesus "the first-born from the dead." Here again Christ is not only the first to rise but also the first in rank since "as in Adam all die, so also in Christ shall all be made alive" (1 Cor 15:22). Salvation means essentially return to God, and this Christ has accomplished in a way for all when he returned to the Father as the head of redeemed humanity.

Perhaps the earliest occurrence of *plêrôma*, "fullness," in the Christological sense, is found in the Colossian hymn (v. 19), but the term is used also in Col 1:19; 2:9f, as well as in Ep 1:22f; 3:19;

4:8-13, texts which Ernst has analyzed in detail.[29] "In him all the fullness was pleased to dwell." In Judaism the visible and glorious presence of God was called the *Shekinâh*, from the verb *shākan*, "to dwell" (see Ex 40:35). In a true sense, in Colossians "Christ replaces the Jewish temple," that is, "the divine fullness of love and power acts and rules in all its perfection through Christ" (*TDNT* 6, p. 303). Unusual is the absolute use of *plêrôma* in Col 1:19 (*RSV*'s "the fullness of God" adds to the text). It is possible, however, to supply "God" as the subject of the sentence, and read: "God was pleased to let all the fullness dwell in him" (Lohse 56), and God would also be the subject in v. 20, "and through him to reconcile all things toward him, making peace through him, whether on earth or in the heavens." According to Lohse, "there can be no doubt that in the Christ-hymn, God himself is called 'pleroma' " (p. 57). The formulation of Col 1:19 calls to mind OT texts which, for example, say that Zion is "the mountain on which it pleases God to dwell" (Ps 68:17 LXX). Other examples would include Ps 132:13f, and also several texts from Deuteronomy, in which God is said to have chosen a place where he wants his name to dwell (see 12:5, 11). Christ's humanity is now the place where God has chosen to dwell.

Col 1:20 explains that God reconciles all things through Christ (see Rm 5:10; 2 Cor 5:18f), who is thus the universal Peacemaker (see also Ep 2:15). "Toward him" refers to Christ, not to God. The cosmic unity is accomplished through the rulership of Christ, who now exercises sovereignty over all the cosmic powers (see v. 16 and the exposition of 1 P 3:18-22). By adding to the original hymn "through the blood of his cross" the author of the epistle has brought the statement closer to the mainstream conception of redemption (see Rm 3:25; Ep 1:7). The cosmological statements of the first strophe of the hymn are singularly illumined by the soteriological statements found in the second strophe. Having stated that God raised Christ far above all the cosmic powers, Ephesians continues: "And he has put all things under his feet and has made him the head over all things for the church, which is his body, the fullness of him who fills all in all'' (1:22-23).

The Logos Incarnate (Jn 1:1-18)

There is no need for our purpose to attempt any extensive discussion of the Johannine prologue. It seems acceptable to formulate thus the links between it and the rest of the gospel: the author of the whole work must have used a primitive Christian hymn which celebrated the pre-existence and incarnation of Christ, but added his own comments to link more closely the prologue with the rest of the gospel. Thus Jn 1:6-8 can be considered as an insertion regarding John the Baptist which prepares the reader for the rather abrupt beginning of the narrative proper in v. 19. Also stylistic criteria suggest that the evangelist redacted these three verses. In addition, v. 15 fulfills an apologetical as well as a theological purpose: ''the contemplation of the *doxa* of the Logos incarnate remains possible even for later believers through the 'testimony' of those who have experienced the event of his historical coming.''[30] By disclosing the origin and the divine status of the Revealer the prologue as a whole sheds light on the entire gospel. Several reasons can be given for considering the prologue (Jn 1:1-18) to consist largely of a Logos-hymn which was used as a preface to the gospel.

As compared to the other verses, which look like prose, the following verses could have formed the original hymn, in three strophes: 1-3, 4-5, 10-12 (see Richter). We can read them in the *RSV* translation:

> 1 *In the beginning was the Word*
>   *and the Word was with God,*
>   *and the Word was God.*
> 2 *He was in the beginning with God;*
> 3 *all things were made through him,*

> *and without him was not any thing*
> *made that was made.*
>
> 4 *In him was life,*
> *and the life was the light of men.*
> 5 *The light shines in the darkness,*
> *and the darkness has not overcome it.*
>
> 10 *He was in the world,*
> *and the world was made through him,*
> *yet the world knew him not.*
> 11 *He came to his own home,*
> *and his own people received him not.*
> 12 *But to all who received him,*
> *who believed in his name,*
> *he gave power to become children of God.*

All three strophes begin in Greek with *en*, ''in,'' which could very well, here as elsewhere, serve a structural function. The strophes proclaim the Word's pre-existence and mediation in creation (I), his manifestation to humanity as life and light (II), the response he received in the world and the corresponding effect on the believers (III). It appears, however, difficult to leave v. 14 out of the original hymn, since the mention of the incarnation would seem so much to be the expected climactic conclusion of what precedes. Schnackenburg has proposed another reconstruction of the hymn, in four strophes, composed of vs. 1 and 3, 4 and 9, 10 and 11, 14 and 16 (see pp. 226-28). For Boismard (p. 74) the primitive hymn consisted only of vs. 1, 3, 4, 5, and with P. Borgen, he underlines its dependence on the first narrative of creation (Gn 1:1-2:4a).

Several authors have argued, after Bultmann, that the Logos-hymn originated in a pre-Christian Baptist group. However, ''it is problematical in the extreme that the disciples of John (in competition with Christians) should have applied the Gnostic myth of the heavenly envoy to their master at an early date, and have considered the son of Zechariah as the pre-existent revealer and redeemer who became flesh'' (Schnackenburg 231). The Logos-hymn is likely to have originated among converts from Hellenistic Judaism, because of the title ''Logos'' on the one hand, and on the other the presence of motifs related to the Old Testament and to Jewish speculation on Wisdom and the Torah (if vs. 17 was part of the original composition), for the Old Testament already connected creation with the word of God, as will be seen, and several verses of Si 24 have some correspondence with the Johannine prologue.

Schnackenburg has presented quite well the ongoing discussion and his own conclusions on ''the origin and nature of the Johannine concept of the Logos'' (vol. 1, pp. 481-93). It should be clear, he states, that the closest parallels in thought are to be found in Jewish wisdom speculation, but the Johannine Logos-doctrine stands on a different, higher level, ''by reason of the personal character of the Logos, his real personal pre-existence and above all his incarnation'' (p. 481). The sub-titles of Schnackenburg's survey show the different areas of recent investigation regarding the background of John's Logos-conception: the Logos in Greek philosophy, the theology of the Word of God in the Bible, ''Word of God,'' Wisdom, Torah and Memra of Yahweh in Judaism, the Logos in Philo, the Logos and the Gnostic myth. My own review article of Muñoz León's book, almost 800 pages, on the Memra of God, began with the following observation: ''The expression *Memra di Yhwh*, 'the Word of Yahweh,' occurs more than 600 times in the different Aramaic Targums of the Pentateuch. An unending debate has been going on in the last decades around the following questions: was this Memra considered as an hypostasis (or autonomous substance, being); can it be equated with the 'Word' of creation or the 'Word' of revelation; is it to be connected with the logos of Philo or of the Fourth Gospel; can the Targums be used to illustrate the thought of intertestamental Judaism?'' It would seem that the Memra of the Targums is simply a periphrasis for God, used to avoid pronouncing the sacred name, and has little, if anything, in common with the Johannine Logos, a divine being in his own right. However, it is quite possible that the author of the prologue or of the hymn was brought to speak of the Logos the way he did from hearing the reading of the Targum which spoke of the Memra of God as shining forth through darkness at the moment of creation (see McNamara).

In Philo's Hellenistic Judaism, wisdom speculation combined with the notion of Logos. John's Logos-hymn originated in the same cultural background, but its composition depends directly on Christian faith. It can be argued that the author of the hymn opted for the masculine *Logos* as more appropriate than the feminine *Sophia*, "wisdom," to represent Christ. Superficially, writes Schnackenburg, "the Gnostic saviour may seem to be more clearly and definitely a person than the Jewish Wisdom or Torah, or the Logos of Philo. In reality, it is however only a mythical figure and hence far less a person." In conclusion, "the fundamental problem of the roots of Johannine Christology still remains an open one" (p. 493). The fact that the title "Logos" does not figure in the Fourth Gospel after the prologue suggests that John is not the author of the hymn, but even if he were he could have refrained from applying the title to the incarnate Son, who is for the evangelist the Messiah.

"In the beginning" of v. 1 evokes the first words of Genesis, but, differently from there, here it refers to an absolute beginning, to an eternal beginning, not to the beginning of the world. "The Word was with God," the best equivalent of the French "auprès de Dieu," seems to render correctly enough the Greek *pros ton Theon*, while "the Word was turned towards God," that is, the Father (see *pros ton patera* in 1 Jn 1:2), is the rendering adopted by the French *TOB* in vs. 1 and 2. Jn 1:18 certainly suggests the meaning of v. 1, where it states that the only Son "is in the bosom of the Father," to use the more common translation. "And the Word was God" clearly indicates that the Logos, the Son of God, shares with the Father the divine being, or as *NEB* writes: "what God was the Word was." It is not enough to say that the Logos is

God functionally, since "the function which Christ fulfills is based on his nature, his being" (Boismard, *Prologue* 123).

Already in the Old Testament, creation is attributed to God's word (see Ps 33:6; Ws 9:1), and God's Wisdom is associated with it (Pr 8:27-30). For Paul creation is the work of the Father and the Son (1 Cor 8:6). Possibly, v. 5 refers to the manifestation of the Word as operative in the appearance of light in the world, but darkness has not comprehended what it meant. The other meaning suggested in *RSV* is this: darkness could not conquer light and subjugate it.

Differently from the text given above, it is grammatically possible to follow ancient authorities who read the end of v. 3 with v. 4, as follows: "That which has been made in him was life." However, B.M. Metzger assigns this reading to the Gnostics who found in the text thus read a support for one of their doctrines (pp. 195f). It is therefore preferable to read the text as it usually is, in spite of *The Greek New Testament* and Aland's support for the reading it proposes.

Very few words about the other verses. The Fourth Gospel often raises the question: "Where does Jesus come from?" See 7:27-29; 9:29, 33. Those who read the prologue know who Christ is and where he comes from. The mystery for John is the glory of the Word made flesh (see 1:14). While Moses was not even allowed to see directly the glory of God (Ex 33), this glory was manifested in the person of Jesus, and his miracles (Jn 11:40). Jesus' glory belongs to him as the Son of God, and it is reflected especially where the power of God is at work, in the signs he performs (Jn 2:11), and this glory coincides with that of the Father (11:4, 40). Jesus' passion is also his glorification, because it will lead him to the glory of the resurrection, and because in it the saving power of God is manifested (17:1-2). Finally, it is possible to translate Jn 1:18 as follows: "No one has ever seen God; the only Son, who is turned towards the bosom of the Father, he has made him known." J.P. Louw discovers in this last verse of the prologue a significant title of Johannine Christology: Jesus the Narrator of the Father. Jesus' life, particularly in John, can indeed be seen as a marvelous story in which the intimate life of the Father is made known to the world.

Conclusion

Although the five early Christological hymns we have examined in this chapter belong to different periods and to different *milieux*, they all celebrate the glory of Christ and proclaim his universal sovereignty, over the spirits and over the cosmos. Both the Colossians hymn and the Johannine prologue explicitly suppose Christ's pre-existence, while the Philippians hymn quite probably also presupposes it. Both the Philippians hymn and that of First Peter refer to the redeeming death of Jesus, while the Colossians hymn sees him as the mediator of reconciliation. It is significant that two hymns attribute to Christ a major role in creation, and this obviously under the influence of the attributes of OT Wisdom, and probably also because the Memra of God in the Targums is associated with his creative activity. It can be instructive to note that none of these hymns explicitly calls Christ the Son of God, unless the end of the Johannine prologue is considered to have been part of the primitive hymn. Although these hymns have no proper Christology in common, their different formulations of Christ's mystery do contribute singularly to our knowledge of the early doctrine of the Church expressed in the liturgy.

CHAPTER EIGHT

THE CHRISTOLOGY OF PAUL

This will appear to many as an impossible task: to present in one chapter the Christology of Paul. Within the framework of a larger study on the New Testament, there is less ground for despair, because Paul's Christology reflects in large part that of the early Church, of which he was one of the great leaders. We intend to outline here the more distinctive Pauline traits, and limit ourselves to Christology proper, without including soteriology which most authors tend to confuse with Christology. It is not always possible, however, to describe who Christ is, without saying also what he has done.

There is no marked evolution or progress in Paul's Christological conceptions, but his emphases can be different from the earlier to the later epistles. About 25 years ago Cerfaux found that Paul's writings belong to three levels.[31] In my own adaptation, they would appear as follows:

a) *Archaic level*: Thessalonians and a passage of 1 Cor 15. Here Paul is at his nearest to the outlook of the Jerusalem community, as reflected in the Synoptic gospels and the book of Acts. At this stage Paul insists on Christ's resurrection and his expected return at the *parousia*, the first mystery being the prelude of the second.

b) *Early level*: particularly Romans, Corinthians, Galatians. These epistles stress that Christ's work has put an end to the regime of the Mosaic Law; salvation now comes through faith in Jesus Christ; the advent of the spiritual Christ precludes any further interest in Orphism and the mystery cults of the philosophical religions.

c) *Later level*: which includes in chronological order Philippians, Colossians, Ephesians. At this stage the "mystery" of Christ is stressed, his cosmic role underlined as well as salvation already achieved through sacramental participation in the mystery of his death and resurrection.

a) Texts from the Archaic Level (51 A.D.)

Born at Tarsus in Cilicia about year 10 of the Christian Era, from a Jewish family, but also a Roman citizen, Paul received early—under Gamaliel in Jerusalem—a solid religious education in the Pharisaic tradition. After being fiercely opposed to the Christian movement he was converted to it around the year 36, and became a very successful Christian preacher. Paul had evangelized Thessalonica, a port city of northern Greece, during the summer of the year 50. Compelled to leave the place by opposing Jews, he went to Athens and then to Corinth, from where, during the winter of 50/51, he wrote the First Epistle to the Thessalonians.

"Wait for his Son from Heaven" (1 Th 1:10)

Towards the end of his initial thanksgiving Paul in his first letter to the Thessalonians reminds them of their recent conversion from idolatry, to serve the living God, "and to wait for his Son from heaven, whom he raised from the dead, Jesus who delivers us from the wrath to come" (1:10). This is quite an exceptional text: the return of the Son of God is awaited instead of the Son of man of the

Synoptic tradition (Mk 12:36; Mt 24:44). A contamination between ''Son of man'' and ''Son of God'' appears also in Matthew where it is said that ''the Son of man is to come with his angels in the glory *of his Father*'' (16:27). About 1 Th 1:10 Hahn writes that ''the coming 'from heaven' indicates fusion with the Son of man tradition, as does also the function of Jesus as 'Redeemer' (*ruomenos*) from 'the wrath to come,' which has to be understood in the sense of the apocalyptic judicature of the world'' (p. 286). The title ''Son of God'' would of course be more easily understood than ''Son of man'' in the Gentile churches to whom Paul is writing. For G. Friedrich 1 Th 1:9-10 originally concerned the Son of man, and was used in a pre-Pauline baptismal hymn with reference to the Son of God. P.-E. Langevin has extensively defended the pre-Pauline origin of the passage and has brought out its Christological significance: Jesus, the Son of God, is the Lord Jesus of the pre-Pauline tradition (Ph 2:9-11; Rm 10:9), and the eschatological Savior expected on ''the Day of the Lord'' (see 1 Th 5:2).

''At the Coming of our Lord Jesus'' (1 Th 3:13)

The last verse of its ch. 3 can be considered as a typical statement of First Thessalonians. There Paul prays that love may establish the hearts of the faithful ''faultless in holiness before our God and Father, at the coming of our Lord Jesus with all his saints.'' It is remarkable that particularly in his letters to the Thessalonians Paul stresses the unity existing between God, often called ''Father,'' and Jesus Christ, who is predominantly referred to as the Lord. Both epistles are addressed to ''the Church of the Thessalonians in God the Father and the Lord Jesus Christ'' (in 2 Th 1:1 we have ''God *our* Father.'' See also 1 Th 3:11; 2 Th 1:2, 12; 2:16).

Although the saving action of Christ is already in some way present (1 Th 1:10; 2:13; 2 Th 2:16), it is mainly expected in the future, at the *parousia*, the second coming (1 Th 2:19; 3:13; 4:15; 5:23; 2 Th 2:1, 8f). It can be asserted that in Thessalonians Paul sees the title *Kyrios*, "Lord," particularly in association with the *parousia*. Probably on account of his concentration on the future perspective Paul in Thessalonians says nothing of Christ's pre-existence, which of course he does not deny. The term *parousia* existed already but it appears certain that Paul was first to use it in the Christian sense. Since Matthew alone uses the term in the Synoptic tradition (24:3, 27, 37, 39), he probably received it from the early Church, not, however, directly from Paul (see more on *parousia* in *Matthew*, vol. 2, pp. 806f).

A Messianic Kingdom (1 Cor 15:24)?

Like 1 Thessalonians, 1 Cor 15:23-28 reflects the Jewish apocalyptic tradition. This appears particularly in the manner in which Paul mentions in the Corinthian passage the stages in which God's predetermined plan will be fulfilled: the resurrection of Christ, then of the believers, followed by "the end," and the transfer of sovereignty to God and the subjection of the Son to the Father. While in 1 Thessalonians the focal point is the *parousia*, in 1 Cor 15 it is the resurrection.

The general resurrection of the believers marks for Paul a decisive event: "Then comes the end, when he delivers the king-dom (or the sovereignty) to God the Father after destroying every rule and every authority and power" (1 Cor 15:24). Taking first the term *basileia* to mean "kingdom" here, it is perhaps possible to refer the text to a Messianic kingdom here on earth, which some commentators find mentioned in the New Testament. It is no doubt necessary to make a distinction between the eschatological king-dom of God and the kingdom of the Son of man, particularly mentioned in the gospel of Matthew (13:41; 16:28; 20:21). But also see Lk 22:30 and 23:42, where the meaning remains disputed. For the intermediate period, between the resurrection of Christ and his *parousia*, it is permissible to speak of the Messianic ''reign of Christ,'' which will come to an end with the perfect establishment of God's reign (1 Cor 15:24). Only 1 Th 4:16 (cf. 4:17) speaks of the Lord's (Christ's) ''heavenly kingdom,'' while a similar notion appears in 2 P 1:11 (see Col 1:13). Paul speaks at one point of those who have no ''inheritance in the kingdom of Christ and of God'' (Ep 5:5).

Of the NT texts the Apocalypse most clearly foresees a kingdom of Christ's preceding the definitive establishment of God's eschatological kingdom. The millenarists understand literally Rv 20:1-6 as prophesying the establishment on earth of a kingdom over which Christ would rule. More probably the thousand years refer symbolically to the period which separates the first coming from the second coming of Christ.

Albert Schweitzer held that the eschatology of Paul was quite different from that of Jesus: instead of thinking as Jesus did along the lines of the simple eschatology of Daniel and Enoch, Paul followed the twofold eschatology of the Scribes, set forth in the Apocalypses of Baruch and Ezra, but added to it the conception of two resurrections, a first in which believers in Christ attain to a share in the Messianic kingdom, and a second in which all men who have ever lived upon earth will resurrect at the end of the Messianic kingdom, here on earth, and will possess ''the resurrection mode of existence'' (p. 91). Rv 20:5-6 also seems to suppose a ''first resurrection'' leading to participation in the Messianic kingdom. However, it is also possible to understand this ''first resurrection'' spiritually, for life in the Church, Christ's kingdom on earth. No NT text compels one to adopt Schweitzer's viewpoints on the ''Messianic kingdom'' (pp. 66-69, 84-100).[32] *TOB* understands *basileia* in 1 Cor 15:24 as meaning ''kingship'': at the end Christ will deliver the kingship to God the Father.

For Paul, writes Conzelmann, Christ's ''kingdom fills up the period between the resurrection and the consummation of the work of salvation after the parousia . . . It is Christologically speaking the time of the Church, of the proclaiming of the death of Christ, of faith, of hope'' (p. 270). Contrary to what Schweitzer believed ''the kingdom of the messiah does not lie in the future for Paul'' (*ibid.*): it is enjoyed already by believers through faith, hope, and love (the advance gifts of eschatological existence) and through the abiding presence of the Holy Spirit (see Rm 8).

The absolute use of ''the Son'' in 1 Cor 15:28 is quite remarkable and unique in Paul, although ''his Son'' occurs elsewhere (Rm 1:3f). See on ''the Son'' as title Ch. 4, about Mk 13:32. The subjection of the Son to the Father does not seem to have created any particular difficulty for Paul, although he does seem in some texts to consider Christ as God (see next section). St. Augustine explained that the subjection concerns only the human nature of Christ (*De Trinitate* [*The Trinity*] I, 8). ''Christ is God's'' of 1 Cor 3:23 seems to reflect the same desire of not presenting Christ as another God, which of course would gravely offend Jewish monotheism. Imprudent efforts to solve the question theologically will lead later to various subordinationist deviations in Christology. In 1 Cor 15:28 the main thrust of the statement can be seen as follows: when Christ completes his redeeming role, his rulership over the world will cease, and his sovereignty will be absorbed in the universal dominion of God the Father.

b) Early Level Pauline Texts (57/58 A.D.)

According to the majority opinion of NT scholars, as reflected, for example, in the *Jerusalem Bible* chronology, the First Letter to the Corinthians would have been sent about Passover 57, Galatians a month or two later, and Romans and 2 Corinthians during the following winter, 57/58. Philippians could have been written shortly before this group, but traditionally it has been linked with Ephesians and Colossians, and accordingly we will examine it in the third level, although it could belong to the second. A large number of texts could be quoted from these epistles, giving the lead to as many corresponding developments. Considering our purpose, we have selected only a few, which appeared to us as particularly representative of Paul's Christology.

"Established Son of God" (Rm 1:4)

In the prescript to the Epistle to the Romans (1:1-7), Paul presents himself as preacher of "the Gospel of God," promised beforehand through his prophets, "the Gospel concerning his Son, descended from David according to the flesh, and established Son of God in power according to the Spirit of holiness by his resurrection from the dead, Jesus Christ our Lord" (Rm 1:3-4). Quite possibly, from "descended" onwards this text quotes or closely reflects a pre-Pauline confession of faith, as several commentators presuppose.[33] It must be said, however, that "Son of God" and "Lord," to designate Christ are very Pauline indeed, as also is the importance given to his resurrection by God.

Christ's pre-existence is not denied in Rm 1:3-4, but it is not stated—as it is, for example, in Rm 8:3, which represents God as "sending his own Son in the likeness of sinful flesh." Both verses of Rm 1 refer to the person of Jesus Christ with v. 3 focusing on the human condition of his life on earth, while v. 4 shows him endowed with the prerogatives of his divinity. The perspective is similar to that of Ac 2:36 (see Ch. 5 above). For Hahn, Rm 1:3-4 marks the "initiatory acts" of a two-stage Christology: "of the birth as the beginning of the earthly reality as Son of David, of the exaltation as the beginning of the mode of existence *kata pneuma hagiosunês* as Son of God and messianic king, and in this process the resurrection marks the temporal turning-point between the lowliness and the exaltation of Jesus" (*Titles* 251). In his *Commentary on Romans* (1973, E.T. 1980), E. Käsemann observes that the attribution of Christ's resurrection to the power of the Holy Spirit is unusual in Paul, since for the Apostle "the Spirit proceeds from Christ or represents him, but the Spirit does not act upon him'' (p. 11). This appears to be an indication of the pre-Pauline origin of the formula. *Kata pneuma hagiosunês* can be understood also as meaning ''in the sphere of the Holy Spirit,'' that is of ''the heavenly sphere,'' in contrast to the earthly sphere of the flesh (compare with 1 Tm 3:16a). It is true to say that the title ''Son of God'' bestowed on Christ in Rm 1:4 is *functional*, as in most NT texts, when a similar post-resurrectional attribution occurs: at Easter Jesus took up his office as Messianic King over the community (see *TDNT* 8, p. 367).

Christ Called ''God'' (Rm 9:5)

The structure of the sentence and to some degree the context suggest reading Rm 9:5 as follows: ''And the patriarchs . . . from whom, according to the flesh, is the Christ, God who is over all be blessed for ever. Amen.'' The early Latin translators and Christian tradition have understood the text in this way. Of course, such a clear affirmation of Christ's divinity is relatively rare in the NT, but it occurs in Jn 1:1, 18; 20:28; Tt 2:13, and 2 P 1:1 (see also Heb 1:8a). In Rm 9:5 the statement comes from a liturgical acclamation.[34] That the writers of the New Testament and the communities behind them considered Jesus to be God results particularly from their constant application of the title *Kyrios* to Christ, for *Kyrios* is the normal translation of YHWH in the Septuagint. This occurs, for example, where OT texts concerning the Lord are used to describe a mystery regarding Christ (Mk 1:3; Ac 2:2; Rm 10:13). In *The Names and Titles of Jesus* I have argued at length that the New Testament does call Christ ''God'' (pp. 297-304).

It is not certain, however, that Rm 9:5 has to be read as proposed above. Several modern editions of Romans read the verse as follows (*RSV*): ''to them belong the patriarchs, and of their race, according to the flesh, is the Christ. God who is over all be blessed for ever. Amen.'' The doxology would be directed to God the

Father, not to Christ. Perhaps the main argument presented in favor of this relies on the fact that Paul does not elsewhere designate "the Christ" as God. Even if this were so the argument loses much of its weight when it is admitted that the doxology can have been borrowed from a liturgical acclamation and not redacted by Paul himself as his own thought.

One God — One Lord (1 Cor 8:6)

In the course of his instruction on the attitude to adopt regarding meats offered to idols, Paul asserts that idols, of course, have no real existence, as the Christian faith testifies: "For us there is one God, the Father, from whom all things come and for whom we exist; and one Lord, Jesus Christ, through whom everything was made and through whom we exist" (1 Cor 8:6). "Is," "exist" (twice) are added here to the Greek text, which has no verb. It will not be necessary to analyze here the last proposition of the verse, since Christ's role in creation has been discussed in Ch. 7 in connection with Col 1:15-20. On the other hand, two other texts do have special relevance here. One is Rm 10:9, a profession of faith which very likely originated in a baptismal setting: "For if you confess the Lord Jesus with your lips and believe with your heart that God has raised him from the dead, you will be saved." The accent is on Jesus as Lord also in the other text (1 Cor 12:3b): "No one can say 'Jesus is Lord' except by the Holy Spirit." In both Rm 10:9 and 1 Cor 12:3 we have a confession in the form of acclamation. The mention of the Spirit reflects the fact that the early Christian cult was celebrated under the inspiration of the Spirit and consisted essentially in the invocation and acclamation of Christ the Lord (see also Ph 2:11).

In 1 Cor 8:6 the concept "God" is explained in terms of "content," for the pagans, to whom the nature of the one God has to be made known. However "Lord," assumed to be known, is not explained, but defined by naming Jesus Christ, the bearer of the title (see Conzelmann, *First Corinthians* 144). God is not described as Father of our Lord Jesus Christ (Rm 15:6; 2 Cor 1:3; 11:31; Ep 3:14; Col 1:3), but as the Creator (see Rm 1:25; Col 3:10; Heb 3:4), "from whom" all things are. Yet all things are "through" Jesus Christ, for he is the Mediator of creation. The preposition *dia*, "through," is also used for Christ's role in Col 1:16, and his mediatory role supposes pre-existence.

The Last Adam (1 Cor 15:45)

The whole chapter 15 of First Corinthians is devoted to the resurrection of the dead, and the first eleven verses form a basis from which Paul can proceed: the apostolic tradition he has received testifies to the fact that Jesus was seen alive, and Paul's own experience confirms the reported facts of the appearances. The resurrection of Christ is for Paul an indisputable fact on which the hope of a general resurrection of believers (v. 23) is founded. For Christ is not merely the first to be raised; all the others are raised in him (v. 49 and Ph 3:21). This Christological approach also explains why Paul seems interested only in the resurrection of believers, while other biblical authors envisage a general resurrection (Dn 12:2; Jn 5:29; Ac 24:15).

In 1 Cor 15:21f Paul, with the Jewish tradition, considers Adam not merely as the ancestor of men, but as the primal man, in whom the whole of mankind is virtually contained (Conzelmann 268). "All shall be made alive," looking to the future, shows Paul detaching himself from the Gnostic mythical schema, which would say: "All have been made alive" (see also Rm 6:5). The apocalyptic order which follows (v. 23-28) has already been discussed in the last part of the first section. From v. 35 onwards Paul attempts to visualize the condition of the risen body. Again, his approach is Christological, as v. 45 shows: "Thus it is written, 'the first man Adam became a living being'; the last Adam became a life-giving spirit." The first proposition literally refers to Gn 2:7, while the connection of the second with Scripture is not at all clear.[35] The heavenly origin of the "last Adam" should probably be linked in some way to the Son of man of Dn 7, while the vivifying power he possesses calls to mind Ws 7:22: "in wisdom there is a spirit." Thus would Paul's reasoning combine apocalyptic (Daniel) and sapiential ideas to formulate the mystery which links together original creation and eschatological redemption.

Adam and Christ appear as prototypes of two different humanities, one earthly, the other heavenly. While in 1 Corinthians Paul concentrates his attention on the two persons, in Rm 5:12-21 there is a shift rather to their respective work. Here Christ appears clearly as Adam's antitype. Adam, Paul writes, "was a type of the one who was to come" (v. 14). As L. Goppelt explains, *typos* can be the "hollow form" which makes an opposite impression on some other material (*TDNT* 8, p. 252). In fact, the correspondence between Adam and Christ is antithetical. "In the universal havoc he caused Adam is for Paul a *typos*, an advance presentation, through which God intimates the future Adam, namely, Christ in his universal work of salvation" (*ibid.*). Adam represents the old aeon which followed the fall; around Christ is built the new aeon based on redemption and grace.

"The Lord is the Spirit" (2 Cor 3:17)

In the course of a development on the ministry of the new covenant Paul contrasts the limited revelation to Moses with the true glory which marks the new revelation in Christ. Then he explains that only through their conversion to the Lord will the Jews truly understand the Scriptures: "Now the Lord is the Spirit, and where the Spirit is, there is freedom." The more probable interpretation of this difficult statement must be the following: while Moses represents the letter of Scripture, Christ, in contrast, represents the spiritual sense, which liberates from the letter of

Scripture, which leads nowhere. Others say that 2 Cor 3:17 unlocks the meaning of Ex 34:34 cited in 3:16, and *NEB* reflects this in its translation: ''However, as Scripture says of Moses, 'whenever he turns to the Lord the veil is removed.' Now the Lord of whom this passage speaks is the Spirit.'' One has therefore an identification between Yahweh and the Spirit. There is little doubt, however, that ''the Lord'' in v. 16 is Christ, so that in v. 17 *Kyrios* must refer to him also. But it can be held that Christ stands here for the presence of God: Christians always live in the presence of the Spirit of Christ and therefore do not need to turn or to put the veil on or off.[36]

c) Texts of a Later Level (61-63 A.D.)

There is no consensus on the date of the composition of Ephesians, Philippians and Colossians. A few commentators would place Colossians last, as a post-apostolic writing of the end of the first century. Others place it with Ephesians and Philippians during Paul's detention in Rome (61-63). But Philippians could, as we have said before, be as early as First Corinthians, or at least have been composed with Colossians during Paul's ministry in Ephesus (54-57). An imprisonment of him there has to be supposed, although no other report of it is available. In any case, Ephesians is certainly later than Philippians and was very probably composed, either by Paul or by a disciple, after Colossians. Excepting 2:6-11, already analyzed as a pre-Pauline hymn (Ch. 7), there is no distinctive Christological statement in Philippians. So we pass immediately to Colossians.

In Him the Fullness of Deity Dwells Bodily (Col 2:9)

In Colossians Paul has to combat, among other things, the tendency to attach an excessive importance to the heavenly powers (see 2:8). He opposes this deviation by underlining the supremacy of Christ (see 1:16) and his closeness to the being of God. In Ch. 7 we already examined the statement found in 1:19 on the dwelling of the *plêrôma* in Christ. In Col 2:9 the affirmation is more precise and invites further study. We are now told that in Christ "the entire fullness (*plêrôma*) of the deity dwells bodily." *Theotês*, "deity," used only here in the entire NT, refers to God's being, and is to be distinguished from *theiotês*, "divine nature."

Sômatikôs, "bodily," is diversely interpreted. It certainly underlines the reality of this dwelling of the deity in Christ. For E. Schweizer *sômatikôs* "means the corporeality in which God encounters man in the world in which he lives. It means the full humanity of Jesus, not a humanity which is a mere cloak for deity" (*TDNT* 7, p. 1077). It can be said that statements like Col 2:9 suppose that Christ exercises divine functions, but do not answer the question if he is to be equated with the Godhead. In 1:13 Paul had written: "He has delivered us from the dominion of darkness and transferred us to the kingdom of his beloved Son." Christ's closeness to deity itself assures that "whoever has been transferred into the domain of his kingdom is free from the powers which rule in the cosmos and which want to force their enslaving yoke upon men" (E. Lohse, *Colossians and Philemon* 101).

"Recapitulate all things in Christ" (Ep 1:10)

In Ephesians—an epistle addressed in fact to all the churches of Asia Minor—Paul insists even more than in Colossians on the sense of mystery and on the spiritual understanding which it requires. If Ephesians was the work of a disciple, he has in a rather unclever fashion resumed some of the themes found in Colossians. Still, Ephesians bears the marks of Paul's genial way of pursuing homogeneously an original understanding of God's revelation. The crisis in Colossae had brought him to give more attention to cosmic salvation, already referred to in Rm 8:22. In Ephesians, as in Colossians, sin appears connected with the influence of cosmic forces, seen more than before as evil powers, "potentates of this dark world," "superhuman forces of evil in the heavens" (Ep 6:12 in the *NEB* version, not literal, but accurate). Christ has conquered the cosmos through a descent followed by an ascension (4:8-10). As in Colossians, this triumph is not future but already present, a thought formulated in the perspective of "realized eschatology," more boldly expressed than previously: not only are the baptized already risen (Col 2:12), they are already enthroned in heaven (Ep 2:6).

Although the main thrust of Ephesians will subsequently appear to center around the Church, the long opening sentence (1:3-14) focuses on Jesus Christ, in whom and through whom God bestows all his blessings. The divine plan of salvation includes the "recapitulation" of all things in him (1:10), a new and perhaps better formulation than the universal reconciliation referred to in Col 1:20. The term *anakephalaioun* (lit. "recapitulate") seems to mean in the present context "to sum up/comprehend all things in Christ as head."[37] H. Schlier explains: "The summing up of the totality takes place in its subjection to the Head. The subjection of the totality to the Head takes place in the co-ordinating of the Head and the Church" (*TDNT*, 3, p. 682). In fact, in Ephesians the Church is now explicitly identified with the Body of Christ, who is the Head (1:22f; 5:23) through whose influence the Body builds itself up (4:15f). The Church is even equated with the *plêrôma*, the fullness of all, discussed in Ch. 7 in connection with Col 1:19 (see also 2:9 and Ep 3:19; 4:13). To the same context belongs Ep 4:10, which says that Christ has ascended far above all the heavens, "that he might fill all things." He does so because he fills the Church (see 1:22f). Finally the mention of the "kingdom of Christ" in Ep 5:5 is quite remarkable, and has to be explained in the same way as the related texts (see on 1 Cor 15:24 in the first section of the present chapter).

Conclusion

It is not necessary to repeat here the sketch of ideas characterizing the three levels of Pauline thought (see the beginning of this chapter). The first level, mainly represented by Thessalonians, shows the application to the return of Christ of the apocalyptic schema regarding the heavenly Son of man. It was thought appropriate to discuss here the references to an earthly Messianic kingdom. At the second level Paul's Christian theology appears in full light, with the representation of Christ as the transcendent Son of God, even as God, and also as Lord beside God the Father. As ''the Last Adam'' Christ in his glorified humanity embodies the newly redeemed mankind, and the new economy of grace. In him Scripture becomes totally intelligible, since the Spirit of God dwells in him fully. The third level of Pauline thought extols even more the hold Christ has over the universe, particularly through the Church, his Body, because in him the fullness of the Deity dwells in a real way. In some true sense it can be said that ''Christ is God's nature.'' Conzelmann wrote this about Paul's statement that Christ is ''the power of God and the wisdom of God'' (1 Cor 1:24), meaning that the power and the wisdom of God are in Christ. The combination of ''power'' and ''wisdom'' shows that the latter is not considered here as an hypostasis, but as a conceptual term, although in other writings Christ is represented as fulfilling the task of divine Wisdom (see Ch. 7 about Col 1:15-20 and Jn 1:1-14). In a word, we can say that Paul's Christology involved above all else the proclamation of Jesus as Lord and the confession that God has raised Jesus from the dead.[38]

CHAPTER NINE

HEBREWS, FIRST PETER AND THE PASTORAL EPISTLES

Of course, to each of these writings a full chapter could be devoted, but for a rapid overview of NT Christology it appeared best to put them together. And these writings have a number of concepts in common which will be pointed out. Hebrews is probably the earliest of them, and a few authors, with good reasons, place its origin well before the destruction of the temple (70 A.D.).[39] In spite of several arguments to the contrary, it is still possible to retain the Petrine authorship of First Peter, perhaps actually written down by Silvanus (5:12), called Silas (Greek) in Ac 15:22, 40. That would put the composition of the letter at the latest shortly before the persecution under Nero (64 A.D.) and the death of Peter. Although no decisive proof has yet been offered against the Pauline authenticity of the Pastoral Epistles (1-2 Timothy and Titus), the question remains unsolved, and so also the date of the origin of these letters. In any case the Christology they reflect, as we shall see, appears to belong on several points to post-Pauline developments.

God Has Spoken to Us by a Son (Heb 1:2)

A few commentators, Dunn included, suggest that Heb 1:1-3 could incorporate at least part of an early Christian hymn, characterized by a Wisdom Christology.[40] This appears difficult to prove, however, because the author of Hebrews shows throughout the letter that he is capable of the kinds of developments as are found in the first verses. We know, for example, that Christ is often called ''Son of God'' in the epistle (also 3:6; 4:14; 5:8; 6:6; 7:3, 28; 10:29), and references to Ps 110:1, as here in 1:3, occur elsewhere in the epistle (5:5f; 7:17; 8:1; 10:13).

Having said that God spoke of old in many ways, the author continues: ''But in these last days *he has spoken to us by a Son*, whom he appointed the heir of all things, through whom also he created the world'' (1:2). This last proposition echoes the common early Christian belief, as it is also reflected in two early Christological hymns (see Ch. 7 on Col 1:15-17 and Jn 1:1-3). In the opening statements of Hebrews, Christ appears as the ultimate Messenger and Revealer of God and his word enjoys the unique authority of being that of the Son. But the verses also announce developments that will spell out other central roles to be played by the Son.

In view of Jesus' pre-existence, Cullmann writes, the author of Hebrews is interested in connecting ''High Priest'' very closely with ''Son of God,'' for he quotes the confessional formula and makes it expressly recognizable as such: ''Having therefore a great High Priest who has gone through the heavens, Jesus, the Son of God, let us hold fast to the confession'' (4:14).[41] This Son, by whom he created, ''after having effected purification from sins, took his seat to the right of the majesty on high'' (1:2-3). What is here stated of the Son applies to the sacrificial work and to the exaltation of our High Priest (see 8:1-2). Again, what he writes of the Son, quoting Ps 110:1, ''Sit at my right until I have placed your enemies as a footstool of your feet,'' he states also of Jesus as High Priest (10:13). The two texts, one about the Son (Ps 2:7), the other on the High Priest (Ps 110:4) are quoted together in Heb 5:5-6: ''So also Christ did not exalt himself to be made a high priest, but was appointed by him who said to him, 'Thou art my Son, today I have begotten thee'; as he says also in another place, 'Thou art a priest for ever, after the order of Melchizedek.' '' Elsewhere, as in 7:28, the combination of the two texts is suggested rather than expressed. In another passage, Christ, the Son (Heb 3:6), is declared faithful over his (or God's) house, which he edified as High Priest (3:1) by his redemptive work. Finally, 7:3 has also to be referred to: there Melchizedek, a prophetic type of our High Priest, is likened to the Son of God.

''Pioneer of their Salvation'' (Heb 2:10)

Setting the passion of Jesus in the divine plan of salvation the author of Hebrews writes: ''For it was fitting that God, for whom and by whom all things exist, in bringing many sons to glory, should make the pioneer (*archêgos*) of their salvation perfect through suffering'' (2:10). In the Septuagint *archêgos* is usually a political or military ''leader'' of the whole people, or of a part of it (see *TDNT* 1, p. 487). In Philo the cognate term *archêgêtês* is often predicated of Adam, Noah, or the patriarchs, especially Abraham. The notion behind *archêgos*, independently of the term, is one which suits well leaders like Moses and Joshua, whose vocation it was to bring the chosen people to the Promised Land. Moses is in effect called ''ruler and deliverer'' (*archôn kai lutrôtês*) in Ac 7:35, but he was *archêgos* only imperfectly since he did not introduce his people into the Land, while Joshua was leader only in the last phase of the journey. It is a different, superior leadership that applies to Jesus, called in Acts ''Leader and Savior'' (*archêgos kai sôtêr*, 5:31), or ''the Author of life'' (*ho archêgos tês zôês* 3:15). He it is who has opened for us by his blood, by the *teleiôsis* of his humanity, the new and living way leading to God (Heb 10:19f), and in this he was also ''the pioneer and perfecter of our faith'' (12:2), he ''who inspires our faith from the beginning to the end'' (H. Montefiore, *A Commentary on the Epistle to the Hebrews, in loc.*).

Paul exhorted his readers to self-discipline by citing the example of runners who compete for earthly prizes (see 1 Cor 9:24; Gal 2:2). In Heb 12:1 the imagery recurs in the form of a ''gigantic relay race'' (Montefiore), a challenge for the last competitors to ''run with endurance the race that lies before us,'' knowing that as Forerunner (*prodromos*) Jesus entered the sanctuary on our behalf, having become High Priest for ever according to the order of Melchizedek (6:20). In fact, these two titles, *archêgos* and *prodromos* apply to our High Priest in his essential function: by means of his sacrifice he has entered into heaven itself, to appear before God for us (9:24).

''So also the Christ . . .'' (Heb 5:5)

Since Hebrews explicitly recognizes the royal and the priestly character of Jesus, it has two basic reasons for calling him also ''the Christ,'' the Anointed One. In the Old Testament the high priest is called also ''the anointed priest'' (Lv 4:16). In Hebrews, as elsewhere in the NT, ''the Christ'' (with the article, see 3:14, 5:5, 6:1, 9:14, 28, 13:21b) designates Jesus rather as the Messiah, while ''Christ'' alone (3:6, 9:11, 24) is more of a personal name, like Jesus Christ (10:10, 13:8, 21), although the meaning still affects its use. Thus where ''Christ'' occurs for the first time in Hebrews, the context has changed from the earthly life of Jesus to that of his glorious state as the Son now ruling over his house (3:6). In the other two texts (9:11, 24) ''Christ'' designates the exalted High Priest entering into the sanctuary (in 9:14, 28 the article points to the same person as in 9:11, 24).

The author of Hebrews thought of ''Christ'' as being the Messianic king. This is already clear from his use of Ps 2:7 and Ps 110:1, combined with Ps 110:4 and the figure of Melchizedek, the Priest-King of Salem (Heb 7:1-3). He does not call Christ ''King'' but alludes to such a title by describing his exaltation in terms of royal enthronement: ''But of the Son he says, 'Thy throne, O God, is for ever and ever, the righteous scepter is the scepter of thy kingdom' '' (1:8). It is almost certain that in ''O God'' the divine appellative is understood in its full sense, although in Ps 45:7, quoted here, it does not necessarily have a transcendent meaning. The idea of rest after completing a work (cf. Heb 4:10) and the use of royal imagery appear combined in the following very distinctive text: ''But when Christ has offered for all time a single sacrifice for sins, he sat down at the right hand of God, then to wait until his enemies should be made a stool for his feet'' (10:12-13; cf. Ps 110:1). The Messianic expectation, both royal and priestly, was fulfilled in Jesus and this the Epistle to the Hebrews has admirably expressed by describing as an *enthronement* the exaltation of Christ our *High Priest.*

''Proclaimed High Priest'' (Heb 5:9)

In Cullmann's words ''the Christology of the High Priest is combined with that of the Son of God throughout Hebrews. The writer does not forget that the theme of *obedience* belongs with the ideal of Jesus' sonship, especially since it can be related easily to the High Priest concept'' (p. 305). Although he was Son, Hebrews asserts, Christ learned obedience from the things he suffered (5:8). This is also the context in which we read that having been given fulfillment, Christ became for all those who obey him a cause of everlasting salvation, ''proclaimed by God high priest according to the order of Melchizedek'' (5:9-10). This can be compared to the exaltation which according to Paul Christ was granted as a consequence of his extreme self-denial (Ph 2:5-11). They are two examples, among many, of the ''New Testament dialectic between deepest humiliation and highest majesty'' (Cullmann, *Christology* 92). The proclamation of Christ as High Priest in connection with his *teleiôsis*, ''perfecting,'' may also be related to John's notion of the Cross as an exaltation (see Jn 13:31, 17:1). As God-man Christ by his very being was destined to be High Priest, which he effectively became gradually during his lifetime, and especially in his sacrificial *transitus* to God as head and representative of redeemed mankind. He is proclaimed High Priest upon achieving his mediatorial work. Being the Son of God, his Priesthood could only be unique and incomparable.

The Chief Shepherd (1 P 5:4)

Both Hebrews and First Peter seem to be addressed to Christians undergoing some kind of persecution, and both offer encouragement with Scripture references. Closer resemblances are noticeable: the addressees are afflicted with various trials (1 P 1:6; Heb 12:11), they are exhorted to recall the coming judgment (1 P 1:17; Heb 11:6), and not to forget that Christ has died for our sins (1 P 3:18; Heb 9:26-28); that through the sprinkling of his blood (1 P 1:2; Heb 12:24), we are cleansed (Heb 9:18-22); and baptism brings to us this salvation (1 P 3:21; Heb 10:22). No direct contact between the two writings has to be supposed, but both reflect some aspects of early Christian preaching.[42]

The Christological use of the Shepherd figure is not found in the Pauline epistles, but it is quite well represented in other writings of the New Testament, particularly in Matthew, as we have seen in Ch. 6 above. Not too surprisingly, since Peter had been appointed chief deputy shepherd (Jn 21:15-17), the First Epistle attributed to him introduces the theme already in 2:25, where it says of the faithful that after straying like sheep they have returned to Christ, "the Shepherd and Guardian" of their lives (lit. "souls"). A discrete allusion can be seen here to Zc 13:7-9, a text explicitly referred to in Mk 14:27. In Zc 13 the trials of the Shepherd-King precede those of the purified people (Spicq 114). The theme recurs in Jn 10:15-17, where Jesus himself says he is the good Shepherd who gives his life for his sheep.

Both Hebrews and First Peter refer to Christ as the sovereign Shepherd, using different words: *megas poimên*, "great Shepherd," in Heb 13:20; *archipoimenos*, "chief Shepherd," in 1

P 5:4. In a concluding development the author of Hebrews express-es the hope that his addressees will find themselves perfectly equipped by the gifts they will receive from ''the God of peace who brought again from the dead our Lord Jesus, the great Shepherd of the sheep, by the blood of the eternal covenant'' (13:20). Through his blood, his sacrifice, Jesus has become the Mediator of the better covenant (7:22; 8:6) and the great Bringer of Peace (Ep 2:13-16). Heb 13:20 quite explicitly reflects Is 63:11b: ''Where is he who brought up out of the sea the shepherd of his flock?'' Although the plural ''shepherds'' can also be read, more probably the singular is meant, referring to Moses (Ps 77:21), saved from the waters of the Nile (Ex 2:10) and of the Sea of Reeds (Ex 14:21-29). Pursuing his exhortation, the author of First Peter reminds the elders to tend properly the flock of God (compare Ac 20:28), for in so doing they will qualify to obtain the unfading crown of glory ''when the chief Shepherd is manifested'' (1 P 5:4). The term *archipoimenos*, ''chief Shepherd,'' occurs only here in the whole New Testament. As chief Shepherd Jesus is the supreme Overseer above all the other shepherds of the flock, who are his deputies on earth and are expected to fulfill their duties on the model of the chief Shepherd and with the help of his grace.

''Our Savior Jesus Christ'' (2 Tm 1:10)

The Pastoral Epistles do not offer any distinctive Christology. This may be due to the unspeculative nature of these writings, which insist rather on the meaning of salvation for the present (2 Tm 1:9),[43] and on piety (*eusebeia*) as the rule of life (1 Tm 4:7 and often). There are two texts, however, Christologically significant: 2 Tm 1:10 and Tt 2:13.

Purportedly exhorting Timothy to carry on faithfully the good fight for the Gospel, Paul reminds him of the grace of God, given us in Christ Jesus ages ago, and now ''manifested through the appearance (*epiphaneia*) of *our Savior Jesus Christ,* who abrogated death and brought life and immortality to light through the Gospel'' (2 Tm 1:9b-10). In the Pastoral Epistles we find little speculation on Christ's pre-existence: ''given us in Christ Jesus ages ago'' rather signifies that the present revelation of salvation in Christ Jesus responds to the salvation history plan made by God ages ago (see Tt 1:2; Col 1:26).[44] The term *epiphaneia* and the underlying concept receives special stress in the Pastorals (also 1 Tm 6:14; 2 Tm 4:1, 8; Tt 2:13). ''Strictly speaking, the religious term 'epiphany' means the appearance of a divinity that is otherwise hidden, manifested as a *deus presens* either in a vision, by a healing or some other helping action, or by any manifestation of power. In any of these instances, the emphasis is not on revelation in myth, but rather on events in history and in the present'' (Dibelius 104). The manifestation of the god's presence or power can also take place in the cult. *Epiphaneia*, already used by Paul in 2 Th 2:8 with reference to ''the lawless one,'' is adopted in the Pastoral Letters in preference to *parousia*, ''coming'' (1 Cor 15:23). But *epiphaneia* occurs in the Pastoral Letters both for Christ's second coming (2 Tm 4:1, 8) and for his coming into the world in the incarnation, as here in 2 Tm 1:10.

In ch. 18 of *The Names and Titles of Jesus* I have discussed the origin and meaning of the theme ''salvation'' and also the pre-Christian, as well as the Christian use of the title SAVIOR, noting this in particular: if the function of Savior is rarely attributed to the Messiah (see Zc 9:9 LXX), it must be due to the Old Testament habit of reserving the title and role of Savior to God himself, as in Is 12:2, 45:21 and in the Psalms: ''Shall my soul not give itself to the Lord? For with him is my salvation. He is my God and my Savior (*sôtêr*), my refuge; I shall not falter'' (Ps 60:1f, LXX). See more on the pre-Christian and Christian use of the title ''Savior'' in Ch. 5, under Lk 2:11. The only properly Pauline text which calls Jesus ''Savior'' can be appropriately quoted here: ''But our citizenship is in heaven from which also we eagerly await a Savior, our Lord Jesus Christ, who will refashion the body of our lowliness, conforming it to the body of his glory by exerting the power by which he is able also to subject all things to himself'' (Ph 3:20f). As also this text indicates, in Paul's own letters salvation is a reality of the future, even though it is founded in the already past redemptive work of Christ. With the increasingly Hellenized formulations of Christian faith, as they are found in the Pastoral Epistles, Jesus is frequently there acknowledged as ''Savior'' (2 Tm 1:10; Tt 1:4; 2:13; 3:6), like God himself (see 1 Tm 1:1; 2:3; Tt 1:3; 2:10).

''Our Great God and Savior Christ Jesus'' (Tt 2:13)

Under Rm 9:5 in Ch. 8 the question has been raised: does the New Testament call Christ ''God''? It may be doubtful in Rm 9:5, but the divinity of Christ is clearly asserted in Jn 1:1, 18; 20:28, while the Second Epistle of Peter does seem to present Christ as the Savior-God of humanity in 1:1, perhaps also in 1:11; 2:20; 3:18 with words like ''our Lord and Savior Jesus Christ.''

Chapter two of the Letter to Titus consists mainly of ''rules for the household,'' to serve as guidelines for daily conduct.[45] The first section ends curiously with the statement that ''slaves'' ought to be faithful and worthy, so as to be in everything a credit ''to the teaching of God our Savior'' (2:10). It is tempting to say that reference here is made to the teaching of Christ. But the rather strange formulation could point to the pre-Christian origin of the list of rules for the household (Dibelius *in loc.*). A clearer motivation for good conduct immediately follows: ''because we await the blessed hope and the manifestation of the glory of our great God and Savior Jesus Christ'' (2:13). This is the more probable translation of a verse which is somewhat ambiguous in the Greek. Having carefully studied the OT and NT use of the expression ''Great God,'' W. Grundmann concludes that in Tt 2:13 ''we have to take Jesus Christ as the *megas Theos*. This is demanded by the position of the article, by the term *epiphaneia* (the return of Jesus Christ will be an epiphany), and by the stereotyped nature of the expression.

With its cultic and polytheistic background the phrase is better adapted to refer to Jesus Christ as God than to God the Father in the narrower monotheistic sense'' (*TDNT* 4, p. 540). In their commentary, Dibelius and Conzelmann, however, read ''the appearance of the glory of the great God and of our Savior Christ Jesus,'' basing their reading on the fact, they claim, that the subordination of Christ to God is consistently retained precisely in the ''epiphany passages'' of the Pastoral Epistles. This reason does not appear strong enough to upset Grundmann's argumentation just presented, and the more obvious understanding of the Greek sentence as it stands. In the same line of thought, the Second Letter of Peter, a writing which represents the apostolic tradition as understood at the end of the first century or even later, speaks of ''the righteousness of our God and Savior Jesus Christ'' (2 P 1:1). Spicq defends this reading (p. 208) and refers to both Tt 2:13 and 3:4 as texts which call Jesus Christ ''God.''

Conclusion

After a brief reference to the debated date of composition of these later writings, I have chosen a few texts from Hebrews, First Peter, and the Pastoral Epistles as a basis for a discussion of their contribution to Christology. Hebrews underlines the title ''Son'' and breaks new ground with the titles ''Pioneer'' and, of course, ''High Priest,'' which is intimately connected with the epistle's manifest interest in the sacrificial approach to God. The two latter titles also fit well in the general framework of the writing: an exhortation to a pilgrim people on its way to the true Promised Land. That the First Letter of Peter should refer to Christ as the Chief Shepherd is not at all surprising, since the letter is attributed to, if not written by, precisely the apostle to whom was entrusted the task of looking after the entire flock of the Lord. The Pastoral

Epistles insist on the epiphany of Christ the Savior, and very probably represent him as the Savior-God. This was in response to all the Hellenistic claims about divine and human saviors, which for the Christian believer amount to little more than empty speculation, where spiritual salvation is concerned.

CHAPTER TEN

THE FOURTH GOSPEL AND THE JOHANNINE LETTERS

With the presentation of Jn 1:1-18 in Ch. 7 important aspects of Johannine Christology have already been examined, and the *Logos* theme will not be explicitly taken up again. As was said there, for the evangelist John the incarnate Logos is the Messiah. Before passing to particular texts and their distinctive significance, it seems appropriate to recall a few generalities regarding the Fourth Gospel and its presentation of Jesus of Nazareth.[46]

In the Preface to his commentary, R. Schnackenburg states that John's gospel stands among the most mature, and at the same time among the most controverted products of early Christianity. It took some time to recognize its full orthodoxy, because its language had some affinity with dualistic and even Gnostic ways of expression. Having originated in Palestine, the Johannine tradition absorbed elements of Hellenistic Judaism in its passage through Antioch, before reaching Ephesus, in Asia Minor, where it was fixed and edited (see vol. 1, p. 155). In this gospel, equally, if not more, than in the other gospels, Jesus appears insistingly as a human person, whose activity on earth is described by precise annotations regarding place and time. At the same time, the person and story of Jesus Christ clearly transcend in John the historical situation to which they are referred by concrete threads. Progressive development is certainly lacking in John's gospel from chapter to chapter, and the different persons involved—John the Baptist, Nicodemus, the Samaritan woman, the man born blind, Mary and Martha, Pilate, Jesus himself, the Jews—all have a characteristically Johannine way of expressing themselves. This occurs because John speaks with their voices, and because several persons, who intervene in dialogue with Jesus, are types representing attitudes as well as historical figures. Even indications of time and space can have figurative meanings: "Siloam" (9:7 = "sent"), "winter" (10:22), "night" (13:30). But, of course, the historical Jesus is the central figure and is irreplaceable since in his voice and in his works of power the Word expresses itself.

It is the nature of its central thought that John's gospel should contain so much of dramatic presentation. Rudolf Bultmann has stressed what he considers, and rightly so, to be the central theme of John's gospel: the impact on the world of the Incarnation of the Word. Before the coming of the REVEALER darkness existed, as well as death, and untruth. But they were situations of a temporary character, a period of expectation. When he comes, however, everything becomes definitive (12:35-36). Henceforth those who do not believe in the Revealer definitively choose darkness instead of light, falsehood instead of truth, death instead of life (see 3:18; 5:24; 8:51). The appearance of the Revealer initiates a process of authenticity. Will it confirm one's full acceptance of God or reveal one's latent belonging to the opposite camp? The presence of the Revealer constitutes a continual "interpellation," a challenge to verify one's true standing before God. Bultmann failed, however, to recognize well enough that revelation is not only intimately linked to the person of Jesus, but that Christ himself is, also for John, the object of faith.

"Seeing" in John is very important, but it is not purely human: it penetrates beyond the appearances to discover the true reality, God's presence in Jesus. The object of the Johannine vision is of course Christ. Having come as the Revealer he had to publicly manifest himself, in the clarity and in the concreteness of history

(Mollat 217). He spoke openly (7:26; 18:20); everybody saw his signs (11:47-48) and his works (5:20; 10:32). His death is an "elevation" (3:14; 8:28; 12:32). Pilate presents him to the crowds, "Here is the man!" (19:5), the king (19:14). The reason of his condemnation is affixed to the cross in three languages (19:19f), for the whole world to know what happened. Examples of "seeing" abound particularly in Chs. 19 and 20.

For John "listening" is also very important. Jesus has come to "bear witness to what he has seen and heard" (3:32). He "had heard" the truth from God (8:40), and made known to the disciples, as to "friends," all that he "heard" from his Father (15:15). He himself is constantly on the listening line with his Father. So should the disciples be with respect to Christ. The voice listened to is that of the Son of God (5:25), of the transcendent Son of man (5:27-29), of the Shepherd (ch. 10), of the King who bears witness to the truth (18:37). Christ's *voice* does more than pronounce words: it "calls," as to gather the sheep (ch. 10); it "commands" the dead back to life (5:27-29; 11:43). Mary of Bethany appears as a model; she listened earnestly to his teaching (Lk 10:39) and answered promptly to his call (Jn 11:29).

"Behold, the Lamb of God" (Jn 1:29)

Several authors recognize that the Baptist's presentation of Jesus in Jn 1:29 as "the lamb of God"—which really expresses the theology of the Fourth Evangelist—should be referred primarily to the Passover Lamb (see Barrett 147), as Johannine texts connected with the passion would indicate. John sees the fulfillment of Scripture in an episode of Jesus' death on the cross: "Not even a bone of him shall be broken" (19:36). This ritual custom (Ex 12:46) reflects an old belief in a certain revivification—at least in the perpetuation of the flock—of the victim offered to the divinity. Its Johannine symbolism is that Jesus was destined to resurrect. There exists at least a possibility that the similarity between *pas-*

chein, "to suffer," "to die" (see Ac 1:3; 3:18), and *pascha*, "Passover," may have influenced the paschal formulation of Jesus's sacrifice, so that Paul could write: "Christ, our paschal lamb, has been sacrificed" (1 Cor 5:7). According to First Peter Christ is the new Paschal Lamb who redeemed mankind from a slavery prefigured by the oppression of the Hebrews in Egypt (1:18-20).

Behind Jn 1:29 some commentators also correctly see the figure of Isaac, especially as it was referred to in Jewish tradition—namely as the *Aqeda* or the "binding" of Isaac, mentioned in Gn 22:9. It is noteworthy that in later Judaism, about the time of Christ, "the sacrificial character of the Aqeda" was stressed.[47] Being the "only-begotten" son of the Promise, Isaac could easily appear as a figure of Jesus, called the "only-begotten" son of the Father (Jn 1:18). Like Isaac Jesus was not spared by a loving Father (Rm 8:32). That Abraham "received Isaac back as a symbol" (Heb 11:19) can be understood as meaning that because of God's timely intervention the son escaped from death, as it were, miraculously—a sort of prefiguration, the Church Fathers explain, of the other Son who truly rose from the dead.

"Savior of the World" (Jn 4:42)

The title "Savior" came up for consideration first in Ch. 5, about Lk 2:11, then in Ch. 9 in connection with 2 Tm 1:10 and Tt 2:13 "our Great God and Savior." In Jn 4:42 the Samaritans tell the woman who had encountered Jesus: "We know that this is indeed the Savior of the world." For W. Foerster, "the Samaritans, whom the Jews regarded as Gentiles, represent the whole world here" (*TDNT* 7, p. 1016). The same phrase occurs at an emphatic point in 1 Jn 4:14: "And we have seen and testify that the Father has sent his Son as the Savior of the world." We have in addition here the very Johannine theme of the sending of the Son, and of the testifying by the Son. In Jn 4:42 the Samaritans give a universalist interpretation to the title ''Messiah'' or ''Christ,'' previously used (4:25-29). As Schnackenburg remarks (vol. 1, p. 458), John felt that ''Savior of the world'' was a well adapted title to use for the public preaching of the Gospel. It was known in Hellenistic circles, and it occurs in emperor worship (especially about Hadrian) and for the healing god Asclepius. For all this, the title does not seem to be used by John in a polemical perspective. Like *Kyrios*, the title ''Savior'' also contains an element of majesty and royalty. The Savior of the world exercises *a saving sovereignty* over the world (see also 17:2).

The Son as Judge (Jn 5:27)

The title ''Son of man'' has already been discussed, under different aspects: the origin and meaning of the name (Ch. 2, under Lk 9:58), the suffering Son of man (Ch. 3, under Mk 8:31), the kingdom of the Son of man (Ch. 6, under Mt 16:27). A fusion of the titles ''Son of man'' and ''Son of God'' has been noted particularly in 1 Th 1:10 (see Ch. 8). In this respect it is noteworthy that John can easily mention in three successive verses ''the Son of God,'' ''the Son,'' ''the Son of man'' (5:25-27). The hour is coming, John writes, when the dead will hear the voice of the Son of God, and those who hear will live (5:25). The calling of Lazarus out of the tomb will illustrate this (11:43f), but the meaning is mainly symbolical and spiritual: those will gain life who hear the Son's voice in faith and obedience (see 18:37). The voice that the dead will hear, Schnackenburg writes (vol. 2, p. 111), is that of the Son of God, who ''calls'' the words of God into the world (7:28, 37; 12:44).

The Son has in full the power to give life, and the Father has also ''given him authority to execute judgment, because he is the *Son of man*'' (5:27). John had already stated that the Father ''has given all judgment to the Son'' (5:22). As said above, the presence of the Revealer is in itself already a judgment, because it compels those confronted with him to a choice: the Son's word will on the last day be the judge of unbelievers (12:48); no explicit sentencing will be necessary. In judging, the Son only does what he is told (5:30).

Only in 5:27 does John explicitly ascribe judgment to the Son of man. The connection is often found, however, in the figurative discourses of the *Book of Enoch* (chs. 37-41). In the early Q logion of Lk 12:8f the connection is at least implicit, while it is explicit in Mt 25:31, and probably assumed in other texts, dependent on Dn 7, like Mk 14:62 par. See also Rv 1:13; 14:14; Ac 7:56, where the Son of man appears to be pictured as Judge. As mentioned above (Ch. 2), the tradition represented by Q recognized in Jesus a prophet of the end-time and identified him with the Son of man, the eschatological Judge. Recent studies have shown that it is unnecessary to ascribe to another redactor than John the reference in 5:27b-29 to future eschatological events. Realized eschatology, predominant in the Fourth Gospel, does not exclude the future judgment, which will solemnize for the whole world the fates the individuals have brought on themselves in accepting or refusing the call of the Son of God. It is, however, possible that references to the future judgment in the Fourth Gospel represent an addition by a different representative of the Johannine school, who wished to indicate that realized eschatology did not exclude future eschatology (see also 1 Jn 4:17). It was, of course, traditional teaching that Jesus would return to judge the living and the dead (see Ac 10:42; 2 Cor 5:10; 1 P 4:5; 2 Tm 4:1). Judgment certainly has to be taken into account in assigning distinctive traits to ''the Johannine Son of man,'' but further characterization of this figure does not appear easy in the studies published till now.[48]

''The Holy One of God'' (Jn 6:69)

Jesus is referred to as ''the Holy and Righteous One'' in Peter's kerygmatic discourse (Ac 3:14), and also as ''your Holy One'' in a quotation (2:27). Expelled demons declared Jesus to be ''the Holy One of God'' (see Ch. 3 under Mk 1:24). In the Fourth Gospel Peter makes the following confession: ''We have believed, and have come to know, that you are the Holy One of God'' (6:69). This could be an echo of the confession at Caesarea Philippi, especially as found in Luke, where Peter defines Jesus as ''the Christ of God'' (9:20), and in Matthew, who further explains Jesus' Messiahship in terms of Sonship (16:16). According to Jn 10:36 the Father made the Son ''holy'' when he sent him into the world. In Jn 17:11 Jesus addresses as ''holy Father'' the God who has given him his name, his divine nature. ''The Holy One'' of 1 Jn 2:20 is probably Christ, since in Rv 3:7 he is referred to as ''the holy one, the true one.'' ''Holy,'' writes Schnackenburg, ''expresses the closest possible intimacy with God, a participation in God's deepest and most essential being'' (vol. 2, p. 77). Jesus' sanctification is also his *teleiôsis*, his ''perfecting'' (Heb 5:9), and it is connected with his sacrifice, as Jn 17:19 clearly indicates: ''I sanctify myself, that they also may be sanctified in truth.''

Anthrôpos (Jn 8:40)

In the introduction to this chapter the insistence of John on the humanity of Jesus has been noted. This follows logically from the emphasized declaration that the *Logos* became ''flesh'' and dwelt among us (1:14). It can even be said that *anthrôpos*, ''man,'' almost takes the value of a title when applied to Christ in John. Jesus told the unbelieving Jews that they descend from Abraham, but are not truly his children, since they want to do what Abraham never thought of doing: ''You seek to kill me, a MAN who has told you the truth which I heard from God'' (8:40). It seems implied here that the Jews want to kill Jesus precisely because they will not accept that a simple man can reveal to them directly the truth from God. Jesus the man is set in contrast with God. Jn 8:40 is the only NT text in which Jesus explicitly describes *himself* as ''man.'' In

Rm 5:15 the emphasis is on contrasting the first and the second Adam, and 1 Tm 2:5 stresses the unique mediating role of "the man Christ Jesus." Unlike in Jn 8:40 the emphasis is not on the contrast between God and the man Jesus. Possibly, John's statement is antidocetic: Jesus is not man in appearance only. He does not say, however, that he is *only* man. The same contrast between God and the man Jesus can be read in Jn 10:33: "We stone you . . . because you, being a man, make yourself God." Jesus answers with a reference to Ps 82:6, which he says, does bring together the two terms, "God" and "man," suggesting this is what happens in his own person (see also Jn 5:18).

According to Jn 19:5, with the words "Behold the man!" Pilate showed the accusing Jews Jesus crowned with thorns and wearing the purple robe. Historically, if the event actually took place, derision is meant, directed against the Jews, who claimed that this man pretended to be king. For John the scene is meant to show that in his extreme humiliation Christ is still in truth the glorious King, for the passion in John is an elevation, a glorification (Jn 17:1). Possibly an influence of Daniel can also be read into the scene: to the Son of man, "the Man" *par excellence*, "was given dominion and glory and kingdom" (7:14). The Danielic figure lies also behind the first words of the final proclamation in Matthew (28:18). Jn 19:5 can therefore be seen as a royal epiphany, perhaps also connected with the marvelous transformation of the Man of Sorrows in Is 53. Several texts of the Gospel tradition do combine the Son of man and the Suffering Servant with regard to the person of Jesus.[49]

Egô Eimi Sayings

The Johannine Christ often has recourse to the formula *egô eimi*, "I am," to attribute metaphorical or symbolic titles to himself: "I am the bread of life" (Jn 6:35), "I am the light of the world" (8:12), "I am the door of the sheep" (10:7), "I am the good shepherd'' (10:11), ''I am the resurrection'' (11:25), ''I am the way, the truth, and the life'' (14:6), ''I am the vine'' (15:1). Even more strikingly Christ in the Fourth Gospel uses *egô eimi* about himself in an absolute sense, with no predicate following. In Jn 6:20 and 18:5, 6, 8 the phrase is certainly more than an identifying formula, because of what follows its utterance: ''It is also a unique expression of authority, as can be seen from the epiphany on the lake and the collapse of the soldiers on hearing the words'' (Schnackenburg, vol. 2, p. 80). In 8:24, 28 and 13:19 *egô eimi* epitomizes the full content of faith and knowledge, while in 8:58 by saying ''I am,'' not ''I was,'' Jesus clearly asserts the unique nature of his pre-existent being.

A Gnostic origin for the self-revelation formula has been proposed in learned studies,[50] but there is no need for this, since the Old Testament provides an adequate background, and the formula is, for John, a way of asserting his belief in the divinity of Christ. Obviously some of the *egô eimi* sayings do go back to Jesus himself. The most obvious case, outside John, occurs in Mk 6:50, where Jesus tells the disciples on the lake: ''Take heart, it is I; have no fear.'' In the Old Testament, ''I am'' is a formula peculiar to Yahweh *who reveals himself* and who commands. Of the original phrase, ''I am who I am'' (Ex 3:14), often only the first part has been retained, ''I am'' (see Dt 32:39; Is 43:10 LXX), as in the command to Moses: ''Say to the people of Israel: *I am* sent me to you'' (Ex 3:14).

It is clear, writes Schnackenburg, ''that the Johannine *egô eimi* sayings are completely and utterly expressions of John's Christology and doctrine of salvation'' (p. 88). More than the ''Son, Son of man, Son of God'' titles, also important in a different way, they make the saving character of Jesus' mission visible in striking images and symbols. Their predicates—life, bread, light, door, shepherd, way, truth, vine—are all concerned with the meaning Jesus' person and work have for those who accept him and his message: ''that they may have life, and have it abundantly''

(10:10). Although the *egô eimi* sayings make sense only when uttered by one having divine status, their immediate purpose is not to define Christ as a divine person in two natures, divine and human. Other texts in John (mainly 1:1, 18; 20:28) and in the New Testament expressly declare that Jesus is God (see Ch. 8, under Rm 9:5 and Ch. 9 under Tt 2:13). It is not doubtful that in 1 Jn 5:20 "this is the true God and eternal life" refers to Jesus Christ, and not to God, of whom it has twice been said in the preceding sentence that he is "true."

Fellowship with God and Christ (1 Jn 1:3)

Strictly speaking no new Christological development is found in the First Johannine letter, which forcibly reiterates against heretics the common beliefs in Jesus Christ recognized as the Son of God in a transcendent sense. *Koinônia*, "communion, fellowship," constitutes a central theme of the epistle, and the doctrine is already formulated in the prologue: "That which we have seen and heard we proclaim also to you, that you may have *fellowship with us* and *our fellowship* is with the Father and with his Son Jesus Christ" (1 Jn 1:3; see also 1:6). The fellowship theme was introduced to combat the threat of division in the community resulting from a lack of unity in doctrine and teaching.

Paul had written: "Faithful is God, through whom you were called to the fellowship of his Son, Jesus Christ our Lord" (1 Cor 1:9). Ac 2:42 speaks of the *koinônia* which united the Christian brethren. Also John refers to the fellowship among the brethren ("with us" in 1 Jn 1:3), and with Jesus Christ. John stresses what Paul (whose theology is particularly Christocentric) did not: fellowship with the Father. This is not surprising, since the Father plays such an important role in Johannine theology. But John does not speak, as Paul does (especially 2 Cor 13:13; Ph 2:1) of *koinônia* in the Holy Spirit. May it be suggested that the perfect *koinônia* formulation could be: ''And our fellowship is with the Father and his Son Jesus Christ in the Holy Spirit.''[51]

A Paraclete, Jesus Christ (1 Jn 2:1)

''My little children, I am writing this to you that you may not sin; but if any one does sin, we have an advocate (*paraklêtos*) with the Father, Jesus Christ the righteous'' (1 Jn 2:1). In the Fourth Gospel, of course, *ho paraklêtos*, ''the Paraclete,'' or ''the Advocate,'' is the Holy Spirit (14:16, 26; 15:26; 16:7). The sending of the Spirit, mentioned in 14:26, has a kind of parallel in Gal 4:6 and 1 P 1:12. *Paraklêtos* existed as a term before John, who used it to express in the Gospel the role of the Spirit which Christ would send. It appears at least probable that the Paraclete of the Fourth Gospel ''was above all experienced as the community's teacher and interpreter,''[52] a role which the evangelist himself felt he was fulfilling, interpreting Jesus' person, his words, and his actions: ''He will teach you all things, and bring to your remembrance all that I have said to you'' (Jn 14:26).

The etymology (passive form) of the term *paraklêtos* suggests the meaning *advocate*, ''he who is called'' (Latin: *ad-vocatus*). In the legal language a *paraklêtos* fulfills the role of defender, mediator, intercessor. According to Heb 7:25 Jesus is always alive to ''intercede'' for sinners, but the verb *parakalein*, ''to summon, exhort, entreat,'' is not used in this text. Intercession is also implied in Heb 9:24, which says that having entered heaven Christ ''will appear in the presence of God on behalf of us.'' He will do this as High Priest who through his sacrifice has gained access to the Father, for himself, and for all those ''who obey him'' (5:9). The context of 1 Jn 2:1 clearly suggests a similar intercessorial meaning for the Paraclete Jesus Christ. In Schnackenburg's words *paraklêtos* in 1 Jn 2:1 has the meaning of ''intercessor'' or ''advocate,'' ''in accordance with classical and Jewish linguistic usage''

(p. 148). Not by chance is the expiatory role of Christ recalled in the following verse.

An Hilasmos for our Sins (1 Jn 2:2)

Twice First John calls Christ *hilasmos*, which should be translated "expiation," or "victim of expiation," not "propitiation," as I have explained fully elsewhere.[53] The first text says that Christ "is *the expiation for our sins*, and not for ours only but also for the sins of the whole world." The meaning is that Christ is a sin-offering, or a victim of expiation, a divinely supplied means of cancelling guilt and purifying the sinner (Dodd 360). Through the mediation of his Son, *hilasmos*, God forgave our sins and freed us from our iniquities (see Rm 5:8f).

Although the second *hilasmos* text (1 Jn 4:10) is, like the first, Johannine, its similarity with Rm 8:3 is striking: "God sent his own Son . . . as a sacrifice for sin (*peri hamartias*)" (Rm 8:3); "God sent his Son as *hilasmos* for our sins (*peri tôn hamartiôn hêmôn*)" (1 Jn 4:10). Also Rm 3:24-25 belongs to the same context. It is said there that we are justified by God's grace, through the redemption which is in Christ Jesus, whom God put forward as an expiation (*Hilastêrion*) by his blood, to be received by faith. The First Epistle of John recalls almost simultaneously the dual role of Christ, intercession and expiation. At the *hilastêrion*, the mercy-seat (Ex 25:17-22), both intercession and expiation took place. Also the Suffering Servant fulfills both the role of expiation and intercession (Is 53:10, 12).

"The Son of the Father" (2 Jn 3)

In the Roman Catholic mass the faithful recite or sing every Sunday the *Gloria in Excelsis Deo*, "Glory to God in the Highest," which in the English missal calls Jesus Christ "only Son of the Father." But in the Latin we have simply "*filius Patris*," "Son of the Father,'' which the French *Gloria* renders correctly as "*le Fils du Père*.'' It would be interesting to know how many faithful, and even celebrants, know that Christ is explicitly called "the Son of the Father'' only once in the New Testament, in verse 3 of the only chapter of the Second Johannine Epistle: "Grace, mercy, and peace will be with us, from God Father, and from Jesus Christ the Son of the Father, in truth and love.'' However, in 1 Jn 2:22f the Father and the Son are each mentioned three times. Of course, in the Fourth Gospel and elsewhere Jesus very often calls God his Father, particularly in the so-called "hymn of jubilation'' (see our Ch. 4). This must be the reason why the NT authors willingly speak of Christ as the Son of God. Only the author of Second John thought of calling him "the Son of the Father.'' I have more than once in this work referred to Christ as "Son of God,'' but see particularly in Ch. 3 our analysis of Mk 1:11; 3:11; 13:32; 15:39 (see also Booknote 16 and the next to last section of Ch. 4).

Conclusion

This brief Johannine trajectory has led us from an overview of John's method and orientation to specific texts concerning Christ the Revealer, the Lamb of God, the Savior of the world, the Son as Judge, the Holy One of God, the Man, and his extraordinary claims in the *ego eimi* sayings. The Johannine Epistles distinctively call Christ a Paraclete, an *hilasmos*, and "the Son of the Father.''

The Fourth Gospel attaches great importance to the figure of God the Father (read Chs. 6, 8, 10, 14). At the same time it is very Christocentric, because for John, as for Paul to a certain degree, God is mainly the Father of Jesus Christ. The Christocentricity of John's theology is reflected in several ways. In the Fourth Gospel, for example, the "kingdom'' of the Synoptics is relegated to the background by the radiant figure of the King; the Vineyard is no longer the field of the gospel laborers (see Mt 12:1f), but Christ himself and all his disciples incorporated in him (Jn 15:1-11); the

Light is more than a ray illuminating the faces of Christians (Mt
5:14), it shines forth in the very person of Christ, who says, ''I am
the Light of the world'' (Jn 8:12). John seldom analyzes; he
contemplates, and it is the fullness of the mystery of Christ that he
contemplates. Beyond the visible and changing world his vision
penetrates the supernatural world, dominated by the figure of
Christ, whose eternal, hieratic features are often reflected in the
Evangelist's remarkable serenity of thought and language.Two
new studies have underlined the fact that Christ for John is ''the one
sent.'' Given all authority he makes the Father known and returns
to the Father. See J. Becker, ''Ich bin die Auferstehung und das
Leben. Eine Skizze der johanneischen Christologie,'' *TZ* 39
(1983) 138-51; W.R.G. Loader, ''The Central Structure of Johannine Christology,'' *NTS* 30 (1984) 188-216. J. Painter holds that
the evangelist John would have substituted the term *logos* for
sophia, ''wisdom,'' found in the pre-existing text he used
(''Christology and the Fourth Gospel. A Study of the Prologue,''
Australian Biblical Review 31, 1983, 45-62).

CHAPTER ELEVEN

THE CHRIST OF THE APOCALYPSE

Apocalyptic literature dominated among the Jewish writings from 150 B.C. to about 130 A.D. It has left important traces in the New Testament. One thinks immediately of the prophetic discourse Jesus pronounced during his last stay in Jerusalem, of which Mark 13 certainly represents the most primitive version. Some exegetes believe that this chapter is constituted by words of Jesus joined to a little Jewish apocalypse which took its departure from the book of Daniel.[54] John's Apocalypse or the book of Revelation obviously also belongs to a religious view of the world related to that of Jewish apocalypticism. Less obvious are the apocalyptic features of other NT books, which have been repeatedly pointed out in the present work (see Index). Of the gospels Matthew as a whole is certainly the most apocalyptic, as this writer has demonstrated in a recent study (see *Religious Studies Bulletin* 1983, pp. 19-36).

Recent research agrees in recognizing that the interpretation of history lies in the center of apocalyptic thought. As their name itself suggests—''apocalypsis'' means ''revelation''—the apocalyptists claim to have received a ''revelation'' from God: the ruler of history makes known to them, in visions (Dn 10:1; Rv 4:1), what course history will follow in the decisive stage that will lead the world to its end; he tells them, in particular, how the great empires that persecute God's people are heading towards their own destruction. God has revealed his plan for the world to one of his faithful servants—Enoch, Abraham, Moses, or Daniel—to whom the writings are attributed. The time has come to reveal the secrets, for the end is near and inevitable. The revelation is made through images and symbols, which is appropriate for visions and suits the supernatural and mysterious character of the message to be transmitted. In the apocalyptic perspective evil fills the world, which lies under the dominion of evil powers. But when God will intervene, he will fully reestablish his own right; the just will be rewarded and the wicked punished. Apocalyptic ethic consists therefore in this: expect in faith the salvation which is at hand: "Now when these things begin to take place, look up and raise your heads, because your redemption is drawing near" (Lk 21:28).

Apocalyptic owes a lot to the OT prophecies, say the more recent commentaries. It would result from a long process of development, which would go back even to pre-exilic times. This is particularly true of apocalyptic eschatology, which has its roots in prophetic soil. The contribution of Iranian dualism and of Hellenism would have been only marginal, as additional to a doctrine already constituted in its essential traits. The book of Daniel is the first and the greatest of Jewish apocalypses, redacted in a climate of persecution, of terror, and of death—the climate that characterized for the Jews the rule of Antiochus IV Epiphanes (175-165 B.C.). It is in a similar atmosphere, during another persecution, that the Christian book of Revelation was born.

John's Apocalypse borrows a lot from the images and the symbols of the book of Ezekiel, and resembles in several ways the Jewish apocalypses. The differences have also to be pointed out. First of all, the author of the Christian writing identifies himself and the circumstances in which he received the revelation, and he also indicates the situation of his addressees (1:9-11). The central role it assigns to the person and to the work of Jesus Christ distinguishes John's apocalypse from the Jewish writings of the same type. The Savior does not appear in Revelation simply as the heavenly Son of man of the apocalypses, but as the slain Lamb (5:6, 12), returned to life (1:18), and present among the witnesses of God in the world. It is not enough to interpret the teaching of Jesus in the light of apocalyptic; it is especially necessary, as John does in Revelation, to reread apocalyptic in the light of Jesus. "THE CHRIST OF THE APOCALYPSE" is not radically different from the Christ known through the other NT writings, but some features are characteristically underlined in Revelation. The essential message of the Apocalypse can be expressed as follows: God brings to fulfillment in Christ and his redemption the plan of salvation prepared and announced in the Old Testament. The abundant use of OT formulas to convey the Christian message reflects precisely this overall orientation of the writing.

Like a Son of Man (1:13)

Hearing a voice "like a trumpet," the seer of Patmos turned to see whose voice it was, and he saw seven golden lampstands, "and in the midst of the lampstands *one like a son of man*, clothed with a long robe and with a golden girdle round his breast" (1:13). The seven lampstands apparently refer to the temple lamps described in Ex 25:31-40 and 27:20f, to which allusion is also found in Zechariah's visions (Zc 4:2), used also elsewhere in Revelation (compare Rv 5:6 and Zc 4:10; Rv 11:4 and Zc 4:3, 14).

"Like a son of man" obviously comes from Dn 7:13, where *kebar 'enash* is rendered in Greek as *hôs huios anthrôpou* (here the genitive instead of the expected dative can be influenced by the phrase with *hôs*; same in 14:14).[55] In Jewish apocalyptic "Son of man" referred to a mysterious figure invested with royal and judicial authority, who at the end-time would execute God's design for salvation and judgment. In Rv 1:13-16 the majesty and transcendence of the "One like a Son of Man" are underlined with various symbols, also borrowed from Dn 7:9 and 10:5-6. "I am the first and the last, and the living one" refers also to Christ the Son of man in Rv 1:18f; 2:8; 22:13. In Is 44:6 and 48:12 this description applies to the Lord. It can be said that the figure of the Son of man in his role of eschatological Judge (Rv 1:16-19; 14:14-20) "is somehow merged with God" (Dunn 91).

In Rv 1:5 Jesus Christ the faithful witness (see on 3:14) is called "the first-born of the dead" (see Col 1:18), and the ruler of kings on earth: three designations which can be referred to the passion, the resurrection, and Christ's exaltation as Lord. "Behold, he is coming with the clouds . . ." obviously points to the Son of man, as in 1:13, while the rest of vs. 7 is dependent on Zc 12:10. The mourning in Rv 1:7 seems caused by the sight of the wounded Christ. In Mt 24:30 it is the terrifying effect of the sudden appearance of the Son of man "with power and great glory." In the discussion of 1 Th 1:10 in Ch. 8 some texts have been referred to, in which "Son of God" appears where "Son of man" is expected. An additional case is Rv 2:18, where the "Son of God"—the only mention of this title in Revelation—is described in terms that recall the One like a Son of man in 1:13-15: "The words of *the Son of God*, who has eyes like a flame of fire, and whose feet are like burnished bronze" (2:18). As Loader observes, the description of Jesus as Son comes to carry with it the idea of Jesus exercising the kind of apocalyptic functions mostly associated with the Son of man motif (p. 528). The apocalyptic model of sonship is prominent in Mt 19:28; 28:18f; 1 Cor 15:24, 28; Col 1:12-20 and Rv 2:18.

The Key of David (3:7)

Christ is called "He who has the Key of David" in a verse which describes him with other appellations as well: "The words of the holy one, the true one, who has the key of David, who opens and no one shall shut, who shuts and no one opens" (3:7). The whole context clearly indicates that Christ is meant here. "The Holy One" is a usual name for God in the Old Testament and in Jewish tradition: "God came from Teman, and the Holy One from

Mount Paran'' (Hab 3:3). In Is 49:7 God is called both "the Holy One" and "the True One."

The description of the exalted Christ as the One Having the Key of David is based on Is 22:22, where the appointment of Eliakim as royal treasurer is announced with the following words: "And I will place on his shoulder the key of the house of David; he shall open, and none shall shut; and he shall shut, and none shall open." Unknown to Judaism, Revelation's Messianic interpretation rests on the mention of the Davidic line, whose representative is ultimately Christ (Rv 22:16). Is 22:22 had in view the royal palace; Rv 3:7 says that Christ has the key to God's eternal palace. "The meaning of the description is that Christ has unlimited sovereignty over the future world. He alone controls grace and judgment. He decides irrevocably whether a man will have access to the salvation of the last age or whether it will be withheld from him" (*TDNT* 3, pp. 748f). The liturgy of Advent evokes Rv 3:7 in the great antiphon for Dec. 20: "O Key of David and Scepter of the house of Israel: you open and no man closes; you close and no man opens. Come, and deliver him from the chains of prison who sits in darkness and in the shadow of death."

The Amen (3:14)

The expression "Amen" (Greek *amên*) is used once as a properly Christological title: "And to the angel of the church at Laodicea write: Thus says *the Amen*, the faithful and true witness, who is the beginning of the creation of God" (Rv 3:14). Greek and Latin have taken up the Hebrew word just as it was. In this passage from an eschatological discourse of Deutero-Isaiah the word is applied to God as an epithet: "He will be blessed on whom a blessing is invoked in the land [see Gn 14:19]; he who takes an oath in the land shall swear by the God of *truth* [lit.: by Elohim *Amen*], for the hardships of the past shall be forgotten, and hidden from my eyes" (Is 65:16). The seer of the Christian Apocalypse was think-

ing not only of this text but of the Old Testament and Judaism,
when he attributed his message to the *Amen* and immediately
explained the word by adding: ''the faithful and true witness who is
the beginning of the creation of God'' (3:14; see also 1:5).[56]

The primitive sense of the Hebrew root of *Amen* was ''to bear
or carry'' in the physical sense, which led to the idea of ''security,'' ''steadfastness,'' ''certainty,'' especially in relation to the
fidelity of God (see Dt 7:9). In a Messianic context concerning the
Servant, the fidelity of God is again recalled by the use of a word
similar to *Amen*, that is ''faithful'' (Is 49:7). The same terminology
reappears in an oracle associated with the new covenant (Is 55:3). It
is not surprising, then, that the causative form of the root *amen*
means ''to believe'': ''Abram *believed* the Lord, who credited the
act to him as justice'' (Gn 15:6). In its *liturgical use, Amen* is a
response proclaiming a community's complete adherence to what
has just been said, and a wish for its fulfillment. The doxological
amens that end three books of the Psalms (41:14; 72:19; 89:53)
attest its liturgical use, as does the First Book of Chronicles:
''Blessed be the Lord the God of Israel from eternity to eternity!
Let all the people say, *Amen*'' (16:36).

The frequent New Testament mention of *Amen* at the end of the
doxologies (cf. Rm 1:25; Heb 13:21) shows its ancient use in the
Christian community as a *liturgical response* (see also 1 Cor
14:16). In Revelation the *Amen* often concludes the heavenly
hymns (see 1:7; 5:14), presumably modeled on earthly acclama-
tions. St. Jerome records that the faithful of Rome used to answer
''Amen'' so loudly and in such great numbers that it resembled the
rumbling of thunder. The importance of the Christian *Amen* flows
from its connection with the person of Jesus Christ. St. Paul said so
in an astonishingly deep theological statement: ''For all the promises of God find their 'Yes' (*nai* in Greek) in him; and therefore
through him also rises our 'Amen' to the glory of God'' (2 Cor
1:20). The person of Jesus and his work are, in fact, the ground of
our certitude in the fulfillment of the divine promises proclaimed

by the liturgical response "Amen." For that reason the Christian liturgy ordinarily has the faithful's *Amen* follow the formula "through Jesus Christ Our Lord."

The term *nai* from 2 Cor 1:20, translated "yes" is practically synonymous with "Amen." In the beginning of Revelation the two terms are linked: *nai, amên* (1:7). So too in the gospels, "*Amen*, I say to you" is often replaced by "*nai*, I say to you" (Mt 11:9; Lk 7:26). The use that Jesus made of the formula "Amen, I say to you" (see Mk 3:28) is very unusual: in the Old Testament "Amen" approves what precedes; in Jesus' sayings, it stresses what follows. The Son speaks with the authority (Mk 1:27) of one whom God "appointed heir of all things" (Heb 1:2) and in whom promises are fulfilled (Rm 15:8; Gal 3:16). In the Synoptics the *Amen* is never doubled, while it always is in the Fourth Gospel, where it is equivalent to a superlative and is found more than twenty times (see Jn 1:51). A similar duplication is found in the Old Testament both in a rite of imprecation (Nb 5:22) and in a doxological response (Ne 8:6). In the ritual prayers recited at Qumran for admittance to the Covenant a redoubled *Amen* was also said (see *The Community Rule* I, 20; II, 18).

This review of connected themes allows us to appreciate the entire range of the unique affirmation: "Thus says the *Amen*, the faithful and true witness, who is the beginning of the creation of God" (Rv 3:14). Here three titles are united, the last two explaining the first, whose origin is complex: Jesus' frequent use of the formula with "amen"; the text of Isaiah (65:16); and Paul's teaching in 2 Cor 1:20 on the final fulfillment of the divine promises in Jesus. The title "Beginning of the creation of God" calls to mind the Christological title "Firstborn of every creature" (Col 1:15, 18). The affinity is not too surprising, for the Christological *Amen* is recalled (Rv 3:14) by the angel of the church at Laodicea, a community associated by Paul with that of the Colossians (see Col 4:16). Perhaps the author of Rv 3:14 knew the Epistle to the Colossians.

The *glorified* Christ is the one that the Apocalypse calls the *Amen*, for this title belongs to one who has finished his work or rather to one whose presence in heaven as the immolated lamb (5:6) testifies to the perfect fulfillment of the saving plan of God. This shall be the subject of eternal praise by the elect, and in this sense Augustine was right to affirm that the occupation of the blessed in heaven consists in saying unendingly: *Amen! Alleluia!*

The Redeeming and Conquering Lamb (17:14)

Christ is called "Lamb" almost 30 times in the book of Revelation, but the term used is *arnion*, not *amnos* as in Jn 1:29 (see Ch. 10 on this text). However, the Exodus context is not absent, as 5:9f suggest. As the Hebrews were redeemed or delivered from the land of sin and slavery (Ex 20:2; Dt 5:6), so Christ's disciples, marked with the blood of the Lamb (Rv 14:1), are redeemed, purchased from the earth (14:3) or the Johannine world of rebellion against God, and won for God (see Ep 1:14; 1 P 2:9).

Other texts from Revelation reveal a different feature of the Lamb, that of the victorious Leader. In his train, for example, walk the 144,000 virgins (14:4), those, that is, who are not defiled with that prostitute, idolatry (see Ho 1:2), by worshipping the Beast (14:9; 20:4). They shall be invited to the marriage feast of the Lamb (19:9). The Lamb of the Apocalypse is both the triumphant Messiah, who leads his people to victory, and the suffering Messiah who gave his life for his followers. In the Servant figure the sacrificial interpretation of the Savior's death was already announced and prepared (Is 53:7).

The translation of *arnion* by "lamb" has to be maintained in Revelation, at least in ch. 5 and related passages. In the Septuagint *arnion* occurs four times and always means "lamb," as it does also in Jn 21:15. It has been argued that "ram" should be adopted to translate *arnion*, where wrath (6:16f), warfare and triumph (17:14) are involved. Dn 8:3 speaks of the two-horned ram, representing the Persian power. However, since the *arnion* of the Apocalypse is described as "slain," we cannot separate the statements of Revelation from what the NT says about Jesus as the sacrificial Lamb (*TDNT* vol. 1, p. 341). As Victor, the Lamb is Lord of lords and King of kings (17:14; 19:16), like the God of Daniel (Dn 2:47).

The Christ of Revelation

Revelation, we have seen, represents Christ as One like a Son of man (1:13), as the One Holding the Key of David (3:7), as the Amen, the true Witness (3:14), and as the redeeming and conquering Lamb (17:14). In many ways the Christ of the Apocalypse seems to share the power and glory of God his Father (1:6), the throne of God being also the throne of the Lamb (3:21; 22:1), who shares the same kingship (11:15). The Christ of Revelation is, like the Johannine Christ, the *Logos* of God (19:13) who stands at the beginning of God's creation (3:14). He enjoys some prerogatives of the OT God, searching mind and heart (2:23; Jr 11:20), judging justly (19:11; Is 11:4), dispensing what every one deserves (2:23; Ps 62:13), being the Shepherd who guides the sheep to springs of living water (7:17; Ezk 34:23), and his is the book of life (3:5; 13:8; 17:8; 20:12, 15; 21:27)—known in the Old Testament as God's book (Ex 32:32; Ps 69:29; Dn 12:1), and also referred to by Paul (Ph 4:3). The Christ of the Apocalypse enjoys other divine attributes: he is "the First and the Last" (1:17), "the Alpha and the Omega, the Beginning and the End" (22:13), descriptions used for God in 1:8; he is "the One Alive for evermore" (1:18), as God himself is (4:9f; 10:6; 15:7), and like him he is "Lord of lords, King of kings" (17:14; 19:16).

PART TWO
THE LATER DEVELOPMENTS

The present work is primarily concerned with Christology in the New Testament. Part One has presented the essential documentation on this. Part Two can serve as a complement, providing some data on the relatively early interpretation of New Testament texts and testimony to the growing fixation of the Church's Christological doctrine. No comprehensive treatment of this complex question will be attempted, but the texts presented and briefly discussed should provide a useful survey of early Christian developments leading to the definition of Chalcedon. The last chapter will be a very restricted survey of some recent studies devoted to Christology.

CHAPTER TWELVE

SOME EARLY CHRISTIAN WRITINGS

The New Testament writers predominantly focus on what is today called a functional theology, tending to address the following question: ''What is Christ for the salvation of the world and for me?'' The medieval theologians, on the other hand, like to deal with the nature of things, like the Greek philosophers, and attempt to answer questions regarding Christ's unique being. The texts will indicate that the early postapostolic Christian writers were close to the NT period, and yet in many ways foreshadow the later scholastic developments. The texts we have chosen are Christological in the proper sense, providing answers to the question ''Who is Christ?'' and are not predominantly soteriological, as would be texts regarding salvation, or the work of Christ.[57]

Jewish-Christian Christology

Having elsewhere written about the origin and meaning of Jewish or Judaistic Christianity, I will not here develop this general aspect again.[58] A short word of introduction does, however, appear necessary. ''Jewish Christianity'' is an ambiguous term which can apply (1) to the Jews who acknowledged Christ as a prophet or a Messiah, but not as the Son of God. They would include the Ebionites and several other groups, like the Elkesaites; (2) to James and his Christian community in Jerusalem, perfectly orthodox but still clinging to certain Jewish forms of life, though not imposing them on converts from paganism; (3) to a type of Christian thought expressing itself in forms largely borrowed from Judaism, especially in its apocalyptic approach. What follows would rather belong to Jewish Christianity in this broader view.

According to an abstract of his study (see Booknote 58), Vivian recognizes in early Jewish Christianity three typical schemas of its Christology. One schema is Messianic, developing in two stages, one earthly and the other heavenly. Traces of this schema are found in Gal 4:4-5, and in the kerygma of Acts (2:22-25; 3:13-15; 3:22; 4:10; 5:30; 7:56). The second schema is that of humiliation/exaltation, as in Ph 2:5-11, and the third would be the priestly schema of Hebrews. It is quite clear from this that Vivian includes under Jewish Christianity also some conceptions of the New Testament. He does, however, point out that these Christians quite consistently make use of concepts of the Name, Angelology, and the Sitting at the Right Hand (of God), when speaking of Christ.

Referring to Daniélou's work, A. Grillmeier asserts: "The first archaic element we encounter (in Jewish Christianity) is a pre-Pauline and pre-Johannine 'name-Christology' " (p. 46). Perhaps non-Pauline, and non-Johannine would express his thought better, because a chronology of these early conceptions is difficult to verify. He goes on to explain that the old-established *shēm* (="name")-theology of the later OT books appears to have been continued and applied to Christ. In *Ethiopian Enoch* (= 1 En) this Name-theology is primarily associated with the "Son of man" concept. According to this Jewish apocalyptic book, at the last judgment the Son of man will be brought before God and his Name before the Ancient of Days. Before the creation of the stars, we are told, his Name was pronounced in front of the Lord of spirits (1 En 48:2f). For H. Bietenhard "the pre-existence of the Name herein mentioned denotes the pre-existence of the Son of man himself, since name and person are very closely related" (*TDNT* 5, p. 267). The 2nd-century A.D. ethical treatise called *Shepherd of Hermas*, partly Jewish and partly Christian, seems to equate ''Name'' with ''Son of God'': ''If then the whole creation is supported by the Son of God, what do you think of those who are called by him, who bear the name of the Son of God and walk in his commandments?'' (IX, 14).

If *angelology* marks most dogmas in Jewish Christian theology, it is especially important in the explanation of the Trinity. The sources could be: ''the Angel of Yahweh'' of the Old Testament, the late Jewish idea of the angels as intermediaries between God and men, or the ''Angel of Light'' of the Essenes, divinely appointed to direct history. In the *Shepherd of Hermas*, the *Ascension of Isaiah*, the *Testaments of the Twelve Patriarchs*, and elsewhere, Christ is called MICHAEL. This is the development of the Jewish tradition according to which Michael received in charge the people of Israel, while the other angels were appointed for other peoples, at the time of the division of languages. This theme developed in different ways among the Ebionites and in the main Church, showing the difference of perspectives. For the former, Christ is a new manifestation of the Angel of Israel; for the Church he is the Word of God who strips the angels of their functions and unites all nations under his sceptre. In the *Pseudo-Clementine Homilies* (18:4), Michael, who gave the Law to Israel, is represented as reappearing in Christ, but the New Testament (see Gal 3:19; Ac 7:53) sets in contrast the Law, given by the angels, and the Gospel, given by the Word (see Heb 2:2f).

The Epistle of Clement of Rome

It is Irenaeus of Lyons (130-202) who supplies the earliest accurate information on the early leadership of the church of Rome. Having founded and edified the church, he writes, the apostles Peter and Paul transmitted to Linus the office of episcopacy; Anacletus was his successor, and then Clement. *The Letter to the Corinthians* attributed to Clement seems to have been a collectively written document with which the church of Rome wished to strengthen the church of Corinth in its difficulties (*Adversus Haereses* [*Against Heresies*] 3:3). In his *Church History* (IV, 22), Eusebius of Caesarea identified Clement of Rome with the Clement of Ph 4:3, but the identity of the two persons remains a conjecture, as Clement was quite a common name in Rome then. On the other hand, it is very probable that Clement's *Letter to the Corinthians* should be dated between 95 and 98.

In many ways the Letter appears as quite a Jewish writing, although it would be an exaggeration to say, with Adolf von Harnack (1851-1930) that Clement's is a religion of the Old Testament. Not only is Christ for Clement the end of salvation history, he is the present mediator of salvation, although this mediation is not always expressed (Jaubert 73). Is 53 and Ps 22 directly described, for Clement, the passion of Christ, about whom all the prophets prophesied. Although Clement certainly knew Paul's First Epistle to the Corinthians, he gives little prominence to Christ's resurrection. For him hope is founded rather on God's promises and on his faithfulness, and in this also Clement reveals his Jewish frame of mind. Only once does the Letter call Christ "Son," when in 36:4 Ps 2 is quoted. The pre-existent Son of God, the brightness of the Father, was sent into the world as man, and is the High Priest of mankind and mankind's way to blessedness (ch. 36; see Grillmeier 103). For Clement Christ is also "the high priest of our sufferings, our protector and rescue in our weakness" (36:1), "the high priest and protector of our souls" (61:3). Unlike Hebrews, however, Clement never connects Christ's priesthood with the priesthood of Melchizedek, although it insists, like Hebrews, on the blood of Christ. It cannot be said that the *Letter to the Corinthians* attributed to Clement of Rome contains a very distinctive Christology.

Ignatius of Antioch

On his way to martyrdom, around 110 A.D., Ignatius of

Antioch wrote a number of letters to the Christian communities, warning them particularly against the false doctrine of docetism, a form of Gnostic dualism which denied the reality of the human body, birth, suffering and death of Jesus Christ the Savior. To the Ephesians he used about Christ expressions that almost anticipate the later conception of the two natures:

> "There is but one physician (*iatros*), carnal and spiritual, generated and not generated, God come in the flesh, in death true life, (born) of Mary and (born) of God, first passible, now impassible, Jesus Christ, our Lord" (7:2).

To call Christ *agennêtos*, "not generated," is surprising, since the Father does generate the Word. It seems that before the clarification of Nicaea (see below) "not generated" referred to the divine essence, not to the divine person (Camelot 31). *Agennêtos* did characterize divine transcendence in the Greek philosophy of the time. For Ignatius Christ is truly man, but he is also *pneuma*, "Spirit," which for him and other early Christian writers *designates Christ's divine nature*. In this sense Ignatius can speak of the flesh and the Spirit of Christ (*Magnesians* 1:2). The same early writers very often connect with his resurrection the mention of Christ's divinity, because it is in the resurrection that Christ's true being was decisively manifested. This view could have been influenced by Ac 2:36 and Rm 1:3-4.

Justin Martyr

One of the second century apologists, Justin, died a martyr around the year 150. "His Christology, in fact his entire theology, focused on the conception of the Word, then current among stoics and others" (Carmody 15). In his *Second Apology* he writes:

> "The Christ who has appeared for us men represents the Logos principle in its totality, that is both body and *Logos*, and soul" (10:13).

The great philosophers and holy men may have been partial instruments of the *Logos*, but the divine Word is present in full only in Christ. Justin's formulation is better understood in the light of what the Platonists said: the world-soul is the principle at work in ordering the world, both at creation and in sustaining the world. According to Justin, Christ as *Logos* has taken over the working of this cosmological principle. In the Incarnation he has appeared in history, as "body, reason, and soul." This division, Grillmeier explains, is made after the same pattern as the trichotomy of the Platonist school; it expresses no more than the reality of the *Logos* as a man in history (p. 110).

Melito of Sardis

Melito, bishop of Sardis in Asia Minor (see Rv 3:1), was known for having written an apology to Emperor Marcus Aurelius (161-180) in defense of Christianity. In 1940 a lost paschal homily of which he is very probably the author (new edition in 1960) was recovered. In it he shows how the Exodus events have been fulfilled in Christ. Both the body and the Spirit—that is, the divinity of Christ—played a role in destroying suffering and death.

> "In place of the lamb there came God, and in place of the sheep a man; and, in the man, Christ, who contains all things . . . For born as a son, and led forth as a lamb, and sacrificed as a sheep, and buried as a man, he rose from the dead as God, being by nature God and man" (*Peri Pascha* [*On the Pasch*] 8).

As Carmody notes (p. 18), the phrase "by nature" foreshadows the terminology of Chalcedon, but in Melito it does not yet have the later philosophical meaning. It means little more than that Christ is *truly* God and man. In line with the Exodus theme Melito also states that the divine-human being of Jesus Christ is the guarantee of our salvation and of man's return to his original home with God (Grillmeier 111). Justin used about Christ the expression *sarkopoiêtheis*, ''being made flesh'' (I *Apol.* 32), not much earlier than Melito's adoption of the formula *sarkôtheis*, ''incarnated'', and Hippolytus of Rome will in the early 3rd century speak of the Logos' *sarkôsis*, ''incarnation'' (*Contra Noetum* [*Against Noetus*] 16). When Melito speaks of God as being *corporatus* he means *incarnatus*; he does not defend ''the corporeality of God.''

In Melito's typological theology, all things of the Old Testament events—persons, institutions, words of Scripture—are oriented towards Christ, ''for whose sake everything happened in the old Law'' (*Peri Pascha* 6). It is Christ, he writes, ''who is the *pascha* of our salvation, who endured a lot in many, who was murdered in Abel, bound in Isaac, exploited in Jacob, exposed in Moses, sacrificed in the lamb, persecuted in David, dishonored in the prophets'' (69). How is it possible, he asks, that the Jews have rejected him who has created the world, elected Israel, rescued her from Egypt, made her a nation, nourished her in the desert, and gave her the promised land in heritage (81-86)? More on Melito's *Peri Pascha* can be read in my review of a book by R. Cantalamessa, in *Religious Studies Bulletin* 1982, pp. 26f.

Irenaeus of Lyons

Born in 130, thirty years before Tertullian, Irenaeus had learned through Polycarp many traditions handed down by John the Apostle. In his main writing, *Adversus Haereses*, he principally defends orthodox Christian thought against the errors of Gnosticism, which gave excessive salvific value to ''knowledge,'' saw matter as inimical to spirit, and showed little interest in sacrificial redemption. On the other hand, Irenaeus insists on the continuity between the two Testaments, between creation and redemption, expressing this especially in his doctrine of *anakephalaiôsis* or ''recapitulation,'' which sees the consummation of all things in Christ: ''Christ the God-man came as the second Adam to restore and renew the plan of salvation which had been deprived of fulfillment by Adam's sin'' (Carmody 21). He also insisted on the necessity of a real Incarnation if mankind was to be truly redeemed. His formulations are impregnated with expressions taken from the New Testament, as the following extract shows. In this he writes as a biblical theologian, ''the first intentionally biblical theologian of the Christian Church.''[59]

> ''For the mediator between God and man had to bring both parties into friendship and concord through his kinship with both; and to present man to God, and make God known to man. In what way could we share in the adoption of the sons of God unless through the Son we had received fellowship with the Father, unless the Word of God was made flesh and entered into communion with us? Therefore he passed through every stage of life, restoring to each age fellowship with God'' (*Adv. Haer.* III, 18).

When he speaks of ''fellowship with the Father,'' Irenaeus is obviously using a Johannine concept and formulation (see above Ch. 10, on 1 Jn 1:3). In his battle against the Gnostic dissolution, and its separation of God and the world, Irenaeus resolutely defended the unity of God, Christ and salvation, developing the idea of a universal *oikonomia* (''economy,'' that is, an ordered plan of salvation), which embraces both Creation and the End, while it puts the Christ-event in the middle (Grillmeier 119). The *oikonomia* works through the ''recapitulation'' mentioned above.

Tertullian and Other Early Christian Writers

A Latin writer who died in 220, Tertullian used expressions in defining Christ that will re-echo during the Chalcedonian period. He recognizes two ''substances'' in Christ, which will later be called ''natures.'' There is, however, only one divine substance, which the Son ''shares'' with the Father, just as sunbeams can be seen as the extension of the substance of the sun. Tertullian would speak of *monarchia* in describing the role of Christ in carrying out the rule of God in the world. When, however, Praxeas began to defend deviating and exaggerated views on *monarchia*, Tertullian became almost anti-monarchian, and stressed rather the notion that the *Logos* is a person, while remaining one with the Father as ''substance.'' The following is probably the most often quoted passage from Tertullian, but the original Latin wording is in some details diversely interpreted (the parentheses are my own additions):

''We observe a double *status* (''state of being''), not confused but combined in one person, God and the man Jesus (or Jesus in one person God and man)—I am not speaking of Christ—and to such a degree is the proper being of each substance (understand ''nature'') kept intact; that in him the Spirit (that is, the divine nature) carried out its own acts, that is, powers, works, and signs, while the flesh (that is, the human nature) accomplished its own passions (human emotions and feelings), hungering in the company of the devil (Jesus' temptations in the desert), thirsting in the company of the Samaritan woman, weeping for Lazarus, sorrowful even to death (agony in the garden), and finally tasting death itself'' (*Adversus Praxean* [*Against Praxeas*] 27:6).

It has to be noted here, with Grillmeier (p. 154), that Tertullian does not wish to explain the unity of Godhead and manhood in Christ, but he attempts rather to correct the Christology of the monarchians. They said that Christ was a composite being made up of God the Father and the man Jesus, in one person. Against them Tertullian asserts that Godhead and manhood may not be divided between Father and Son in this way, but he does not yet have, in explicit terms, the Chalcedonian explanation. He has, however, succeeded in saving, for the time being, the unity of subject in Christ.

One generation after Tertullian, Novatian was already speaking of Christ, the Son of God, as the *Verbum Dei incarnatum* (*''Word of God incarnate''*) (*De Trinitate* [*The Trinity*] 24:138). As for Origen (185-253), a great Scripture scholar and prolific

writer, he was not particularly interested in the ontological constitution of Christ. "He sees Christ above all as mediator of the
mystical union of the soul with the hidden God, as mediator
between Church and God, and all this from the viewpoint of the
union in knowledge and in love" (Grillmeier 164). Origen discussed principally the *epinoiai*, "titles, expressions," which in Christ
represent objective realities defining aspects of his person. Origen
is above all the theologian of the soul of Christ, but his speculations
in this area have not proven very fruitful for a permanent formulation of Christology. He did, however, forcefully and with great
learning oppose the pagan Celsus, who held that there was no other
alternative in defining the person of Christ than either to admit
docetism or a change in the Godhead (see Origen's *Contra Celsum*
[*Against Celsus*] 4:18). Only gradually would the other alternative
come clearly to light and be appropriately formulated: one person,
two natures.

Three Church Councils

At the first council of Nicaea, in 325, Arianism was condemned. Arius (ca. 250-336), the initiator of the doctrine, denied
the divinity of Jesus Christ, regarding the Son of God as standing
midway between God and creature. The main adversary of the
doctrine, Athanasius (296-373), defended vigorously the use of the
term *homoousion*, "one and the same," or "consubstantial"—as
against *homoiousion*, "like only"—to express the identity of the
Son in essence, nature and substance with the Father. And this
formulation was adopted at the council of Nicaea.

On the other hand, Apollinaris the Younger (variant spelling:
Apollinarius), bishop of Laodicea around 376, taught that Christ
had a human sensitive soul, but no human rational mind, since its
place was taken by the divine *Logos*. Apollinarianism was condemned by the first council of Constantinople in 381, which
approved the formulation of the Nicene Creed. This is used on

every Sunday of the year as well as on certain feast days at the Catholic mass, including the following Christological formulation: ''We believe in one Lord, Jesus Christ, the only Son of God, eternally begotten of the Father, God from God, Light from Light, true God from true God, begotten, not made, one in Being with the Father.'' Arianism and Apollinarianism, noted Grillmeier, ''represent probably the most serious and dangerous influx of Hellenistic ideas into the traditional conception of Christ'' (p. 235).

The third ecumenical council, that of Ephesus, in 431, was presided over by St. Cyril, patriarch of Alexandria. It condemned Nestorius, bishop of Constantinople, for teaching that Mary did not bring forth the Word of God, but the man who became the temple of the Godhead. While combating the Arians, Nestorius came to accept the view that in Christ the two natures stand for personalities united in one moral person. Like his master, Theodore of Mopsuestia (died 428), Nestorius refused to admit that Mary was the Mother of God, claiming she is only the mother of Christ. This may be, however, a simplistic and as such inaccurate representation of Theodore's complex views on the person of Christ, including his notion of *prosôpon*.[60] In any case, according to the fathers of the Council of Ephesus, ''one and the same is the eternal Son of the Father and the Son of the Virgin Mary, born in time according to the flesh; therefore she may rightly be called Mother of God.'' The council did not, however, formulate how this takes place. This was to be the task of the council of Chalcedon (451).

Conclusion

In this chapter we have examined ''some early Christian writings'' which have contributed significantly to the search for a better intellectual understanding of the propositions of faith. Jewish Christianity developed a Name-Christology and an Angel-Christology, which attempted to express the new faith with Jewish apocalyptic conceptions. Clement's *Letter to the Corinthians* is in many ways a Jewish writing. It is dependent for several of its concepts on the Epistle to the Hebrews. But it can also be different, as when it represents Christ as the High Priest of mankind, and makes no mention of the order of Melchizedek.

Against docetism Ignatius of Antioch upheld the reality of Christ's humanness and began calling *pneuma* his divine nature. A philosopher himself, Justin discussed the philosophical doctrine of the Logos in the light of the Incarnation and proposed ecumenical views in Christology. In the *Peri Pascha* attributed to Melito of Sardis we encounter about Christ the expression ''by nature God and man,'' but this has to be explained in its own context. The writing speaks beautifully of the prefiguration of Christ in the Exodus events.

Irenaeus' doctrine of ''recapitulation'' expresses well the unity of the two Testaments and an important aspect of the Christian *oikonomia*. Tertullian formulated quite clearly in Latin Jesus' status as combining in one person God and man, without confusion of the ''substances'' or natures, the term to be used later. In the field of Christology Origen is particularly remembered as the theologian of the soul of Christ. Finally we mentioned three ecumenical councils, in which Arianism, Apollinarianism, and Nestorianism were condemned. The stage was set for another and decisive advance in the search for permanent formulations of the mystery of the person of Christ.

CHAPTER THIRTEEN

TOWARDS THE DEFINITION
OF CHALCEDON

The definition of Chalcedon came as the end result of a series of laborious clarifications brought about by controversies in which great pastors and theologians of both the East and of the West were involved. We have already all too briefly discussed some of their writings. We still have to hear from a few outstanding figures of the second half of the fourth century and the first half of the fifth.

The Cappadocian Contribution

Known as the Cappadocians from the region of their origin, in ancient Asia Minor (today Turkey), Gregory of Nazianzus and the two brothers, Basil of Caesarea and Gregory of Nyssa, have several theological perspectives in common. In Letter 101, the first to Cledonius, Gregory of Nazianzus (ca. 325-389) rejects the Apollinarian denial of a human mind in Christ, which would leave the main part of man unsaved, because of the following soteriological principle: ''That which Christ has not assumed he has not healed.'' Elsewhere Gregory's argumentation implies that the body is assumed through the mediation of the soul. Adam's transgression, he also argues, proceeded from the mind. It is therefore the mind that needs most to be saved.

Gregory of Nyssa (ca. 331-394) is particularly remembered for his bold simile: Christ's humanity is totally transformed into divinity, like a drop of vinegar falling into the sea! A transformation even greater takes place after Jesus' death: Christ's manhood seems to disappear and his second coming will not take place in human form. The Cappadocians found it difficult to formulate correctly the constitution of Christ's person and of a "spiritual" being, partly because they were Platonists, and as such could not appreciate the permanent value of matter or of the body. Epistle 38 of the Epistles attributed to St. Basil is now held to be from Gregory of Nyssa. In it we find developed the theory that the *idiômata* or "particularizing characteristics" make the "universal substance" a hypostasis, and this leads to complex applications in Christology, as Grillmeier attempts to explain (see pp. 286-291).

Contribution from the West

We have referred to Tertullian, a Latin writer, in Ch. 12, and found that he especially insisted on the distinction between two "substances" in Christ. Almost two centuries later, Pope Damasus, recapitulating what had been discussed at the Roman synod of 382, expressed his views on some Christological disputes going on in the East. In his Letter to Eastern Bishops he declares himself amazed that some can "say that our Lord and Savior assumed an imperfect man from the Virgin Mary, that is, one without a mind," and continues: "How close they are to the Arians! The Arians say that the Godhead is imperfect in the Son of man. Surely, if an imperfect humanity was assumed, God's gift is imperfect, our salvation is imperfect, because the whole man is not saved." It is easy to recognize here a reasoning used by Gregory of Nazianzus.

Hilary, bishop of Poitiers from 350 to 368, wrote forcefully against the Arian heresy, but in his efforts to uphold Christ's divinity he tends to weaken the reality of the humanity he assumed. So strongly does Hilary emphasize the influence of the Logos on his human nature that in his view the body and the soul of Jesus are capable of suffering "only by a divine miracle" (Grillmeier 309). "Christ," Hilary writes, "had a body to suffer, and he suffered: but he had not a nature which could feel pain. For his body possessed a unique nature of its own; it was transformed into heavenly glory on the mount, it put fevers to flight by its touch, it gave new eyesight by its spittle" (*The Trinity* X, 23; Carmody 69). In his commentary on Ps 68:25 Hilary puts the question: "Who could exist in the form of man while remaining in the form of God?" Although his answer is not altogether clear, it shows that Hilary does not fall into the kenotic doctrine, according to which the divine nature disappeared when the human nature was assumed.

A great Scripture translator (in Latin) and commentator, St. Jerome (ca. 340-420), defended in a homily on Ps 108:31 the assumption by the Word of both soul and body, in much the same way as Gregory of Nazianzus and Pope Damasus, two men with whom he had a close personal relationship. Marius Victorinus Afer, who died after 362, shared the same idea but brought it further. The Logos, he proposes, assumes not merely an *individual* with soul and body but in a way the *totality* of souls and bodies, thus delivering all of them. "Here the orator stands in the larger tradition of the so-called mystical doctrine of redemption, which is represented in Irenaeus and Hilary" (Grillmeier 320). But Victorinus also points forward to Augustine's idea of the total Christ, and develops his own cosmic view: through Christ's first descent in the Incarnation, and his second descent, at his death, to the underworld, all the realms of the world came into contact with the power and activity of the divine spirit (*Adversus Arium* [*Against Arius*] III, 12). Seen in the light of traditional Christology some formulations found in Victorinus can appear both monophysite and adoptionist.[61]

Augustine (354-430) had adopted in his youth the dualistic theory of Manichaeism. It professed the existence from the begin-

ning of two more or less autonomous principles: God on the one
hand, the creator of man's spirit; and on the other, Satan from
whom the human body originates. After he became a Christian,
Augustine combatted Manichaeism and celebrated in his writings
the marvel of God's grace.

Much of Augustine's own thought in Christology is a recapitulation of earlier discussion. In some passages Augustine's notion of
persona reflects that of the Antiochene *prosôpon* (see Booknote
60). Later on, the bishop of Hippo expressed more clearly the
difference in Christ between person and nature: the pre-existent
person of the Word assumes the human nature into the unity of his
person. Commenting on John's gospel (*Treatise* 99:1) he speaks of
one person resulting from two substances (*"persona una ex duabus
substantiis constans"*), while in his letter 137, to Volusian, he uses
the body-soul unity to illustrate the union of God and man in Christ.
He believes that the union of soul and body, of the spiritual with the
corporeal, is more difficult than the union of God and man, where
two spiritual entities are involved, since Christ's body is joined to
the Godhead *anima mediante*, "by means of the soul." In *De Fide
et Symbolo* (*Faith and the Creed*) (IV, 10) he further explains that
the Godhead is not contaminated, even less "polluted," through
the union with the material body, precisely because of the mediatory role of the soul (the Manichean position can be seen here in the
background). Augustine does not always distinguish clearly between Christ as an individual person and as the mystical person
embodying all believers (*Christus totus*). Still, he does profess that
the historical Christ truly suffered and died.

Reconciling Divergent Views

As noted in the last section of Ch. 12, Cyril, patriarch of
Alexandria, presided over the council of Ephesus, which condemned Nestorius, whose doctrine represented the extreme posi-

tion of the Antiochene tendency to see two personalities in Christ. Cyril's doctrine, on the other hand, comes close to that of Apollinaris in its insistence on the *mia phusis*, "one nature," formula. However, "one thing clearly distinguishes Cyril from Apollinarius: the giving of the *natural* life which the body needs is no longer derived from the Logos *qua* Logos, but is attributed to the soul. So although he uses the same language and terminology, the content of Cyril's writings is far removed from that of the writings of Apollinarius" (Grillmeier 404). Archimandrite Eutyches was also monophysitically inclined, and some canonical proceedings were held against him in November 448. The following confession of faith was read at one of the assemblies: "We acknowledge that Christ is from two natures after the Incarnation, in one hypostasis and one person confessing one Christ, one Son, one Lord" (Greek text in Grillmeier 457, no. 1). The formula attempts to reconcile the Alexandrian and the Antiochene viewpoints. *Ek duo phuseôn* can be understood here as meaning "*in* two natures."

Eutyches, however, accepted the profession only halfway, acknowledging that the Lord was "from two natures" before the union, but had only one nature after the union. He managed to have "the Robber Synod of Ephesus" convened in 449 to vindicate his views. In it both Flavian, patriarch of Constantinople, and Theodoret, bishop of Cyrus, were condemned without hearings. Their appeal to Rome led Pope Leo (440-61) to declare null all the acts of that Synod, and to send a dogmatic letter restating the true belief. In this "Tome to Flavian" Pope Leo declares that each of the two natures in Christ retains its own characteristics even though they join to form a single person: "He who is true God is also true man; there is no falsity in this union, wherein the lowliness of man and the greatness of the divinity are mutually united . . . Each aspect (*forma*) performs its own acts in cooperation with the other; that is, the Word doing what is proper to the Word, the flesh pursuing what pertains to the flesh." As Carmody notes (p. 103), this was later frequently quoted during the monothelite (one will)

controversy, in support of two distinct wills and operations in
Christ.

The Council of Chalcedon

This particularly important council for Christology met in 451
at Chalcedon, a city of Bithynia in Asia Minor. The principal
purpose of the council was to define the Catholic doctrine on the
two natures of Christ, against the Monophysite heresy. The Fathers
of the council were slow at first to propose a new formula that
would be agreeable to the various factions. Using Pope Leo's
formulas twenty-three bishops assembled with the imperial com-
missioners and produced a long declaration of faith which was then
approved by the council. It is worth giving a long quotation from
the declaration, in the English translation of R.V. Sellers, *The
Council of Chalcedon* (London 1953) 210f.

> "Following, then, the holy Fathers, we all with one voice teach
> that it should be confessed that our Lord Jesus Christ is one and the
> same Son, the Same perfect in Godhead, the Same perfect in
> manhood, truly God and truly man, the Same (consisting) of a
> rational soul and a body; *homoousios* with the Father as to his
> Godhead, and the Same *homoousios* with us as to his manhood; in
> all things like unto us, sin only excepted; begotten of the Father
> before ages as to his Godhead, and in the last days, the Same, for us
> and for our salvation, of Mary the Virgin *Theotokos* as to his
> manhood.
>
> One and the same Christ, Son, Lord, Only begotten, made known
> in two natures (which exist) without confusion, without change,
> without division, without separation; the difference of the natures
> having been in no wise taken away by reason of the union, but
> rather the properties of each being preserved, and (both) concurring
> into one Person (*prosôpon*) and one *hypostasis*—not parted or
> divided into two persons (*prosôpa*), but one and the same Son and
> Only-begotten, the divine Logos, the Lord Jesus Christ; even as the
> prophets from of old (have spoken) concerning him, and as the

Lord Jesus Christ himself has taught us, and as the Symbol of the
Fathers has delivered to us.''

No distinction is to be read in this text between *prosôpon* (see
Booknote 60) and *hypostasis*, both terms being referred to because
they had been in the past, perhaps with different shades of meaning
in the mind of their protagonists. Chalcedon, writes Grillmeier,
sought to discover the solution of just *one* disputed question: *how*
the confession of the ''one Christ'' may be reconciled with belief in
the ''true God and true man,'' perfect in Godhead, perfect in
manhood (p. 482). The assembled bishops were not concerned
with finding abstract philosophical concepts; the formulas they
used would be the expression of the Christian faith in the full reality
of the Incarnation. This is achieved by clearly asserting the distinction and the completeness in Christ of Godhead and manhood. The
Alexandrians had been shouting ''one nature,'' the Antiochenes
''two natures''! Chalcedon says: Christ is one in two natures.

Conclusion

This chapter was meant to give a clearer picture of the controversies that preceded the council of Chalcedon. We have seen
that Gregory of Nazianzus rejected the Apollinarian denial of a
human mind in Christ and explained that it is through the mediation
of the soul that the Logos assumed his humanity. Gregory of Nyssa
has not perhaps preserved the permanency of a true humanity in
Christ with his comparison of a drop of vinegar in the sea, but other
statements of his show what he really meant. Both Pope Damasus
and bishop Hilary in the West opposed the erroneous claims of the
Arians, but the bishop of Poitiers so much enhanced Christ's
divinity that his humanity does not seem to function entirely in a
human way. Augustine stated more clearly what others had already
proposed, and he particularly emphasized the role of Christ's

humanity as representing the whole of mankind. Pope Leo contributed greatly to clarify several issues and indicated what was to be retained as expressing the true faith. Several of his formulations are incorporated in the declaration of the council of Chalcedon.

CHAPTER FOURTEEN

NEW ISSUES IN CHRISTOLOGY

As we have seen, a more precise formulation of Christology gradually took place, reaching its first climax in 451, with Chalcedon. Several recent authors have raised their voice against Chalcedon's ''Hellenization'' of Christian doctrine. It is true that a certain Hellenic coloring of the dogmatic formulations did take place. This was hardly avoidable since the language of the learned in this remote period—and this is also true today—was molded by the vocabulary of the times which was that of the Greek philosophers. If a dividing line was to be drawn between doctrinal deviations and right beliefs, then more technical formulations had to be worked out with the available expressions, like ''nature'' and ''person.'' It should be pointed out, however, that the truly censurable Hellenization is rather to be found among those heresies which sought a compromise between Christianity and existing non-Christian, mainly Gnostic beliefs. To a certain degree this is true also for certain deviations noticed in Jewish Christianity, where ''Judaizing,'' not ''Hellenizing'' is involved.

The exact formulation of Chalcedon should not be seen as an absolute ''end,'' but rather as a sort of ''beginning,'' since it allows a more secure investigation of the revealed datum. It provides a guiding light in the research process understood as *intellectus quaerens fidem*, which can be paraphrased as ''the intellect's examination of the propositions of faith.'' The ''development of dogma'' is involved in this process, but this is too vast a subject to be examined here. We shall rather concentrate on a few issues which today are the object of discussion among qualified theologians.[62]

The Limitations of Classical Christology

In vol. XVII of *Theological Investigations* K. Rahner insists first on the permanent value of classical Christology, as formulated in particular at Chalcedon: ''Consequently, the Christology of the early Church and the Fathers cannot be merely the object of an antiquarian historical interest; it must be binding to us'' (p. 26). On the other hand, he ventures to write: ''Any Christological formulation which on the one hand allows Jesus to be quite objectively man, in the most radical sense, and which on the other hand allows him to be, in his life and death, the unsurpassable Word of God for us, could be enough; because it would then also be stating what is really meant by the classical Christological formulations'' (p. 27). He does not say if ''the unsurpassable Word of God for us'' necessarily points to a divine being, but the context allows us to suppose it does, if the Chalcedon definition is permanently binding and is not simply one of many possible interpretations of the person of Christ.

One limitation of classical Christology can be linked to its stress of one type of Christology, a *vertical incarnational Christology*. Although this Christology recognizes in Jesus a true man (and fought docetism which tended to deny it), this ''descending'' Christology ''did in fact tend to so idealize this true man—and to idealize his human dimension especially—that *even here* he appeared as a kind of semi-god, instead of being the Word of God for us *just because* he shared in the very reality and fate of a real historical person, including his death'' (p. 28). In addition, an incarnational Christology ''does not sufficiently and directly make clear the connection between the incarnate Logos and his function as the mediator of salvation'' (p. 29). In other words it does not clearly express the soteriological significance of the Christ-event. It must be said, however, that some Fathers, like Irenaeus with his theory of recapitulation, did understand the redemptive value of the Incarnation, saying, for example, as we have seen above, that only that which has been assumed is saved. An existentially minded Christology, on the other hand, does not appreciate, for what it is worth, that too abstractly conceived understanding of Christ's mediation and finds fulfillment rather in a direct encounter with Jesus of Nazareth, in his life, preaching, healings, sufferings, death, and resurrection. Do those who favor this approach realize that Jesus' ministry and death have salvific value ''for us'' mainly because he is the Son of God, precisely as the councils have said he is?

In this type of Christology, which is called ''descending'' or metaphysical, Christ's attributes, pre-existence as Logos, transcendent divine Sonship, even divinity, are regarded as belonging to him from the first; while in the other type of Christology, the ''ascending'' Christology or ''saving history'' Christology, viewed from below, the reflection begins with the man Jesus of Nazareth, with his experience of faith in God, and his love for the Father and his own fellowmen. In this Jesus God spoke to mankind, and bestowed salvation, embodied in the representative resurrection of his Son. It is rather this type of Christology that emerges from the following passage of Vatican II's dogmatic constitution on Divine Revelation:

> ''In His goodness and wisdom, God chose to reveal Himself and to make known to us the hidden purpose of His will (cf. Ep 1:9) by which through Christ, the Word made flesh, man has access to the Father in the Holy Spirit and comes to share in the divine nature (see Ep 2:28; 2 P 1:4). Through this revelation, therefore, the invisible God (see Col 1:15; 1 Tm 1:17) out of the abundance of His love speaks to men as friends and lives among them, so that He may

> invite and take them into fellowship with Himself. This plan of
> revelation is realized by deeds and words having an inner unity: the
> deeds wrought by God in the history of salvation manifest and
> confirm the teaching and realities signified by the words, while the
> words proclaim the deeds and clarify the mystery contained in
> them. By this revelation then, the deepest truth about God and the
> salvation of man is made clear to us in Christ, who is the Mediator
> and at the same time the fullness of all revelation'' (*Dei Verbum* 2,
> in *The Documents of Vatican II*, New York, 1966. W.M. Abbott,
> ed., p. 112).

Traditional Christology has played a necessary role in clarifying
permanently the essential issues involved in the early propositions
of faith concerning the pre-existence, incarnation, life, death, and
exaltation of Jesus the Christ. It would be wrong, however, to
assume that continued reflection on the data of revelation cannot
add significantly to our understanding of Christ, especially of his
meaning for us. No time limit is set for the fulfillment of the
promise he made to the disciples: ''When the Spirit of truth comes,
he will guide you into all the truth'' (Jn 16:13).

Bonhoeffer and Chalcedon

It is well known that Dietrich Bonhoeffer, a German theologian
executed by the Nazis in 1945, stressed the existential approach to
Christology. What counts above all for him is the meaning of
Christ ''for me,'' for this is the real foundation for hope. Still, he
recognized the essential role of Jesus Christ vis-à-vis the whole of
salvation history and thus Bonhoeffer preserves his theology from
being a purely personal experience. For him, as for the New
Testament, Christ provides an interpretation of history. Against
certain liberal theologians he holds that the formulation of Chalcedon has not ''Hellenized'' the Gospel understanding of Jesus
Christ. He blames Chalcedon, however, for not representing the

mystery of God incarnate in terms of ''personal relationship'' between God and man (p. 105). To this it must be said that Chalcedon was convened to deal with specific issues, to be discussed in philosophical terms. It had no intention of excluding other approaches more existential in character.

Some of Bonhoeffer's assertions demand clarification. ''The statement 'This man is God' touches on Jesus vertically from above. It takes nothing from him and adds nothing to him. It simply qualifies the whole man Jesus as God. It is God's judgment and Word on this man. But this qualification, this judgment and Word of God which 'comes from above' is in turn not to be thought of as something which is added. Rather than being understood as an addition, this Word of God coming from above is in fact the man Jesus Christ himself'' (p. 107). In Christology, we are told, ''one looks at the whole historical man Jesus and says of him, 'He is God.' One does not first look at a human nature and then beyond it to a divine nature; one meets the one man Jesus Christ, who is fully God'' (p. 108). A Chalcedonian Christian can also look at Jesus Christ and say ''this man is fully God,'' since the council recognizes only one person in Jesus Christ. Bonhoeffer unduly insists on the Chalcedonian duality of natures, without pointing out that this is properly interpreted by the one-person affirmation. It can be said in addition: to say that God's judgment makes Jesus what he is according to Christian faith can be seen as a dubious application of the early Reformers' questionable principle of ''forensic imputation'' to explain man's justification. Bonhoeffer is popularly better known for describing Christ as ''the man for others'' (see *BTB* 1974, p. 54). This Christ certainly is, as all good Christians should be. But does that sufficiently account for the New Testament's recognition of the risen Christ as the LORD?

In connection with Bonhoeffer's position, it seems appropriate to report two reflections of Karl Rahner found in the *Encyclopedia of Theology* (see Booknote 62). The first is about the meaning of the term ''person'' used for the hypostatic union of God and man in the incarnation. Objectively, he writes, ''the affirmation of the one divine person in Jesus Christ can with certainty only mean that the (in the modern sense) personal, human reality of Jesus Christ has entered into such a unique, God-given union with God that it became God's real self-utterance and a radical gift of God to us'' (p. 769). The second reflection makes it clear that *an implicit acceptance* of the Chalcedonian definition should be read in the expression of belief through personal experience rather than concepts: ''Consequently anyone who does allow Jesus to convey to him the ultimate truth about his life, and professes that in him and in his death God conveys the ultimate truth in view of which he lives and dies, by that very fact accepts Jesus as the Son whom the Church confesses'' (p. 771). If Jesus is not what the Church believes him to be, such confidence in him could only be delusion.

Abandoning Chalcedon

Jean Galot, a serious Jesuit investigator, who reads Dutch, starts his book (see Booknote 62) *Christ, Faith and Contestation* with a presentation of the ''new Christological approach'' in Holland. There, he writes, originated the new Christological orientation which, turning away from the defined doctrine of Chalcedon, considers Christ *as a human person*, in whom God acts and reveals himself. He then takes a closer look at three Catholic theologians who have particularly contributed to the expression and diffusion of this new trend.

In an article published in 1964 in *Bijdragen* (pp. 166-86), Jesuit P. Schoonenberg proposed that Catholic theology would do well to consider seriously the views which J.A.T. Robinson was spreading in Anglicanism. Influenced by Bonhoeffer, Robinson did not see Christ's transcendence in the pre-existence of the eternal Son of the Father but in his *pro-existence* as ''the man for others.'' Schoonenberg himself expressly rejects Chalcedon's statement on two natures in Christ. More precisely, he argues that at least in the original proposal for Chalcedon "nature" was not seen as confronting "person," but as designating the whole reality of Christ, human and divine, so that it would be unnecessary to speak of "two" natures. In *Tijdschrift voor Theologie* 1972, Schoonenberg wrote: "I have inverted the model: it is not the man Jesus who finds his personal center in the Logos, but the Logos who finds his personal center in the man Jesus" (p. 312). And in *The Christ* we read: "Jesus' divine sonship is his humanness to the utmost" (p. 7). A. Hulsbosch moves even farther away from Chalcedon, when he writes: "Jesus is no longer the Son, one with the Father in the divine nature. He is a man exceptionally full of grace" (*Tijdschrift voor Theologie* 1966, p. 254). Jesus, for him, is called "true God" because he is God's revelation. Jesus enjoyed the human experience of being the Son of the Father, and knew he came from the Father. That would explain his speaking of his pre-existence: the subject then of pre-existence is not the Logos, but the man Jesus!

After having written on Christology along traditional lines E. Schillebeeckx began in 1966 to follow the new trend, with an article in *Tijdschrift voor Theologie* 1966, pp. 274-88. He argued that Hulsbosch's position could be brought into line with tradition, since Thomas Aquinas himself has written "Verbum caro factum est, i.e. homo, quasi ipsum Verbum personaliter sit homo" (*De Unione Verbi Incarnati*, art. 1): "The Word became flesh, that is, man, as if the Word were personally man." Already in 1953, Schillebeeckx explains, he had suggested this: the correct Christological formula is not "Christ is God and man" or "the man Jesus is God," but "Jesus, the Christ, is Son of God in his humanity." There is no point in looking for the divinity beyond the man Jesus, because God reveals himself in his human being. The man Jesus is himself the presence of God. It is not in fact at all clear in what sense Schillebeeckx retains the divinity of Christ.[63] In the book *Interim Report* he often complains that he has been misunderstood and misrepresented by reviewers of his works. The origin of this can also be traced to the obscurity and ambiguity of some of his statements. In the Epilogue of *Interim Report* Schillebeeckx proposes to answer the question, posed clearly by others, "In your view, is Jesus still God?" In fact no answer to the question is given, except that God is revealed in Jesus. On p. 142 he writes: "Therefore in the definition of what he is the man Jesus is indeed connected with the nature of God." This, however, is true of every man created in God's image!

To appreciate at its true value the immense labor embodied in Schillebeeckx's two main volumes on Christology, *Jesus* and *Christ*, first published in 1974 and 1977, one must not forget the original readers he had in view: "By retracing and reconstructing the genesis of the apostolic confession of faith, Schillebeeckx hoped to provide a historical guide (*manuductio*) which would help marginal Christians and non-Christians in their encounter with Jesus and with the confession of the Church, and could help disconcerted Christians in their faith" (Swidler 249). It would be a mistake to seek in these complicated books a clear and complete exposition of the Church's understanding of Christ. His investigation and reflections cannot be dismissed as irrelevant. On the other hand, I do not personally believe they contain an acceptable breakthrough in Christology. Used with caution they can serve to stimulate further research by those having the necessary training and knowledge to tackle subjects that involve long-past controversies and difficult exegetical as well as theological problems. Several authors, including Christian Duquoc, Hans Küng, Ortensio da Spinetoli, David Tracy, and J.J. Gonzalez Faus have written helpful studies, but not without ambiguities, which Galot has pointed out (pp. 30-54, 66-77). It does not seem necessary in our synthesis to comment on them in detail, especially because they tend to repeat the same positions in different formulations.[64]

Christ the Liberator

Latin American theologians did not invent the notion of salvation as liberation. The term *apolutrôsis*, with roots in the Old Testament, like *pedût*, "redemption" (Ps 111:9; 130:7), is usually translated "redemption," which etymologically means "buying back," normally through ransom, and this leads to "liberation." The notion occurs often to express the salvation wrought by Christ, for example in Lk 21:28; Rm 8:23; Ep 1:14, and Col 1:14. In the New Testament "liberation" is mainly from sin and the spiritual powers of evil.[65] In the Old Testament, God listens to "the cry of the oppressed": "I have seen the affliction of my people in Egypt, and I have heard their cry for liberation from their slave drivers ..." (Ex 3:7-9). The prophets particularly have been the spokesmen of the cry for social justice (Is 19:20; Hab 1:2), but it is heard also in the Psalms (19:13; 107:6, 28) and in other books (Jb 34:28; Ex 22:21f). See this writer's presentation of J. Miranda's book *Marx and the Bible* (New York 1974), in *Religious Studies Bulletin* 1 (1981) 66-74.

In 1971, G. Gutiérrez produced in Lima, Peru, a quite successful study, *Teología de la liberación* (English title: *A Theology of Liberation*), which originated a movement intended to develop, especially in Central and South America, a theology and a Christology having the particular purpose of discovering in revelation the foundations for the demand of deep social changes in favor of the poor classes, too often oppressed by unconcerned individuals and regimes. In 1976, a Jesuit theologian from San Salvador, John Sobrino, came out with a substantive study on Christology oriented by the need of liberation from poverty and oppression. In it he (Booknote 65) correctly insists on the fact that Jesus reveals a God who acts, one who has concern for people.

"That is why the Gospels place Jesus in the midst of situations embodying divisiveness and oppression, where the good news and salvation can only be understood as being in total discontinuity with them. The freedom that Jesus preaches and effects in practice cannot help but take the form of liberation. Jesus appears in the very midst of those who are positively despised by society and segregated from its life. It is to such people that he addresses his proclamation of the coming kingdom: to the sick, who are helpless in themselves and dominated by a stronger force; to the lepers, who are cultically separated from the rest of society; to the Samaritan woman, who is regarded as a schismatic; to the Roman centurion, who is a foreigner; and to others of this sort. Jesus allows women to follow in his company and tend to his needs, though women were allowed only a marginal role in society. He eats meals—a clear sign of the eschatological reality—not only with his friends but also with sinners. He goes out to meet those possessed by demons, which embodied the division existing within people'' (p. 47).

This certainly describes an important aspect of Jesus' ministry. On the other hand, the story of the Lord's concern for Zacchaeus, the rich tax collector, shows that for Jesus the wealthy can also look forward to salvation (Lk 19:9) under certain conditions. And Jesus likewise called tax collectors, e.g., Levi (Mk 2:13-17) or Matthew (Mt 9:9-13), to be his close collaborators. ''The social stance of Jesus'' can in fact be investigated, particularly from the third gospel, as R.J. Cassidy has done (pp. 20-49) with, among many, the following conclusions: Luke's Jesus frequently called upon those with surplus possessions to use them to help the poor (16:19-31; 19:8-10), and to avoid excluding the destitute and infirm from their immediate concerns (14:12-14). Jesus' teaching and actions relative to violence are thoroughly consistent. In some circumstances Jesus appears aggressive (19:45-46), but he never himself sanctions violence acted upon particular persons—in ''the cleansing of the temple,'' zeal for God's house, more than a social stance, is involved—always placing forgiveness above every other less socially minded sentiment (23:34). ''Jesus continually adverts to God's involvement in human affairs, and his social stance is always ultimately related to his belief in God and his judgment about God's concerns'' (p. 49).

For Sobrino, ''Jesus gradually fashioned himself into the Son of God, became the Son of God'' (p. 338). This statement will appear less surprising and shocking, in the light of Hegel's notion of ''person,'' which the author describes as ''self-surrender to another'' (p. 336). For Sobrino again, the ascending model is to be preferred to the descending model of Chalcedon. In the latter ''the eternal Son becomes a human nature,'' while in the first ''the human being, Jesus of Nazareth, becomes the Son of God in and through his concrete history'' (p. 338). The ''distinct and unique relationship'' of Christ with the Father ''can be described as one of filiation or sonship'' (pp. 335f). Sobrino seems to retain the divinity of Jesus, but the way he arrives at this is rather perplexing. Self-surrender to God does not seem, for this writer, to add anything to the actual being of Christ, and this is difficult to reconcile with the traditional dogma, but it does have a strong moral appeal, showing that Jesus is ''the Way to the Father'' (pp. 338-340). The truth of Chalcedon seems to depend, for Sobrino, on what happens afterwards: ''The Chalcedonian formula continues to be true insofar as there really continue to be followers of Jesus, people whose concrete discipleship professes Jesus as the Christ'' (p. 342).

Previously, Sobrino had expressed views more specifically related to the third world's deprived and oppressed people. The oppressed human being, he holds, ''is the mediation of God,'' although, as he admits, the notion is ''complicated'' (p. 196). Bonhoeffer, he recalls, has poetically said: ''Only a God who suffers can save us.'' For this is the only way that God's love will appear ''credible to human beings in an unredeemed world'' (p. 197). References are given here also to J. Moltmann's *The Crucified God* (New York 1974, from German 1972), a book which in its one-sided presentation can certainly not serve throughout as a reliable guide for the correct formulation of the mystery of Christ's salvific work. It is Chalcedon again that tells us how God can be said to suffer, not in his divinity, but in his human nature. There is, however, much truth in this conclusive statement: ''In historical terms God is to be found in the crosses of the oppressed rather than in beauty, power, or wisdom'' (p. 201). Not surprisingly Jesus chose to identify himself with the hungry, the sick, the naked, the prisoners (Mt 25:31-46).

The Myth of God Incarnate

The respectable SCM Press published a book in 1977 which contains both fallacies and some worthwhile reflections. The provocative title, *The Myth of God Incarnate*, contributed more than the contents of the book to the notoriety given it in the media. Written by different authors the book has no true unity. The best I can do is to mention with a few comments some ideas proposed in the controversial work.

The editor of the volume, John Hick, of Birmingham University, believes that ''the significance of Jesus as a model for human life is not directly affected by the way in which his relationship to God is understood'' (p. 8). Anyone would, however, agree, it seems, that such significance *would be* substantially reduced: several saints are great candidates to serve as models for human life, but their significance remains in the moral field. They may lead the way to salvation; they do not give salvation the way Christ does according to Christian faith.

For Frances Young, the Church will sooner or later have to accept pluralism in Christology the way it already does in soteriology, the doctrine of salvation. The reason for this is that both aspects are very closely related: ''Jesus Christ can be all things to all men because each individual or society, in one cultural environment after another, sees him as the embodiment of their salvation. He becomes, as he did for Paul, the unique focus of their perception of and response to God'' (p. 42). The remark made above about Hick's suggestion applies also here. I am sure Young does not believe that Christ is little more than a symbol to help us focus on God! Paul cannot be quoted here, for whom salvation comes through faith in him "who was put to death for our trespasses and raised for our justification" (Rm 4:25). In a subsequent article Young presents documentation tending to show that the cultural atmosphere of the time helped the development of the idea of an incarnate God (p. 117). Fortunately she does not say that this gave origin to the idea, but rather finds A.D. Nock has correctly written that "the impact of the figure of Jesus crystallized elements which were already there" (*Essays on Religion and the Ancient World*, Oxford 1972, vol. 1, p. 35).

Writing on "Myth in Theology" in the same book, M. Wiles recognizes that it is not easy to speak of Christ's incarnation as a myth, because unlike the stories on the creation and the fall the Christ-event is well rooted in history. It is, however, true, he writes, that these "historical happenings" are told to us in a language which has a "metaphorical" or "mythological" quality. "That is to say, they are told in the form which we must necessarily employ when we make God the subject of a verb and discuss in the only terms we possess our relationships to the realm of the divine, the infinite, and the eternal" (p. 154). This is an acceptable comment, since it can hardly be doubted that "myth" is the usual language of religion, which does not mean we have to oppose "myth" and historical reality. But W. Pannenberg would not concede even that: "The idea of the incarnation of the Son of God, regarded as a myth, contains an extremely odd and disturbing element. . . . For what is historically unique is as far as anything possibly can be from myth, which expresses what is archetypal and valid for every age."[66] H.J. Cadbury declared himself not disposed to join those who deny the historicity of Jesus, but added: "One must be prepared to admit that the religion which became the Christianity of the Roman Empire may have had but slight relation to the historical actuality of its founder" (*The Peril of Modernizing Jesus*, London 1962, p. 40). This seems to go beyond the bare minimum a believing Christian is expected to accept as the foundation of his faith.

The Cosmic Christ

The study of ''the early Christological hymns'' (Ch. 7) has led us to examine Col 1:15-20 and parallels under the title ''Head of the Cosmos.'' Back in Ch. 4 we discussed the description of Jesus as ''First-Born of all Creation'' (Col 1:15). A few modern theologians have attempted to determine more precisely the manner of Christ's significance for and insertion into the cosmos. Their reflections merit consideration, even though they may not be directly founded in revelation and may even be defined as unverifiable speculations. We will limit ourselves here to the presentation of a few ideas of Teilhard de Chardin and of Karl Rahner.[67]

Pierre Teilhard de Chardin (1881-1955), Jesuit paleontologist and anthropologist, proposed a new comprehensive synthesis of the physical and especially biological phenomena in the framework of a Christwards-directed evolution of all created beings towards their consummation in God. While the council of Nicaea defined Christ's relationship to God, Teilhard endeavored to define his relationship to the universe. ''The prodigious expanses of time which preceded the first Christmas were not empty of Christ: they were imbued with the influx of his power. It was the ferment of his conception that stirred up the cosmic masses and directed the initial developments of the biosphere. It was the travail preceding his birth that accelerated the development of instinct and the birth of thought upon the earth. . . . When Christ first appeared before men in the arms of Mary he had already stirred up the world'' (*Hymn of the Universe* 76f). He had written back in 1916: ''The movement which aggregates the universe to Christ is in reality a segregation,'' and ''therein lies a formidable mystery'' (*Les noms de la matière*). Much later he stated that through the Incarnation ''God descends into nature to super-animate it and lead it back to him'' (*La mystique de la science*, 1939).

Teilhard de Chardin also reported a vision which ''another

soldier,'' a friend of his, had during the first World War: "I was pondering this in a church near the front and at the same time looking at a painting of Christ on the walls. My eyes were wandering over the outlines of the painter's image, when suddenly I noticed that these very outlines were *melting. . . .* It seemed as though the surface that separated Christ from the world about him was changing into a film of vibration in which all the limits were confounded'' (see Braybrooke 115f). This passage can be read as a piece of autobiography.

Teilhard's mystical interpretations stem from his views on man's spiritual growth. "Around the sphere of the earth's rock-mass there stretches a real layer of animated matter, the layer of living creatures and human beings, the biosphere'' (*Hymn* 82). Superanimating the biosphere is the "noosphere,'' the layer of human thought which covers the earth, the energetic envelope formed by the entire spiritual activity of men. The *Omega* is the point of convergence towards which the whole of evolution and humanity is progressing, the center of attraction and ultimate point of concentration of the reflective psychism of the noosphere. In the final analysis this is God, Center of centers, and more specifically Christ. "Hominization'' represented the passage of evolution from the state of the non-reflective living animal to the human or reflective state. "Man not only knows; he knows that he knows. He reflects. But this power of reflection, when restricted to the individual, is only partial and rudimentary. . . . After the passage of further thousands or even millions of years consciousness can and must super-centrate itself in the bosom of Mankind totally reflexive upon itself'' (*The Future of Man* 133). "And what does this mean if not that, in the last resort, the 'planetization' of humanity presupposes for its proper development not only the contracting of the earth, not only the organizing and condensing of human thought, but also . . . the rising on our inward horizon of some psychic cosmic centre, some supreme pole of consciousness, towards which all the elementary consciousness of the world shall converge and in which they shall be able to love one another: in other words, *the rising of a God*'' (*Hymn* 89f).

Reactions to Teilhard's visions range from almost absolute rejection to almost total acceptance. The difficulty is that few of Teilhard's mental projections can be presently verified, and most do not directly rest on revelation, even though texts like Rm 8:18-25, Ep 1:10, or Ph 3:21 are sometimes offered as relevant references. In the introduction he wrote for the English edition of *The Phenomenon of Man* (1959), Sir Julian Huxley (1887-1975) generally praises Teilhard's synthesis. He regrets, however, that sometimes Teilhard seems ''to equate this future hyperpersonal psychosocial organization with an emergent divinity: at one place, for instance, he speaks of the trend as a Christogenesis; and elsewhere he appears not to be guarding himself sufficiently against the dangers of personifying the non-personal elements of reality.'' In a little book entitled *Teilhard Explained* (1968), the Jesuit patrologist, Henri de Lubac, has naturally high praise for his French confrère, but in a few places he is gently critical of some views, as when he writes: ''However, would it not on the other hand be a very great optimism—and highly disputable—to believe as Père Teilhard did that the triumph of spirit over entropy is assured? This is the second aspect to be envisaged. The answer to this doubt would be tantamount to deciding whether the Teilhardian vision of the universe and its 'spiritualistic evolutionism' is proven or at least likely. We believe that in its essentials it more than holds its own with materialistic theories and that its solidity does not depend on the ultimate prolongations of the system. We will simply note here that this second kind of optimism reproduces exactly—and no more—the 'optimism' of the entire tradition of spiritualistic philosophy which in other ways affirms the immortality of the human soul'' (p. 68). The term ''entropy'' in this context means the decline or diminution of utilizable energy. As everyone can see, de Lubac sets limits to the Teilhardian dream if it is to have credibility.

A Dogmatic Viewpoint

In a study entitled "Christology within an evolutionary world" (*Theological Investigations*, vol. 5), Karl Rahner has implicitly offered some dogmatic approval for evolutionary views similar to those held by Teilhard de Chardin, excluding his more fantastic projections.

Rahner rejects as outdated views which regard man as a weak being produced quite fortuitously by blind Nature. "This contradicts not only metaphysics and Christian thought but also natural science itself" (p. 169). To the contrary, "Nature is planned for him." Nature becomes conscious of itself in man. Even more, it is possible to speak of the "self-transcendence of the cosmos in man" (p. 171). We have to suppose "that the goal of the world consists in God's communicating himself to it" (p. 173). Christ the Savior represents the climax of this self-communication and he also conveys in return the acceptance of his self-communication on the part of the world borne up in the creatures endowed with spirit. Christ then "must not be merely God acting on the world but must be a part of the cosmos itself in its very climax" (p. 176).

Later on, Rahner recapitulates his reflections as follows: "Up till now we have simply tried to fit Christology into the framework of an evolutionary world-view of a cosmos which evolves towards that spirit who attains absolute self-transcendence and perfection through and in an absolute self-communication given by God in grace and glory" (p. 184). He then attempts to situate sin and redemption in this framework. He finds the Scotist position particularly useful here. Following the teaching of Duns Scotus (ca. 1270-1308), many Franciscan theologians, and some others, hold that the first and most basic motive for the Incarnation was not

redemption from sin but the perfecting of the divine plan of creation. From this it can be inferred that the presence of evil and sin
does not have to be an essential part in the meaning of human
existence and of the world. Rahner explicitly refers to Teilhard de
Chardin when he tries to explain that the presence of sin is compati-
ble with an evolutionary view of the world. "In that moment in
which spirit and freedom have been attained in the cosmos, the
history of the cosmos receives its structures and its interpretation
from the spirit and from freedom and not from matter, insofar as
the latter is still in a pre-spiritual way the otherness of the spirit as
such. . . . But wherever there is freedom in and before the reality of
the cosmos as a whole, and in a transcendence towards God, there
can also be a guilt and freedom which closes itself against God:
there can also be sin and the possibility of perdition" (pp. 185f).

New Testament texts like 1 Cor 10:11 and 1 Jn 2:18 suppose
that the advent of Christ took place in the last days (Ac 2:17), and
this does not seem to favor a Christwards evolutionary view. But
these texts primarily state in fact that with Christ began the new
definitive period in the history of the world, that there will be no
new beginning before the end of time. They do not state how long
this last period will endure. This leads Rahner to the following
reflections, which can be seen as reinterpreting a central Teilhardian insight:

> "It is absolutely legitimate to regard this new period as one whose
> ultimate reason is to be found in the faith of Christianity. For only
> the demythologization and secularization of the world which not
> only actually takes place but is willed and carried out by Christian-
> ity has turned the world into a material which man himself can
> manipulate technologically: and only through the Christian mes-
> sage concerning the final self-transcendence of the spirit by grace
> into an absolute God who is totally distinct from the created world,
> has cosmocentricity been turned into an anthropocentricity. View-
> ed in this light, it is perfectly meaningful and understandable that

the Incarnation stands at the beginning of this first really all-human period'' (p. 190).

Concluding Remarks

At the end of every chapter, except the last, we have indicated the main points which have been examined, and these outlines will not be repeated here. It has not, of course, been possible to say everything on Christology in such a short work, but it can claim to contain the essentials of the discipline, what college and seminary students ought to know and can assimilate in one course, with appropriate readings suggested. The work follows a well-defined plan, but was not written to prove pre-conceived notions. We have tried to let the texts speak for themselves, only suggesting their proper interpretation. The work can be said to represent traditional Christology, but it is not fundamentalist in perspective. Perhaps its main interest will be found in the new approach to the NT sources, analytically presented, instead of synthetically, but the Subject Index clearly refers the reader to what he is looking for, such as the NT use of different titles. In any case, the author of this book has learned enormously from his investigation, and is only too willing to share this profit with a large number of students and other prepared readers.

Booknotes

1. Wilhelm Bousset, *Kyrios Christos. A History of the Belief in Christ from the Beginnings of Christianity to Irenaeus*, translated from German by J.E. Steely (Nashville 1970). First published in German in 1913, this translation is made from a more recent edition prefaced by Rudolf Bultmann. See on the book L.W. Hurtado, "New Testament Christology: A Critique of Bousset's Influence," *TS* 40 (1979) 306-17, or more briefly *BTB* 1972, 89-92.

2. The texts published in German by Lidzbarski are now available in English in E.S. Drower, *The Canonical Prayerbook of the Mandaeans* (Leiden 1959). On Reitzenstein see *BTB* 1972, p. 283. In *The Foundations of New Testament Christology* R.H. Fuller states that the theory of the gnostic redeemer myth forms the basic assumption of Bultmann's commentary on John (p. 100, n. 32). New impetus to Gnostic studies arose from the discovery in 1945-46 at Nag-Hammadi (Chenoboskion), in Egypt, and subsequent publication (1956) of the second century (Coptic) *Gospel of Thomas*, which presents Christ as the transcendent Revealer of the unity between the true self and the divine world. This apocryphal "Gospel of Thomas" is in fact a collection of 114 sayings of Jesus, many of which are found in the Synoptic gospels. For a fully documented discussion of the connections of this writing with other ancient writings, see R. North's presentation in *CBQ* 24 (1962) 154-70, and also H.-C. Puech, "The Gospel of Thomas," in E. Hennecke, ed., *New Testament Apocrypha*, vol. 1 (London 1963) 278-307. For the contents, see B. Gärtner, *The Theology of the Gospel of Thomas* (London 1961). More generally see R. McL. Wilson, "Nag-Hammadi and the New Testament," *NTS* 28 (1982) 289-302. On Christology and myth see more below in Booknote 66.

3. In the book edited by R. Laflamme and M. Gervais (see bibliog.), L.J. Richard examines the adoptionist interpretation of the title "Son of God" (pp. 431-65). In his view (p. 439) it is possible to accept an adoptionist *representation* of divine sonship without denying Christ's truly divine nature. A spiritual and personalist way of expressing Jesus' sonship, he claims, should be preferred: it came about through the declaration, the call of the Father. Richard does not sufficiently explain how his position differs from that of the Ebionites (see below Booknote 61). For the NT authors, he also states, "the *model of adoption* is a more adequate analogy than that of generation to describe the 'how' of the divine filiation of Christ" (p. 440).

4. In his book *Interim Report* . . . Schillebeeckx declares: "I see the concept of Mosaic-messianic 'eschatological prophet' as a matrix which gave rise to four pre-New Testament credal models which later came together in the New Testament under the all-embracing title of Easter christology": Maranatha christologies, a "wonder-worker" christology, Wisdom christologies, and "finally, all kinds of forms of Easter christologies in which Jesus' death and resurrection in particular occupy a central place" (p. 69, with a reference to his *Jesus* book, pp. 403-39).

5. See J.A. Fitzmyer, "New Testament *Kyrios* and *Maranatha* and their Aramaic Background," in *To Advance the Gospel* (New York 1981) 218-35. See my presentation of this study in *RSB* 1981, pp. 129f. In *Commentary on Romans* (E.T. 1980), E. Käsemann writes: "It is best to distinguish the Palestinian *Mare-Kyrios* as the returning Son of Man and world judge from the *Kyrios* who is addressed and worshipped in the acclamation *Kyrios Iêsous* as the oldest form of the confession to the cultically present Lord" (p. 13). Fitzmyer (p. 221) mentions, without discussing it, the opinion that *kyrios* as a title for Yahweh would be found only *in Christian copies* of the Septuagint, while non-Christian manuscripts preserved in the Greek text itself the tetragrammaton YHWH. Very few known manuscripts, however, testify to this usage, which can be discounted for our purpose.

6. The notion of Christ's Messianic kingdom will be discussed in Ch. 8 about 1 Cor 15:24.

7. On Christ's self-understanding see the second part of Ch. 4.

8. N. Perrin and D.C. Duling, *The New Testament. An Introduction* (2nd edition, New York 1982), p. 106. The following studies have also significantly contributed to clarify the data on Q: P. Hoffmann, *Studien zur Theologie der Logienquelle* (Münster 1972); S. Schulz, *Q, Die Spruchquelle der Evangelisten* (Zürich 1972); G.N. Stanton, "On the Christology of Q," in B. Lindars and S. Smalley, eds. *Christ and Spirit in the New Testament* (Cambridge 1973) 27-42; R.A. Edwards, *A Theology of Q. Eschatology, Prophecy, and Wisdom* (Philadelphia 1976); J.A. Fitzmyer, "The Priority of Mark and the 'Q' Source in Luke," in D.G. Buttrick, ed., *Jesus and Man's Hope*, vol. 1 (Pittsburgh 1970) 131-70.

9. G. Pidoux, *Le Dieu qui vient, Espérance d'Israel* (Neuchâtel 1947), p. 53. In the Old Testament it is mainly God's own coming which is expected, particularly to judge the world (see Ps 96:12f; 98:9). Christologically very significant is the exclamation heard at the Messianic entry: "Hosanna! Blessed is *he who comes* in the name of the Lord!" (Mk 11:9 par., Ps 118:26). By writing "Blessed is the King who comes," Luke (19:38) has made explicit the application to Christ and emphasized the royal nature of the Jerusalem entry (see my Commentary on Luke, *ad loc.*).

10. I.H. Marshall, "The Synoptic Son of man Sayings in Recent Discussion," *NTS* 12 (1965f) 350f. For a balanced discussion on the issues around the Son of man, see also R.N. Longenecker, *The Christology of Early Jewish Christianity* (London 1970) 82-93; J. Jeremias, *New Testament Theology*, vol. 1 (London 1971) 257-76; M. Black, "Jesus and the Son of Man," *JSNT* 1 (1978) 4-18; C. Colpe, *"Ho huios tou anthrôpou,"* *TDNT*, pp. 400-77; J. Coppens, "Où en est le problème de Jésus 'Fils de l'homme'?" *ETL* 56 (1980) 282-302. Valuable is H.E. Tödt's thorough investigation, *The Son of Man in the Synoptic Tradition* (London 1965, E.T. from German 1959). However, his thesis seems preconceived and basically rests on a disputable interpretation of a few texts (see my *Matthew* 144f). More references on the Son of man can be found in Booknotes 14 and 16 below.

11. In *The Bible and Christ* I have discussed at length, with abundant references, the various issues around typology and about promise and fulfillment. See particularly pp. 39-46, 153-60, and on the prefiguration of Christ pp. 99-126. On the same theme R. Kieffer, "A Christology of Superiority in the Synoptic Gospels," *RSB* 3 (1983) 61-75 can be consulted.

12. N. Perrin, *A Modern Pilgrimage in New Testament Christology* (Philadelphia 1974) 106. We take particular note of the chapter entitled "The Christology of Mark: A Study in Methodology," pp. 104-21.

13. See J.D. Kingsbury, *Jesus Christ in Matthew, Mark, and Luke* (Philadelphia 1981) 28-30; "The Spirit and the Son of God in Mark's Gospel," in D. Durken, ed., *Sin, Salvation, and the Spirit* (Collegeville 1979) 195-201. See also J. Lambrecht, "The Christology of Mark," *BTB* 3 (1973) 256-73, which analyzes mainly Mk 8:27-9:13.

14. C.F.D. Moule, *The Phenomenon of the New Testament* (London 1967) 83 (from a 1952 study). See also M.D. Hooker, *The Son of Man in Mark* (London 1967) 11-32; R.M. Longenecker, *The Christology of Early Jewish Christianity* 87f. A different view is found in M. Casey, *Son of Man. The Interpretation and Influence of Daniel 7* (London 1979) 38f, 205f. On this book see *RSB* 1981, pp. 116f. For an overview of scholarly debate over "the Son of man" until 1973, see L. Goppelt, *Theology of the New Testament*, vol. 1, pp. 178-99.

15. According to the abstract found in *NTA* 25, p. 17. See also A. Feuillet, "Le logion de la rançon," *RSPT* 51 (1967) 365-402; J. Roloff, "Anfänge der soteriologischen Deutung des Todes Jesu (Mk X. 45 and Lk XXII. 27)" *NTS* 19 (1972) (see *NTA* 17, pp. 316f).

16. W. Schneemelcher, art. *Huios*, *TDNT* 8, p. 371. He also refers to W. Grundmann, who believes that the absolute formula, "the Son" is the oldest Christology, which reaches back to the proximity of Jesus himself, and is then developed secondarily into "Son of Man" and "Son of God" (*NTS* 12,

1965f, p. 46). In his book *"Der Sohn" in den synoptischen Jesusworten* (1961), B.M.F. van Iersel maintains similarly that the "Son of God" title arose from authentic "Son" sayings (see Hahn p. 317, but also p. 332, n. 106, where he rejects some of van Iersel's views). In a recent monograph G. Gerleman argues that in the NT several "Son of man" sayings are better understood in the light of the "Son of David" ideology (*Der Menschensohn*, Leiden 1983).

17. K. Rahner—H. Vorgrimler, *Dictionary of Theology* (2nd ed., New York 1981) 408. Several references are given in my text to studies mentioned, in alphabetical order of their authors, in the general bibliography. On the pre-existence of Christ, I wish to add here: H. Merklein, "Zur Entstehung der urchristlichen Aussage vom präexistenten Sohn Gottes," in G. Dautzenberg *et al.*, eds. *Zur Geschichte des Urchristentums* (Freiburg 1979) 33-62; E. Arens, *The êlthon-Sayings in the Synoptic Tradition* (Göttingen 1976); E. Schweizer, "Die Herkunft der Präexistenzvorstellung bei Paulus," *Evangelische Theologie* 19 (1954) 65-70; P.E. Davies, "The Projection of Preexistence," *Biblical Research* 12 (1967) 28-36 (see *NTA* 12, p. 364); F.B. Craddock, *The Pre-existence of Christ in the New Testament* (Nashville 1968). Cf. *NTA* 12, pp. 402f. See also R.G. Hamerton-Kelly's study listed in the bibliography.

18. E. Käsemann, *New Testament Questions of Today* (London 1969) 97, E.T. of an article published in *ZTK* 57 (1960) 167.

19. My translation of P. Benoit, "Préexistence et incarnation," *Revue Biblique* 77 (1970) 29. See the whole article, pp. 5-29, abstracted in *NTA* 15, p. 20. See also A. Contri, "La preesistenza di Gesù Cristo Uomo-Dio alla creazione e alla *sarkôsis*," *Euntes Docete* 27 (1974) 266-310.

20. W. Pannenberg, *Jesus—God and Man* (Philadelphia 1968), p. 326.

21. J. Coppens, *La relève apocalyptique du messianisme royal*: vol. 3, *le fils de l'homme néotestamentaire* (Leuven 1981); M.E. Boismard, *Synopse des quatre évangiles en français*, vol. 2 (Paris 1972); R. Bultmann, *The History of the Synoptic Tradition* (rev. paperback edition, New York 1976); M. Casey, *Son of Man. The Interpretation and Influence of Daniel 7* (London 1979); C. Colpe, *"Ho huios tou anthrôpou,"* *TDNT*, vol. 8, pp. 400-77; M. Dibelius, *From Tradition to Gospel* (New York, no date); R.H. Fuller, *The Mission and Achievement of Jesus* (London 1954)—Fuller has altered his views on the historical Jesus' self-understanding in *The Foundations of NT Christology* 1965, p. 130 (see also pp. 102-41); J. Galot, *La conscience de Jésus*, (Gembloux 1971); J. Hick, ed., *The Myth of God Incarnate* (London 1977); A.M. Hunter, *Introducing New Testament Theology* (London 1957); R. Kieffer, "A Christology of Superiority in the Synoptic Gospels," *RSB* 3

(1973) 61-75; J. Lambrecht, ''The Christology of Mark,'' *BTB* 3 (1973) 61-75; W. Manson, *Jesus the Messiah* (London 1931); W. Marchel, *Abba, Père! La prière du Christ et des chrétiens* (Rome 1971); W. Michaelis, ''*Paschô*,'' *TDNT* 5, pp. 904-23; J. Schmid, *The Regensburg New Testament. The Gospel According to Mark* (New York 1968); E. Schweizer, *The Good News According to Mark* (Richmond 1970).

22. S. Lyonnet, ''Le récit de l'annonciation de la maternité divine de la Ste Vierge,'' *Ami du Clergé* 66 (1956) 33-48. In *NTS* 20 (1973f) 382-407, J.A. Fitzmyer refers to a Qumran fragment which for him undoubtedly applies the titles ''Son of God'' and ''Son of the Most High'' to some human being in an apocalyptic setting of the first century (see also J. Hick, ed., *The Myth of God Incarnate* 105). The text is strikingly similar to that of Lk 1:32, but it is very fragmentary and had to be reconstructed. It can probably, however, be deduced from it that Lk 1:32 does reflect messianic expectations entertained in a Jewish milieu of the time.

23. The French *JB* switched to ''dans la maison de mon Père'' in its second edition (1973). With ''chez mon Père'' *Traduction Oecuménique de la Bible* (*TOB* 1975) has taken advantage of a French idiom, hardly translatable (in Latin *apud Patrem*) which does seem to render well the original Greek, like Lagrange's ''*auprès de*,'' ''close by my Father,'' or simply ''with my Father,'' which in my view could be an acceptable translation. I also refer in the text to R.E. Brown, *The Birth of the Messiah*.

24. In my Introduction to Luke I have discussed quite extensively ''the meaning of Jesus' death'' for Luke, and have attempted to show, with other authors, that Luke does have a particular view on redemption, but that he has not substituted a *theologia gloriae* for a *theologia crucis*, has not reduced Jesus' death to a merely secular event, and has not replaced belief in the mystery of sacrifice by a human morality of imitation. For further study see, for example, F. Schütz, *Der leidende Christus: die angefochtene Gemeinde und das Christuskerygma der lukanischen Schriften* (Stuttgart 1969); R. Zehnle, ''The Salvific Character of Jesus' Death in Lucan Soteriology,'' *TS* 30 (1969) 420-44; A. George, ''Le sens de la mort de Jésus pour Luc,'' *Revue Biblique* 80 (1973) 186-217.

25. R.P. Martin, *Carmen Christi. Philippians ii,5-11 in Recent Interpretation and in the Setting of Early Christian Worship* (Cambridge, 1967); see also E. Käsemann, ''A Critical Analysis of Philippians 2:5-11,'' *JTC* 5 (1968) 45-88 (1950 in the orig. German); P. Henry, ''Kénose,'' *Suppl. Dict. de la Bible*, vol. 5, cc. 1-161; D. Georgi, ''Der vorpaulinische Hymnus Phil. 2,6-11,'' in E. Dinkler, ed., *Zeit und Geschichte* (Tübingen 1964) 263-93; G. Bornkamm, *Early Christian Experience* (London 1969) 112-22; T.A. Thomas,

''The Kenosis Question,'' *Evangelical Quarterly* 42 (1970) 142-51; R.W. Hoover, ''The *Harpagmos* Enigma: a Philological Solution,'' *HTR* 64 (1971) 95-119; J.T. Sanders, *The New Testament Christological Hymns. Their Historical Religious Background* (Cambridge 1971), on Jn 1:1-18; Ph 2:6-11; Col 1:15-20; Ep 2:14-16; Heb 1:3; 1 Tm 3:16; 1 P 3:18-22; A. Feuillet, *Christologie paulinienne et tradition biblique* (Paris 1973) 83-161. J.A. Sanders has argued that Christ is not contrasted with Adam, but with the dissenting deities or angels, unlike whom he did not set himself up as God's rival (see *JBL* 1969, pp. 279-90).

26. On 1 P 3:18-22 see C. Gschwind, *Die Niederfahrt Christi in die Unterwelt* (Münster 1911); W. Bieder, *Die Vorstellung von der Höllenfahrt Jesus Christi* (Zürich 1949); W.J. Dalton, *Christ's Proclamation to the Spirits. A Study of 1 Peter 3:18-4:6* (Rome 1965); ''Interpretation and Tradition: an Example from 1 Peter,'' *Gregorianum* 49 (1968) 11-37.(cf. *NTA* 2, p. 352). In *Christi Abstieg ins Totenreich* . . . (Freiburg 1976), H.-J. Vogels reads in 1 P 3:19 Christ's ''proclamation of forgiveness to the waiting dead.''

27. M. Dibelius and H. Conzelmann, *A Commentary on the Pastoral Epistles* (Philadelphia 1972, from the 1955 German edition). See also W. Stenger, ''Der Christushymnus in 1 Tm 3:16. Aufbau - Christologie - Sitz im Leben,'' *Trierer Theologische Zeitschrift* 78 (1969) 33-48 (see *NTA* 14, p. 77); R.H. Gundry, ''The Form, Meaning and Background of the Hymn quoted in 1 Timothy 3:16,'' in W. Ward Gasque and R.P. Martin, eds. *Apostolic History and the Gospel* (for F.F. Bruce) (Devon 1970) 203-22. See also P. Benoit, ''Pauline Angelology and Demonology,'' *RSB* 3 (1983) 1-18.

28. E. Lohse, *A Commentary on the Epistles to the Colossians and to Philemon* (Philadelphia 1971, from orig. German 1968). See also N. Kehl, *Der Christushymnus im Kolosserbrief: eine motivgeschichtliche Untersuchung zu Kol 1,12-20* (Stuttgart 1967). It is Kehl's view that Paul wrote the hymn himself (see a review of the book in *CBQ* 1968, pp. 106-10). We refer the reader also to E. Testa, ''Gesù Pacificatore universale. Inno liturgico della Chiesa Madre (Col 1, 15-20 + Ef 2,14-16),'' *(Franciscan) Liber Annuus* 19 (1969) 5-64; T.F. Glasson, ''Colossians I 18,15 and Sirach XXIV,'' *Novum Testamentum* 11 (1969) 154-6; B. Vawter, ''The Colossians Hymn and the Principle of Redaction,'' *CBQ* 33 (1971) 62-81; P. Beasley-Murray, ''Colossians 1:15-20: an Early Christian Hymn Celebrating the Lordship of Christ,'' in D.A. Hagner - M.J. Harris, eds, *Pauline Studies* (Grand Rapids 1980), 169-83. E. Käsemann has argued that behind Col 1:15-20 there is a pre-Christian hymn (Wisdom/Archetypal Man) which has been transformed by a liturgical redaction into a Christian homology (see ''A Primitive Christian Baptismal Liturgy,'' in *Essays on New Testament Themes* [London 1964], pp. 149-68, from a text published in German in 1949). For A. Van Roon, there is

no reason to speak of a wisdom Christology in Paul's writings ("The Relation between Christ and the Wisdom of God according to Paul," *Novum Testamentum* 16, 1974, pp. 207-39, see *NTA* 19, p. 201).

29. J. Ernst, *Pleroma und Pleroma Christi. Geschichte und Deutung eines Begriffs der paulinischen Antilegomena* (Regensburg 1970). See also G. Delling's article in *TDNT* 6, pp. 298-305. For A.R. McGlasham, the use of *plêrôma* in Ep 1:23 supposes that Christ fills the Church with his own perfection (*Expository Times* 76, 1965, 132f).

30. R. Schnackenburg, *The Gospel According to St. John*, vol. 1 (New York 1968), p. 233. See also G. Richter, "Ist *en* ein strukturbildendes Element im Logoshymnus Joh 1, 1ff.?" *Biblica* 51 (1970) 539-44; P. Borgen, "Observations on the Targumic Character of the Prologue of John," *NTS* 16 (1970f) 288-95; M.-E. Boismard, *Le Prologue de saint Jean* (Paris 1953); M.-E. Boismard & A. Lamouille, *L'Evangile de Jean* (Paris 1977); 71-79; A. Feuillet, *Le Prologue du Quatrième Evangile* (Paris 1968); M. McNamara, "Logos of the Fourth Gospel and *Memra* of the Palestinian Targum (Ex 12:42)," *Expository Times* 79 (1968) 115-7; L. Sabourin, "The *MEMRA* of God in the Targums," *BTB* 6 (1976) 79-85; K. Aland, "Eine Untersuchung zu Joh 1:3,4. Ueber die Bedeutung eines Punktes," *ZNW* 59 (1968) 174-209; J.P. Louw, "Narrator of the Father—*Exêgeisthai* and Related Terms in Johannine Christology," *Neotestamtentica* 2 (1968) 32-40; B.M. Metzger, *A Textual Commentary on the Greek New Testament* (3rd ed., London/New York 1975); J. Jeremias, *Der Prolog des Johannesevangelium* (Stuttgart 1967); L. Bouyer, *The Eternal Son. A Theology of the Word of God and Christology* (Huntington, IN, 1978).

31. L. Cerfaux, *Christ in the Theology of St. Paul* (New York 1959, from orig. French 1951). See also P. Lamarche, *Christ Vivant* (Paris 1966); A. Feuillet, *Christologie paulinienne et tradition biblique* (Paris 1973); P.-E. Langevin, "Le Seigneur Jésus selon un texte prépaulinien, 1 Th 1,9-10," *ScEcc* 17 (1965) 263-82 and 473-512; G. Friedrich, "Ein Tauflied hellenistischer Judenchristen, 1 Thess. 1.9f," *TZ* 21 (1965) 502-516. In his recent commentary on the epistle, W. Trilling argues that 2 Th is not a Pauline writing. It would have been written by someone who imitated 1 Th. It is admissible that a disciple of Paul wrote 2 Th to rectify incorrect interpretations of 1 Th, and attributed the writing to Paul himself.

32. A. Schweitzer, *The Mysticism of Paul the Apostle* (London 1931). On the Millennium Theory, see Cerfaux (as in Booknote 31) 51f. W.B. Wallis, "The Problem of an Intermediate Kingdom in 1 Corinthians 15:20-28," *JEvTS* 18 (1975) 229-42. In a book length discussion of the problem, H.-A. Wilcke succeeds in establishing that Paul did not believe in a Messianic interregnum, not even in 1 Cor 15:20-28 and 1 Th 4:13-15 (*Das Problem eines messianischen Zwischenreichs bei Paulus*, Zürich 1967). See also J.

Lambrecht, "Paul's Christological Use of Scripture in 1 Cor 15:20-28," *NTS* 28 (1982) 502-27. In *A Commentary on the First Epistle to the Corinthians* (Philadelphia 1975, from German 1969), H. Conzelmann writes that if 1 Cor 15 "Is a self-contained treatise on the resurrection of the dead," it is easier to understand that at least some sections of it can reflect earlier conceptions than the epistle as a whole.

33. See, in particular, P.-E. Langevin, "Une confession prépaulinienne de la 'Seigneurie' du Christ, exégèse de Romains 1,3-4," in R. Laflamme — M. Gervais, *Le Christ hier, aujourd'hui et de main* (Québec 1976) 266-327. For J.D.G. Dunn, the *kata sarka* and *kata pneuma* denote not successive and mutually exclusive stages in Christology but modes of existence and relationship which overlap and coincide in the earthly Jesus: "Jesus—Flesh and Spirit: an Exposition of Romans 1,3-4," *JTS* 24 (1973) 40-68 (see *NTA* 18, p. 52). C. Burger's thesis that Jesus did not see himself as a descendant of David has been justly criticized (see *NTA* 24, p. 348 and 17, p. 202).

34. R.E. Brown observed that the calling of Jesus *Theos*, "God," began in NT times in a liturgical context ("Does the New Testament Call Jesus God?" *TS* 26, 1965, 545-73). H.-J. Winter agrees with this also, noting, besides, that while the combination of "Savior" and "God" in Tt 2:13 and 2 P 1:1 points to an Hellenistic origin, the other instances suggest an OT Jewish background ("Der christologische Hoheitstitel *'Theos'* im Neuen Testament," *BJRL* 50, 1968, 247-61).

35. In his *Excursus* "Adam and Primal Man," Conzelmann refers also to the "special case" of Philo who was confronted by the exegetical problem of two accounts of man's creation (Gn 1:27; 2:7), without the solution later proposed based on different literary sources. So Philo distinguishes (1) two types of man, the heavenly and the earthly, and (2) the ideal man from the historical Adam (*First Corinthians* 286). It is possible, not certain, that this speculation is behind Paul's reasoning. Rather, perhaps, he started from the heavenly man, the risen Christ, and saw him in contrast to Adam, the "earthly-man" (*'adāmâh* means "earth"). To the contents of the "Adam-Christ Analogy" in 1 Cor 15:21f, 45-49 and Rm 5:12-21 corresponds an elaborate literary parallelistic pattern, as Swee-Hwa Quek explains in "Adam and Christ According to Paul," in D.A. Hagner & M.J. Harris, eds, *Pauline Studies* (for F.F. Bruce), Exeter 1980, pp. 67-79. See also H.A. Lombard, "The Adam-Christ 'Typology' in Romans 5:12-21," *Neotestamentica* 15 (1981) 69-100 (see *NTA* 27, p. 158).

36. See *TDNT* 7, p. 728, n. 33, and *CBQ* 34, 1972, 467-72. Another recent study suggests reading *hou*, "where," instead of *ho*, "the," in the beginning of vs. 17, so that a perfect parallelism would be obtained: "Now where the Lord

(Christ) is, the Spirit is also present; but where the Spirit of the Lord is, freedom is also found." The scribe who wrote what Paul dictated misunderstood *ho* for *hou* (A. Giglioli, "Il Signore è lo Spirito," *Rivista Biblica* 20, 1972, 263-76). This, however, supposes that Paul did not check what had been written, and no one expressed surprise at the unusual statement, "The Lord is the Spirit."

37. M. Zerwick - M. Grosvenor, *An Analysis of the Greek Testament*, vol. 2, p. 579. Etymologically "recapitulate" renders well *anakephalaiôsasthai*, since both words are built around the word for "head" (*caput* and *kephalê*), but in its modern usage "recapitulate" is a bit off the mark. For this introduction to Ephesians I have borrowed from a study of P. Benoit on the genesis and evolution of Pauline thought, published in L. De Lorenzi, ed., *Paul de Tarse, apôtre de notre temps* (Rome 1979) 92-100.

38. This would explain, notes H.W. Kuhn, the fact that Paul places so little emphasis on the sayings and deeds of the earthly Jesus ("Der irdische Jesus bei Paulus als traditionsgeschichtliches und theologisches Prcblem," *ZTK* 67 (1970) 295-320 (see *NTA* 15, pp. 186f).

39. The "splendid indifference" of the author of Hebrews with regard to the actual circumstances of Jewish sacrifice in Jerusalem suggests that he had no accurate firsthand knowledge of it and that he wrote before the destruction of the temple in 70 A.D. On the composition of Hebrews see L. Sabourin, *Priesthood* (Brill, Leiden 1973) 178-80. A. Vanhoye in *TOB* (1975) would prefer a date close to Paul's martyrdom, which occurred probably in 67. In his one volume *L'Epitre aux Hébreux*, Paris 1977, C. Spicq proposes a date around 68 for the composition of Heb, which, he believes (p. 31), was written by a Philonian who had become Christian, most likely Apollos (see Ac 18:24-28). Since Clement of Rome used Heb around the year 95, it is not possible to follow the few authors who place its composition at the end of the first century or even later. Very recently R. Jewett has argued for a date around 55/56 (*Letter to Pilgrims. A Commentary on the Epistle to the Hebrews*, New York 1981).

40. J.D.G. Dunn, *Christology in the Making* 206, with reference to German authors, p. 194, particularly to R. Deichgräber, *Gotteshymnus und Christushymnus in der frühen Christenheit: Untersuchungen zu Form, Sprache und Stil der frühchristlichen Hymnen* (Göttingen 1967) 137-40.

41. O. Cullmann, *The Christology of the New Testament* (2nd ed., Philadelphia 1963) 304. On the title "Son" in Heb 1-2, see A. Vanhoye, *Situation du Christ, épitre aux Hébreux 1 et 2* (Paris 1969) 61-227.

42. For a good overview of recent studies on First Peter see D. Sylva, "1 Peter Studies: the State of the Discipline," *BTB* 10 (1980) 155-63. Among the recent studies can be singled out C. Spicq, *Les épitres de Saint Pierre* (Paris

1966); N. Hillyer, "First Peter and the Feast of Tabernacles," *Tyndale Bulletin* 21 (1970) 39-70 (see *NTA* 15, p. 200). On the Shepherd theme in the Bible see Jeremias' article in *TDNT* 6, pp. 485-99, which includes a brief presentation also of the *Shepherd of Hermas*, a second century writing which calls Christ "The Most Holy Shepherd." In this writing an angel of repentance appears in shepherd garb as the mediator of revelations. As Jeremias notes, "there is no root in the NT sphere for the idea of the shepherd as a mediator of revelation" (p. 498).

43. "Salvation is made a present reality in the liturgical recitation and preaching" (M. Dibelius and H. Conzelmann, *A Commentary on the Pastoral Epistles*, Philadelphia 1972, p. 99; see my review of this book in *BTB* 1973, pp. 332-4). See also D. Stanley, "Jesus, Savior of Mankind," *Studia Missionalia* 29 (1980) 57-84, abstracted in *NTA* 27, p. 170.

44. First Peter 1:20 says that Christ "was pre-destined before the foundation of the world but was made manifest at the end of times for your sake." This statement, like similar ones elsewhere (Mt 25:34; Jn 17:24; Ep 1:4; Heb 4:3; 9:26; Rv 13:8; 17:8), underlines the continuity of the divine plan of salvation. *Bible de Jérusalem* (2nd ed.) says of 1 P 1:13-21, "one feels in 1:13-21 the echoes of a catechesis, and even of a liturgy related to Baptism," and of 1 P 2:21-25, "perhaps these verses, which reflect Is 53, derive from an earlier hymn." M.-E. Boismard had previously argued for the presence of four baptismal hymns in 1 Peter, 1:3-5; 2:22-25; 3:18-22; 5:5-9 (*Quatre hymnes baptismales dans la Première Epitre de Pierre*, Paris 1961).

45. The Pastoral Epistles contain an amalgamation of Church order (regulations) and rules for the household, called *Haustafel* in German. In addition to Titus, ch. 2, these are found mainly in Col 3:18-4:1; Ep 5:21-6:9; 1 P 2:18-20. These precepts of ordinary morality are also represented in *Didachê* 4:1 and in Polycarp's *Epistle to the Philippians*, which has affinities with the Pastoral Epistles. On the *Haustafel* see J.E. Crouch, *The Original Intention of the Colossian Haustafel* (Göttingen 1972); L. Goppelt, "Jesus und die 'Haustafel'-Tradition," in *Orientierung an Jesus. Zur Theologie der Synoptiker*, for Josef Schmid (Freiburg i. Br. 1973) 93-106; E. Schüster Fiorenza, "Discipleship and Patriarchy: Early Christian Ethos and Christian Ethics in a Feminist Theological Perspective," *Annual of the Society of Christian Ethics*, 1982, pp. 131-72, which contains a lot on *Haustafel* ethics (see *NTA* 27, p. 63); D. Lührmann, "Neutestamentliche Haustafeln und antike Oekonomie," *NTS* 27 (1980) 83-97; W. Schrage, "Zur Ethik der neutestamentlichen Haustafeln," *NTS* 21 (1975) 1-22, and D.C. Verner, *The Household of God. The Social World of the Pastoral Epistles* (Chico, CA. 1983), esp. ch. III, "The *Haustafel* Tradition in the Pastorals."

46. Most in-depth studies on John have at least a few pages on Johannine Christology. See, for example, R. Bultmann, "The Theology of the Gospel of John and the Johannine Epistles," in *Theology of the New Testament*, vol. 2 (London 1955) 3-92. Rudolf Bultmann's Commentary on the Fourth Gospel was first published in German in 1941. The first English edition appeared in 1971, from the 1964 printing of *Das Evangelium des Johannes*, with the Supplement of 1966. See also C.K. Barrett, *The Gospel According to St. John* (London 1955) 58-62; B. Vawter, "Johannine Christology," *The Jerome Biblical Commentary* (Englewood Cliffs 1968) 830-35; H. Schlier, "La Cristologia del Vangelo di Giovanni," in *La Fine del Tempo* (Brescia 1974) 95-113 (first published in German in 1971); J. Blank, *Krisis. Untersuchungen zur johanneischen Christologie und Eschatologie* (Freiburg i. Br. 1965); D.M. Smith, "The Presentation of Jesus in the Fourth Gospel," *Interpretation* 31 (1977) 367-78; G. Segalla, "Rassegna di cristologia giovannea," *Studia Patavina* 18 (1972) 693-732 (see *NTA* 17, p. 50); W.A. Meeks, "The Man from Heaven in Johannine Sectarianism," *JBL* 91 (1972) 44-72 (see *NTA* 16, p. 307); S. Van Tilborg, " 'Neerdaling' en incarnatie: de Christologie van Johannes," *Tijdschrift voor Theologie* 13 (1973) 20-33 (see *NTA* 18, p. 40); D. Mollat, "Jean l'Evangéliste," *Dictionnaire de Spiritualité*, vol. 8, esp. cc. 202-9, 217-22; B.A. Martin, "A Neglected Feature of the Christology of the Fourth Gospel," *NTS* 22 (1975) 32-51, which studies passages where Jesus is called "God" (Jn 1:1,18; 20:28). These three verses, concludes Martin, describe the pre-existent Logos, the incarnate Logos, and the risen Christ as "God," and so they complement each other to provide an outline of the Church's understanding of Jesus.

47. See G. Vermès, *Scripture and Tradition in Judaism* (Leiden 1961) 204-11. In *RSB* 1 (1981) 37-45 I have discussed various issues regarding "Isaac and Jesus in the Targums and the New Testament," with particular reference to R.J. Daly, *Christian Sacrifice. The Judaeo-Christian Background before Origen* (Washington 1978). A. Negoitsa and C. Daniel have recently proposed that in Jn 1:29 "Lamb of God" refers to the "Word of God," since in Aramaic the similar words for "lamb" and for "word" were probably pronounced *imra (Novum Testamentum* 13, 1971, 24-37). This proposal is ingenious, but unconvincing, since it is so much easier to link the taking away of sin with the paschal lamb and the figure of Isaac than with the Word of God. A more likely, although unnecessary explanation of "the Lamb of God," has been proposed by C.F. Burney, *The Aramaic Origin of the Fourth Gospel* (Oxford 1922) 104-8. The original wording had the Aramaic *talyā'*, which can mean "lamb" and also "lad" (cf. *talitha* in Mk 5:41), or "servant." The original reference would have been to Jesus "the Servant of God" (see *TDNT* 1, p. 339). In Jn 1:34 the reading "Son of God" is much

better attested than "the chosen one," which would indicate a reference to the Servant in the context. See also M. Roberge, "Structures littéraires et christologie dans le IVe Evangile, à propos de Jn 1:29-34," in R. Laflamme and M. Gervais, eds. *Le Christ: hier, aujourd'hui et demain*, pp. 467-77.

48. See S. Schulz, *Untersuchungen zur Menschensohn - Christologie im Johannesevangelium* . . . (Göttingen 1957). A careful examination of all the relevant sayings can be found in Fr. J. Moloney, *The Johannine Son of Man* (Rome 1976). The author has summarized his views in *BTB* 6 (1976) 177-89. See there (p. 177, note 5) other references on the matter. For M. Casey, the Son of man sayings in the Fourth Gospel "say what is said of Jesus elsewhere in this Gospel, without the use of this term" (*Son of Man, The Interpretation and Influence of Daniel 7*, London 1979, p. 197). He believes that even Jn 5:27 derives not from Dn 7:13, but from Christian tradition (p. 199). On " 'The Son' as Jesus' self-designation in the Gospel of John," see R. Schnackenburg, *The Gospel According to St. John*, vol. 2, pp. 172-86.

49. According to Jn 5:27 the Father has given to the Son the authority to judge because he is Son of man. The omission of the article before *huios* and before *anthrôpou* would for some indicate that "man" is meant: Jesus who became man to save humanity would judge humanity also as man. Others explain the omission by the influence of Dn 7:13. However, the Danielic Son of man is not invested with the power to judge.

50. Especially E. Schweizer, *Ego eimi* . . . (Göttingen 1939; second ed. in 1965, with an appendix). To the list of studies given in Schnackenburg, vol. 2, pp. 458f, note 1, can be added: Schnackenburg's own excursus, vol. 2, pp. 79-89; R.E. Brown, *The Gospel According to John*, vol. 1 (New York 1966) 533-8; V. Howard, *Das Ego eimi Jesu in den synoptischen Evangelien. Untersuchungen zum Sprachgebrauch Jesu* (Marburg 1975). According to *NTA* 21, p. 87, Howard concludes from his comprehensive investigation that the *egô*-sayings constitute a claim to an authority analogous to that of the Jewish Messiah and that it cannot be proved with certainty that the *egô*-pronouncement was characteristic of the earthly Jesus.

51. See L. Sabourin, "*Koinônia* in the New Testament," *RSB* 1 (1981) 109-15, with a diagram. The article constitutes a sort of outline of G. Panikulam's published dissertation, *Koinônia in the New Testament. A Dynamic Expression of Christian Life*, Analecta Biblica 85 (Rome 1979).

52. R. Schnackenburg, "The Paraclete and the Sayings about the Paraclete," in *The Gospel According to St. John*, vol. 3 (New York 1983) 149. See the whole *excursus*, pp. 138-54, which includes a discussion of the different theories on the origin of the term "Paraclete" as used by John. See also J. Behm, "*Paraklêtos*," in *TDNT* 5, pp. 800-14.

53. See S. Lyonnet and L. Sabourin, *Sin, Redemption and Sacrifice. A Biblical and Patristic Study*, Analecta Biblica 48 (Rome 1970), especially pp. 256-8. There, in note 50, I have drawn the attention to the possibility of a *rapprochement* between the notions of intercession and expiation, which seems to lie also behind the juxtaposition in 1 Jn 2:1-2 of the two concepts. On *hilasmos* and cognate terms, see also *TDNT* 3, pp. 301-23; C.H. Dodd, "*Hilaskesthai*, its Cognates, Derivatives and Synonyms, in the Septuagint," *JTS* 32 (1931) 352-60. In his commentary on the Johannine Epistles, Bultmann ascribes to an alleged interpolator he calls "the ecclesiastical redactor" 1 Jn 2:2 and 4:10, with the unproven explanation that the concept *hilasmos* "belongs to the ecclesiastical theology" (p. 23). To the contrary, the Epistle does reaffirm against the Gnostic heretics that the glorious Christ is the same person as the Jesus who died on the cross to redeem the world (see 1 Jn 2:22; 5:6-8). On *hilasmos* see also R.E. Brown, *The Epistles of John*, Anchor Bible series (New York 1982) 218-22. "In 1 Jn 2:1-2," he writes, "we move from the setting of an advocate before a heavenly court to that of a high priest in a heavenly temple." Unlike Bultmann he sees no contradiction between forgiveness of sins through intercession and atonement for sins through blood. Those concepts were already joined in intertestamental Judaism (pp. 217f).

54. For a more detailed presentation of apocalyptic see L. Sabourin, "Apocalyptic Traits in Matthew's Gospel," *RSB* 3 (1983) 19-22, and the bibliographical references, pp. 33-36. For this Ch. 11 of *Christology* I must refer particularly to A. Lancellotti, *Apocalisse* (Rome 1975); T. Holtz, *Die Christologie der Apocalypse des Johannes* (Berlin 1962); J. Comblin, *Le Christ dans l'Apocalypse* (Tournai 1965); A. Vanhoye, "L'utilisation du livre d'Ezéchiel dans l'Apocalypse," *Biblica* 43 (1962) 436-76; E. Fiorenza, "The Eschatology and Composition of the Apocalypse," *CBQ* 30 (1968) 537-69; L. Thompson, "Cult and Eschatology in the Apocalypse of John," *Journal of Religion* 49 (1969) 330-50; J. Lambrecht, ed., *L'Apocalypse johannique et l'apocalyptique dans le Nouveau Testament* (Gembloux 1980); W.R.G. Loader, "The Apocalyptic Model of Sonship: its Origin and Development in New Testament Tradition," *JBL* 97 (1978) 525-54; P.S. Minear, *New Testament Apocalyptic* (Nashville 1981); C. Rowland, *The Open Heaven: a Study of Apocalyptic in Judaism and Christianity* (New York 1982; see *RSB* 1983, 148f); U. Vanni, *La struttura letteraria dell' Apocalisse* (Rome 1971). For J.M. Ford, *Revelation*, Anchor Bible series (New York 1975), Rv 4-11 in its oral, not written, form would have originated at the time of *John the Baptist*, while Rv 12-22 could be dated "in the mid-sixties," and the first chapters would be later. More precisely, Revelation is "a composite work from the Baptist School" (p. 56), "Rv 4-11 emanate from the circle of

John the Baptist and reflect his own and his disciples' expectation of 'He that Cometh,' before they could be enlightened by the life of Jesus himself'' (p. 3). For R.H. Mounce, Dr. Ford offers no answer to a major question: how has an essentially (in her view) Jewish apocalypse ever found its way into the Christian canon? (*The Book of Revelation*, Grand Rapids 1977, p. 27).

55. In his book *Son of Man* (see Booknote 48 above), M. Casey maintains with Dalman that ''like a son of man'' in Rv 1:13 and 14:14 is more likely to depend on Dn 10:5-9 than on Dn 7:13. He also argues that the expression means simply ''like a man'' and does not refer to the apocalyptic figure (pp. 144f). Besides, he maintains that in 14:14 the figure ''like a son of man'' does not refer to Christ, but to ''an angelic figure.'' Casey's remarks on these texts follow the line of argumentation he pursues in his book, which is not uniformly convincing (see this writer's review in *RSB* 1981, pp. 116f).

56. My text on *Amen* is partly borrowed from my other work, now out-of-print, *The Names and Titles of Jesus*, pp. 305-8. See also V. Hasler, *Amen. Redaktionsgeschichtliche Untersuchung zur Einführungsformel der Herrenworte ''Wahrlich ich sage euch''* (Zürich 1969). Also concerned with the ''Amen, I say to you'' sayings of Jesus, another work considers them in the light of legitimation formulas in apocalyptic discourse: K. Berger, *Die Amen-Worte Jesu. Eine Untersuchung zum Problem der Legitimation in apokalyptischer Rede* (Berlin 1970). Some critics consider Berger's as ''a fragile hypothesis'' (see *NTA* 17, pp. 13f). Berger has returned to the subject in a substantial article, ''Zur Geschichte der Einleitungsformel 'Amen, ich sage euch,' '' *ZNW* 63 (1972) 45-75 (see *NTA* 17, p. 284). Closer to our subject see P. Trudinger, ''*Ho Amēn* (Rv III:14), and the case for a Semitic original of the Apocalypse,'' *Novum Testamentum* 14 (1972) 277-79. Trudinger does not think that possible allusions to Pr 4:25; 8:22, 30 in the use of ''Amen'' in Rv 3:14 are sufficient to indicate a Semitic original for the Book of Revelation.

57. Works referred to in Ch. 12 include the following: J.M. Carmody and T.E. Clarke, *Word and Redeemer. Christology in the Fathers* (Glen Rock, NJ 1966); J.R. Willis, ed., *The Teachings of the Church Fathers* (New York 1966); P.T. Camelot, *Ignace d'Antioche, Lettres*, Sources Chrétiennes 10 (3rd ed., Paris 1958); A. Jaubert, *Clément de Rome, Epitre aux Corinthiens*, Sources Chrétiennes 167 (Paris 1971); A. Grillmeier, S.J., *Christ in Christian Tradition. From the Apostolic Age to Chalcedon (451)*, London 1965, translated from two long studies included in A. Grillmeier and H. Bacht, *Daz Konzil von Chalkedon I* (Würzburg 1951, 1958, 1963 = 3rd ed.). Good bibliographies of studies before 1965, pp. 506-15. See also Sevenster in the General Bibliography, below.

58. See J.M. Velasco and L. Sabourin, "Jewish Christianity of the First Centuries," *BTB* 6 (1976) 5-26; H.-J. Schoeps, *Jewish Christianity: Factional Disputes in the Early Church* (Philadelphia 1969); A.F.J. Klijn and G.J. Reinink, *Patristic Evidence for Jewish-Christian Sects* (Leiden 1973); I. Mancini, *Archaeological Discoveries Relative to Judeo-Christians. Historical Survey* (Jerusalem 1970); B. Bagatti, *The Church from the Circumcision. History and Archeology of the Judeo-Christians* (Jerusalem 1971); specifically on Jewish-Christian Christology see A. Vivian, "Cristologia dei Giudeo-cristiani," *Rivista Biblica Italiana* 22 (1974) 237-56 (see *NTA* 19, p. 225). Quite an exhaustive classified bibliography will be found in J. Daniélou, *Theology of Jewish Christianity* (London 1964) 411-22. See also B.J. Malina, "Jewish Christianity: a Select Bibliography," *Australian Journal of Biblical Archaeology* 2 (1973) 60-65; R.E. Brown, "Types of Jewish Gentile Christianity," *CBQ* 45 (1983) 74-79; L. Goppelt, *Les origines de l'Eglise. Christianisme et Judaisme aux deux premiers siècles* (Paris 1961). On angel-speculation and Christology, see F. Young's references in J. Hick, ed., *The Myth of God Incarnate* (London 1977) 112f.

    Quite a few studies have been recently published advocating what is called a "SPIRIT CHRISTOLOGY": it starts "from below," with the Synoptic gospels' picture of Jesus as a man inspired by the Spirit. So far so good. But then it tends to deny a real ontological distinction between the Spirit and the risen Christ, relying, for example, on a few ambiguous texts, like 2 Cor 3:17 or 1 Cor 15:45, with an emphasis on Rm 1:3f and Rm 8:9-11. A few authors also claim that Spirit Christology was the first to be formulated among the Fathers. The texts referred to are not, however, clear enough to substantiate such a claim, but statements of *Shepherd of Hermas* in parables 5 and 9 do merit special consideration. In the words of H. Hunter "If Hermas did equate the divine element in Jesus to be the Holy Spirit then this is something like modern day Spirit Christology" (*Heythrop Journal* 24, 1983, p. 268). In Hunter's view the Chalcedonian formula best preserves the integrity of the Spirit (see pp. 270f). I refer in the text to the tendency of some early Christian writers to blur the distinction between the Spirit and the divine nature of Christ. Much of this confusion is reflected also in the apologetic writings of Lactantius in the 4th century (see *Heythrop Journal* 1983, pp. 141-8).

59. Grillmeier 118, quoting G.T. Armstrong, *Die Genesis in der Alten Kirche* (Tübingen 1962), p. 52. On Irenaeus, see A. Benoit, *Saint Irénée. Introduction à l'étude de sa théologie* (Paris 1960).

60. The Greek term *prosôpon* means "face, countenance," and is used, for example, of the face of Christ transfigured (Mt 17:2) or of Moses' face in 2 Cor 3:7, 13. The term occurs also to express that someone is present "in person," as in 1 Th 2:17. *Prosôpon* means directly "person" in 2 Cor 1:11

(*polloi prosôpoi*, "many persons"), and in Clement's *Letter to the Corinthians* 1:1 (*oliga prosôpa*, "a few persons"). For the Antiochene writers, at the level of Theodore of Mopsuestia, *prosôpon* cannot simply be equated with "person," but retains something of its original meaning. *Prosôpon* is the form in which a nature (*physis*) or an hypostasis (person) appears. Every nature and every hypostasis has its own proper *prosôpon*. It gives expression to the reality of the nature with its powers and characteristics. In a fragment belonging to his work on the Incarnation, Theodore writes: "For when we distinguish the natures, we say that the nature of God the Word is complete, and that (his) *prosôpon* is complete (for it is not correct to speak of an hypostasis without its *prosôpon*): and (we say) also that the nature of the man is complete, and likewise (his) *prosôpon*. But when we look to the conjunction, then we say one *prosôpon*." The *prosôpon* issue will surface again at Chalcedon. For the use of the term by Theodore of Mopsuestia see Grillmeier's analysis, pp. 350-6.

61. As was indicated in Ch. 7, about Ph 2:6-11, the Church quite early rejected the Ebionite form of ADOPTIONISM, which denied Christ's pre-existent divinity and claimed he was adopted by God as Son at his baptism in the Jordan. It must be said, however, that the use of Psalm 2 to define Christ could lead to a form of adoptionist language, since in the psalm the king appears adopted as God's son. "But the earliest use of Ps 2:7 in reference to the resurrection of Jesus (Ac 13:33) can hardly be designated *a denial* that Christ was already God's Son before his resurrection. Nor can we say that Mark was intent to *deny* Jesus' divine sonship prior to the Spirit's descent and the heavenly voice at the Jordan. Nor indeed that the birth narratives were deliberately setting their face against the idea of a pre-existent divine sonship" (Dunn 62). On the other hand, the *Shepherd of Hermas*, a Jewish-Christian writing (see our Ch. 12), gives to the parable of the Vineyard (Mk 12:1-12 par.) an adoptionist interpretation: as the reward for extraordinary work a servant is made co-heir with the Son (ch. 5). Later on, however, the servant seems to become the Son himself. Theodore of Mopsuestia, writes Grillmeier, was regarded by some of his contemporaries as a Paul of Samosata *redivivus*, "as a proponent of an anagogic Christology, teaching two persons and two sons, in short of the adoptionist Christology which was seen to be embodied in Paul of Samosata" (p. 348). Probably three synods were held at Antioch between 264 and 269 to condemn Paul of Samosata, bishop and also viceroy for Queen Zenobia of Palmyra, for his unacceptable views: that the Word and the Holy Spirit were not divine persons, but simply attributes of God; and that Christ was a mere man inspired by God in an unusual manner. Adoptionism is closely connected with the concept of Monarchianism, referred to in Ch. 12, about Tertullian. See also Booknote 3.

62. Within the New Testament itself there is a certain development of doctrine, as I have pointed out, with *caveats*, in *RSB* 1982, pp. 68-73. On "The Development of Dogma," see K. Rahner in *Theological Investigations*, vol. 1, pp. 39-77; J.H. Walgrave, *Unfolding Revelation: the Nature of Doctrinal Development* (Philadelphia 1972), anticipated outline in *New Catholic Encyclopedia*, vol. 4, pp. 940-4. The studies referred to in our Ch. 14 include the following: K. Rahner, "The Two Basic Types of Christology," *Theological Investigations* 13 (1975) 213-23; "Christology Today," *Theological Investigations* 17 (1981) 24-38, and "Jesus Christ" in *Encyclopedia of Theology. The Concise Sacramentum Mundi* (New York 1975) 751-72; D. Bonhoeffer, *Christology* [American title: *Christ the Center*], introd. by E.H. Robertson (London 1966); J. Galot, *Le Christ: Foi et Contestation* (Chambray 1981); J. Hick, ed., *The Myth of God Incarnate* (London 1977); M. Green, ed., *The Truth of God Incarnate* (Sydney 1977); A.E. Harvey, ed., *God Incarnate: Story and Belief* (London 1981). See on this *NTA* 26, p. 212. See also P. Schoonenberg, *The Christ* (London 1972). I will not discuss the positions of the American theologian Paul Tillich (1886-1965), but see M. Palmer, "Correlation and Ontology: a Study in Tillich's Christology," *The Downside Review* 96 (1978) 120-31. Tillich's Christology, we are told (p. 123) is formulated around three central themes: Adam's state before the fall (essence); Adam in the state of fallen-ness (existence); the appearance of the Christ as the Last Adam (new being). In his article "New Trends in Christology" (*BTB* 1974, pp. 33-74), B. Mondin has analyzed briefly, with some quotations, the thought of a number of recent authors, whom he classified as follows, according to the type of Christology they defend: the *existential*, Bultmann, Tillich, Rahner; the *historical*, Cullman, Pannenberg, Moltmann, Marxsen; the *secular*, J.A.T. Robinson, Bonhoeffer, van Buren, Schoonenberg, Teilhard de Chardin; the *political*, J.B. Metz, G. Gutierrez.

63. In *Jesus*, writes A. de Valk, Schillebeeckx over and over again "emphasizes Jesus' *humanity* and, in fact, the entire book is one long, incredibly complex juggling of words to avoid what Schillebeeckx calls 'a celestial cult mystery: the great *Ikon* Christ' (p. 267)" ("The *Jesus* of Schillebeeckx," *The Chelsea Journal* 6, 1980, 115). Schillebeeckx's *Jesus, an Experiment in Christology* (London 1979), has four parts: 1. Questions of Method, Hermeneutics and Criteria; 2. The Gospel of Jesus Christ; 3. Christian Interpretation of the Crucified and Risen One; 4. Who Do We Say That He Is? Schillebeeckx's second book, *Christ, the Christian Experience in the Modern World* (London 1980), in spite of its title, has really little to do with Christology as such (except for what concerns the Johannine writings 305-462): it deals predominantly with soteriology; more specifically it is a treatise on grace. In the

third book, *Interim Report*, a small paperback, Schillebeeckx comments on the reactions to his two tomes (see Bibliography).

In *Revue Théologique de Louvain* 6 (1975) 212-23, the late Scripture scholar and bishop A.L. Descamps found Schillebeeckx's exegesis "of good technical quality" but apparently employed "in the service of a pre-established Christology." Descamps finds unacceptable the thesis that the disciples' Easter experience of conversion grew independently of their failure to find Jesus' body. More generally he finds that Schillebeeckx's attempts to establish from NT texts a basically functional Christology and to reconstruct the apostolic faith remain unconvincing (see further in *NTA* 20, p. 70). Other viewpoints are expressed in a review in *JBL* 1981, pp. 293-6).

64. The main works of these authors figure in the Bibliography. For Küng's *On Being a Christian*, see my review article in *RSB* 1981, pp. 2-18. In *Menschwerdung Gottes* he had expressed the wish that a new Christology would be worked out, in which "the becoming of God" would be recognized and studied. He further expressed the view that the traditional doctrines on the Trinity and the Incarnation are in need of being dehellenized and adapted to the modern culture (Galot 66). See also on Küng's Christology the studies of P. Chirico, A.L. Descamps, and J. Dupont. A connection between the so-called *death-of-God theology and Christology* is seen by H.-M. Barth, "Tod-Gottes-Christologie," *Kerygma und Dogma* 17 (1971) 258-72. See also M. Simpson, "The 'Death of God' Theology: some Philosophical Reflections," *Heythrop Journal* 10 (1969) 371-89. Without using the expression, P. Van Buren initiated the movement towards a death-of-God theology in his work *The Secular Meaning of the Gospel* (London 1963), claiming that the word "God" cannot be the object of a cognitive proposition, but serves to express a human attitude based upon the empirical events of the life and death of Jesus and upon the "Easter experience" of the apostles (more on him in *BTB* 1974, 57-59). See also T.J.J. Altizer, *Radical Theology and the Death of God* (Indianapolis 1966). Long before these modern sceptics, Ludwig Feuerbach, a professed atheist, had claimed in *The Essence of Christianity*, published in German in 1841, that *man* has created God in his own image. The least that can be said is that it must have been a very idealized image!

65. See S. Lyonnet, "The Terminology of 'Liberation,' " in S. Lyonnet and L. Sabourin, *Sin, Redemption and Sacrifice* (Rome 1970) 79-103. Studies on liberation theology are too numerous to list. The following can be mentioned: G. Gutierrez, *A Theology of Liberation* (Maryknoll, NY 1973); J. Sobrino, *Christology at the Crossroads. A Latin American Approach* (London 1978); D. Solle, "The Gospel and Liberation," *Commonweal* 1973, pp. 270-5; A. Fernando, "Salvation and Liberation in Buddhism and Christianity,"

Catholic Mind 1973, pp. 30-41; L. Boff, *Jesus Christ Liberator. A Critical Christology for our Time* (Maryknoll 1978); J. Miguez-Bonino, ed., *Faces of Jesus: Latin American Christologies* (Maryknoll 1984). In his notes on the political approach to Christology (*BTB* 1974, pp. 61-68), B. Mondin mentions J.B. Metz in first place for the Christological sections of his work *Theology of the World* (London 1969), in which he criticizes (pp. 107-40) both the traditional (metaphysical) and the existential Christologies. Positively, he defends the public dimension of the cross of Christ, which should not be relegated to the privacy of the human heart.

66. W. Pannenberg in *Basic Questions in Theology*, vol. 3 (London 1973) 71f. On "myth" and its language see also P. Barthel, *Interprétation du langage mythique et théologie biblique* (Leiden 1963); J. Goetz, "Symbole et mythe," *Gregorianum* 61 (1980) 449-60; I. Henderson, *Myth in the New Testament* (London 1952); Br. S. Childs, *Myth and Reality in the Old Testament* (London 1960); W.J. Duggan, *Myth and Christian Belief* (Notre Dame, IN 1971); A. Dulles, "Symbol, Myth, and the Biblical Revelation," *TS* 27 (1966) 1-26; M.F. Wiles, " 'Myth' in Theology," *BJRL* 49 (1976) 226-46; Th. Fawcett, *The Symbolic Language of Religion: an Introductory Study* (Minneapolis 1971); *Revelación y pensar mitico* (Madrid 1970): the 27th Biblical week devoted to revelation and mythic thinking. For an appraisal of Bultmann's demythologizing endeavor, see Ch. H. Talbert, *What is a Gospel? The Genre of the Canonical Gospels* (Philadelphia 1977); D.M. Baillie, *God Was in Christ* . . . (London 1961) 212-27. More particularly on Christology and myth see in the bibliography the books listed under the names H.D. Betz and H. Riesenfeld. In his own contribution to *The Myth of God Incarnate*, "Jesus and the World Religions," J. Hick presents quite a fascinating explanation of the growth of Christology (pp. 167-85), although several of the views he expresses can be disputed. *The Myth of God Incarnate* has led to the publication of other studies, like those listed in the bibliography under the names of M. Green, M. Goulder, and A.E. Harvey.

67. My text on Teilhard de Chardin is mostly taken from students' notes I had prepared for my course on human nature at the University of Calgary, Alberta (1980-81). See the useful (English) bibliography on Teilhard at the end of the article by S. Davis, "Pierre Teilhard de Chardin: the Relevancy of an Experience," *RSB* 1 (1981) 143-50. Add R.W. Kroff, *Teilhard, Scripture, and Revelation: a Study of Teilhard de Chardin's Reinterpretation of Pauline Themes* (Cranbury, NJ 1980), and a bibliography of works mainly in French in *Etudes* (Paris) May 1981, pp. 581-605. K. Almquist offers quite a negative evaluation of Teilhard in "Aspects of Teilhardian Idolatry," *Studies in*

Comparative Religion 12 (1978) 195-203. On the Eucharist as sacrament of the Incarnation, according to Teilhard, see Joseph Kulisz's article in French, in *Collectanea Theologica* (Warsaw) 48, 1978, pp. 141-9. He concludes by saying that Teilhard's conceptions in this matter belong to higher mysticism and cannot totally be harmonized with Thomistic theology. In the text I refer also to N. Braybrooke, ed., *Teilhard de Chardin, Pilgrim of the Future* (London 1964). See also in the bibliography the works listed under the names of J.F. Bonnefoy, J.A. Lyons, G.A. Maloney, C.F. Mooney, and W. Pfeffer.

BIBLIOGRAPHY

Abramowski, L., *Drei christologische Untersuchungen* (Berlin 1981). See on this book *NRT* 104 (1982) 773.

Adam, K., *The Christ of Faith. The Christology of the Church.* (London 1957).

Aldwinkle, R.F., *More than Man: a Study in Christology* (Grand Rapids 1976). See on this book *Gregorianum* 60 (1979) 180.

Arens, E., *The êlthon-Sayings in the Synoptic Tradition* (Freiburg 1976).

Aron, R., *The Jewish Jesus* (Maryknoll, NY, 1971).

Augstein, R., *Jesus Son of Man* (New York 1977, from orig. German 1972). Rejects basic tenets of Christian belief.

Aulen, G., *Jesus in Contemporary Historical Research* (Philadelphia 1976).

Baillie, D.M., *God Was in Christ. An Essay on Incarnation and Atonement* (London 1961). Includes a good appendix on "Christology and Mythology."

Balz, H.R., *Methodische Probleme der neutestamentlichen Christologie* (Neukirchen 1967).

Barclay, W., *Jesus as They Saw Him: New Testament Interpretation of Jesus* (London 1962 and 1977).

Bardler, G., *Wahrer Gott als wahrer Mensch. Entwürfe zu einer narrativen Christologie* (Munich 1977).

Bauckham, R., "The Sonship of the Historical Jesus in Christology," *ScotJT* 31 (1978) 245-60.

Beckerlegge, G., "Jesus' Authority and the Problem of his Self-Consciousness," *Heythrop Journal* 19 (1978) 365-82.

Benoit, P., "Préexistence et Incarnation," *Revue Biblique* 77 (1970) 5-29. See also *NTA* 15, p. 20.

Berkey, R.F. & Edwards, E.A., eds, *Christological Perspectives. Essays in Honor of Harvey K. McArthur* (New York 1982). See *NTA* 27, p. 223.

Betz, H.D., ed., *Christology and a Modern Pilgrimage; an Inquiry into the Character, Extent and Interpretation of the Mythological Element in New Testament Christology* (London 1956).

Black, M., "Jesus and the Son of Man," *JSNT* 1 (1978) 4-18.

Blank, J., *Der Jesus des Evangeliums. Entwürfe zur biblischen Christologie* (Munich 1981). See *NTA* 26, p. 193.

Boers, H., "Where Christology is Real: a Survey of Recent Research on New Testament Christology," *Interpretation* 26 (1972) 300-27.

Boff, L., *Jesus Christ Liberator. A Critical Christology for our Time* (Maryknoll, NY 1978, London 1980, first published in Brazil in 1972). See *TS* 1979, pp. 395f.

Bonhoeffer, D., *Christology*, Introd. by E.H. Robertson (London 1974; also published in New York as *Christ the Center*).

Bonnefoy, J.-F., *Christ and the Cosmos* (Paterson, NJ 1965).

Bornkamm, G., *Jesus of Nazareth* (Sydney 1969).

Borowitz, E.B., *Contemporary Christologies: a Jewish Response* (Ramsey, NJ 1980).

Borsch, F.H., *The Son of Man in Myth and History* (London 1967). By the same, ''Jesus the Wandering Preacher?'' in M. Hooker & C. Hicling, eds, *What About the New Testament? Essays in Honour of Chr. Evans* (London 1975) 45-63. Bousset (next) had characterized Jesus in his ministry as ''the Wandering Preacher'' (p. 175).

Bousset, W. *Kyrios Christos. A History of the Belief in Christ from the Beginnings of Christianity to Irenaeus* (Nashville 1970, from orig. German 1913). On this book see Hurtado and *BTB* 1972, pp. 89-92.

Bouyer, L., *The Eternal Son. A Theology of the Word of God and Christology* (Huntington, IN 1978, from orig. French 1974).

Bowman, D.J., *The Word Made Flesh* (Englewood Cliffs 1965).

Braun, H., ''The Meaning of New Testament Christology,'' *JTC* 5 (1968) 89-127.

Brown, R.E., *Jesus: God and Man. Modern Biblical Reflections* (London 1968).

Bultmann, R., *Jesus Christ and Mythology* (New York 1958).

Burger, C., *Jesus als Davidssohn. Eine traditionsgeschichtliche Untersuchung* (Göttingen 1970). See Booknote 33.

Cahill, P.J., ''The Johannine Logos as Center,'' *CBQ* 38 (1976) 54-72.

Carmody, J.M. & Clarke, T.E., eds, *Christ and His Mission. Christology and Soteriology* (Westminster, MD 1966).

Cegielka, A., *Handbook of Ecclesiology and Christology. A Concise Authoritative Review of the Mystery of the Church and the Incarnation in the Light of Vatican II* (New York 1971).

Cerfaux, L., *Christ in the Theology of St. Paul* (New York 1959, from orig. French 1951).

Chestnut, R.C., *Three Monophysite Christologies: Severus of Antioch, Philoxenus of Mabbug and Jacob of Sarug* (Oxford 1976).

Chirico, P., "Hans Küng's Christology: an Evaluation of its Pre-suppositions," *TS* 40 (1979) 256-72.

Christ, F., *Jesus Sophia. Die Sophia-Christologie bei den Synoptikern* (Zurich 1970). See *Matthew* 153, note 63.

Clark, N.S., "Spirit Christology in the Light of Eucharistic Theology," *Heythrop Journal* 23 (1982) 270-84. See also Hunter.

Cobb, J.B., *Christ in a Pluralistic Age* (Philadelphia 1975).

Congar, Y., *Jesus Christ* (New York 1966).

Contri, A., "La preesistenza di Gesù Cristo Uomo-Dio alla creazione e alla *sarkôsis*," *Euntes Docete* 27 (1974) 266-310. A well documented study published by Università Urbaniana (Rome).

Conzelmann, H., "Jesus Christus," *Die Religion in Geschichte und Gegenwart*, vol. 1 (3rd ed., Tübingen 1957) 619-53. By the same, *An Outline of the Theology of the New Testament* (London 1969).

Cook, M.L., *The Jesus of Faith: a Study in Christology* (Ramsey, NJ 1981).

Coppens, J., "Où en est le problème du Fils dell'homme," *ETL* 56 (1980) 282-302. Contains a comprehensive bibliography.

Cortès, J.B. and Gatti, F.M., "The Son of Man or The Son of Adam," *Biblica* 49 (1968) 457-502.

Cullmann, O., *The Christology of the New Testament* (London 1967).

Dawe, D.G., "A Fresh Look at the Kenotic Christologies," *ScotJT* 15 (1962) 337-49.

Descamps, A.L., "La christologie de Hans Küng. Réflexions exégétiques," *Revue Théologique de Louvain* 10 (1979) 51-75. He also has an article in J. Dupont *et al., Jesus.* . . .

Dibelius, M., *Jesus* (Philadelphia 1949).

Dodd, C.H., *The Founder of Christianity* (London 1974).

Driver, T.F., *Christ in a Changing World: Towards an Ethical Christology* (London 1981).

Dunn, J.D.G., *Christology in the Making. A New Testament Inquiry into the Origins of the Doctrine of the Incarnation* (London 1980). Briefly reviewed in *RSB* 1983, 112f; *CBQ* 1982, 320-22; *The Journal of Religion* 1983, 79-82. Has a good bibliography 354-403.

Dupont, J., *Essai sur la christologie de saint Jean* (Bruges 1951). He has also edited, with others, *Jésus aux origines de la christologie* (Louvain 1975).

Duquoc, C., *Christologie. Essai dogmatique*, I. *L'Homme Jésus* (Paris 1968), II. *Le Messie* (Paris 1972).

Elert, W., *Der Ausgang der altkirchlichen Christologie* (Berlin 1957).

Ernst, J., *Anfänge der Christologie* (Stuttgart 1972).

Ferrier, F., *What Is the Incarnation?* (New York 1962).

Feuillet, A., *Christologie paulinienne et tradition biblique* (Paris 1973).

Fitzmyer, J.A., *A Christological Catechism. New Testament Answers* (Ramsey, NJ 1982). See *RSB* 1983, pp. 167f.

Fuller, R.H., *The Foundations of New Testament Christology* (London 1969) and "The Conception/Birth of Jesus as a Christological Moment," *JSNT* 1 (1978) 37-52.

Galot, J., *La conscience de Jésus* (Gembloux 1971); *Who is Christ? A Theology of the Incarnation* (Rome 1980); *Le Christ, Foi et Contestation* (Chambray 1981).

Gelin, A., ed., *Son and Savior: the Divinity of Jesus Christ in the Scriptures, a Symposium* (London 1960).

George, A., *Etudes sur l'oeuvre de Luc* (Paris 1978).

Gerleman, G., *Der Menschensohn* (Leiden 1983). See Booknote 16.

Gese, H., ''Wisdom, Son of Man, and the Origins of Christology: the Consistent Development of Biblical Theology,'' *Horizons in Biblical Theology* 3 (1981) 23-57 (from orig. German 1979).

Gonzalez Faus, J.I., *La Humanidad Nueva. Ensayo de cristologia* (Madrid 1974).

Goppelt, A., *Christologie und Ethik: Aufsätze zum Neuen Testament* (Göttingen 1968). Also ''The Self-Understanding of Jesus,'' in *Theology of the New Testament*, vol. 1 (Grand Rapids 1981) 159-205.

Goulder, M., ed., *Incarnation and Myth: the Debate Continued* (London 1979).

Green, M., ed., *The Truth of God Incarnate* (Sydney 1977).

Griffin, D.R., *A Process Christology* (Philadelphia 1973).

Grillmeier, A., *Christ in Christian Tradition. Vol. 1, From the Apostolic Age to Chalcedon (451)*, (London 1965 and 1975). See Booknote 57.

Gruenler, R.G., *New Approaches to Jesus and the Gospels. A Phenomenological and Exegetical Study of Synoptic Christology* (Grand Rapids 1982). See *NTA* 27, p. 208.

Grundmann, W., *Das Evangelium nach Markus* (3rd ed., Berlin 1968); *Das Evangelium nach Lukas* (5th ed., Berlin 1969).

Hahn, F., *The Titles of Jesus in Christology* (London 1969, from orig. German 1963).

Hall, S.G., "Christology, Prophecy and Scripture," in E.A. Livingstone, ed., *Studia Biblica* III (1978) 157-71.

Hamerton-Kelly, R.G., *Pre-Existence, Wisdom, and the Son of Man. A Study of the Idea of Pre-Existence in the New Testament* (Cambridge 1973).

Hardy, E.R. and Richardson, C.C., eds, *Christology of the Later Fathers* (Philadelphia 1954).

Harl, M., *Origène et la fonction révélatrice du Verbe Incarné* (Paris 1958).

Harvey, A.E., ed., *God Incarnate: Story and Belief* (London 1981). See *NTA* 26, p. 212.

Hatch, H.G., *The Messianic Consciousness of Jesus. An Investigation of Christological Data in the Synoptic Gospels* (London 1939).

Hengel, M., *The Son of God. The Origin of Christology and the History of Jewish-Hellenistic Religion* (Philadelphia 1976).

Hermann, I., *Kyrios und Pneuma: Studien zur Christologie der paulinischen Hauptbriefe* (Munich 1961).

Hengstenberg, E.W., *Christology of the Old Testament, and a Commentary on the Messianic Predictions . . .* in four volumes (Edinburgh 1864-72, E.T. from German).

Hick, J., ed., *The Myth of God Incarnate* (London 1977). See Booknote 66.

Higgins, A.J.B., *The Son of Man in the Teaching of Jesus* (Cambridge 1980). See on this book *CBQ* 1982, pp. 678f.

Hodgson, P.C., *Jesus—Word and Presence. An Essay in Christology* (Philadelphia 1971).

Holtz, T., *Die Christologie der Apocalypse des Johannes* (Berlin 1962).

Hooker, M.D., *The Son of Man in Mark* (London 1967).

Hunter, H., "Spirit Christology: Dilemma and Promise," *Heythrop Journal* 24 (1983) 127-40, 266-77. See Booknote 58.

Hurtado, L.W., "New Testament Christology: a Critique of Bousset's Influence," *TS* 40 (1979) 306-17.

Johnson, M.D., "Reflections on a Wisdom Approach to Matthew's Christology," *CBQ* 36 (1974) 44-64. Mainly a discussion of Suggs.

Kasper, W., *Jesus the Christ* (London 1976). By the same, *Christologische Schwerpunkte* (Düsseldorf 1980).

Kearns, R., *Vorfragen zur Christologie*, 3 vols. (Tübingen 1978-1982). Vols. 1 and 2 deal mainly with the Son of Man (see *Gregorianum* 1981, p. 612).

Keck, L.E., "Jesus in New Testament Christology," *Australian Biblical Review* 28 (1980) 1-20.

Kelly, B., "Current Problems in Christology," *IrTQ* 37 (1970) 280-91.

Ketcham, C.B., *A Theology of Encounter. The Ontological Ground for a New Christology* (Philadelphia 1978).

Kieffer, R., "A Christology of Superiority in the Synoptic Gospels," *RSB* 3 (1983) 61-75.

Kingsbury, J.D., *Jesus Christ in Matthew, Mark and Luke* (Philadelphia 1981).

Küng, H., *Menschwerdung Gottes. Eine Einführung in Hegels theologisches Denken als Prolegomena zu einer künftiger Christologie* (Freiburg 1970). Also published in French in 1973.

Lafferty, O.J., "Acts 2:14-36: a Study in Christology," *Dunwoodie Review* 6 (1966) 235-53.

Laflamme, R. and Gervais, M., eds. *Le Christ hier, aujourd'hui et demain* (Québec 1976). A congress volume.

Latourelle, R., *Christ and the Church, Signs of Revelation* (New York 1972).

Lawton, J.S., *Conflict in Christology. A Study of British and American Christology, from 1889-1914* (London 1947).

Lindars, B. and Smalley, S.S., eds. *Christ and Spirit in the New Testament. In Honor of C.F.D. Moule* (Cambridge 1973). Includes also articles by J.A.T. Robinson, E. Trocmé, G.N. Stanton. Of Lindars see also "The New Look on the Son of Man," *BJRL* 63 (1980f) 437-62. In the collective volume Lindars' contribution is "The Son of Man in the Johannine Christology" (pp. 43-60).

Loader, W.R.G., "The Apocalyptic Model of Sonship: its Origin and Development in New Testament Tradition," *JBL* 97 (1978) 525-54. By the same, *Sohn und Hoherpriester. Eine traditionsgeschichtliche Untersuchung zur Christologie des Hebräerbriefes* (Neukirchen 1981). See *CBQ* 1983, pp. 496-8.

Longenecker, R.N., *The Christology of Early Jewish Christianity* (London 1970).

Lütgert, W., *Die Johanneische Christologie* (2nd ed., Gütersloh 1916).

Lyons, J.A., *The Cosmic Christ in Origen and Teilhard de Chardin. A Comparative Study* (Oxford 1982).

Lyonnet, S., and Sabourin, L., *Sin, Redemption and Sacrifice. A Biblical and Patristic Study*, Analecta Biblica 48 (Rome 1970).

Mackey, J.P., *Jesus. The Man and the Myth. A Contemporary Christology* (London 1979).

Maloney, G.A., *The Cosmic Christ: from Paul to Teilhard* (New York 1968).

Marchesi, G., *La cristologia di Hans Urs von Balthasar. La figura di Gesù Cristo espressione visibile di Dio* (Rome 1977).

Marshall, I.H., *The Origins of New Testament Christology* (Downers Grove, IL 1976).

Marxsen, W., *The Beginnings of Christology, together with the Lord's Supper as a Christological Problem* (Philadelphia 1979, from orig. German 1960).

Matera, F.J., *The Kingship of Jesus. Composition and Theology in Mark 15* (Chico, CA, 1982).

McIntyre, J., *The Shape of Christology* (Philadelphia 1966).

Matsunaga, K., ''The *'Theos'* Christology as the Ultimate Confession of the Fourth Gospel,'' *Annual of the Japanese Biblical Institute* 7 (1981) 124-45. See *NTA* 26, p. 254.

Meeks, W.A., *The Prophet-King. Moses Traditions and the Johannine Christology* (Leiden 1967).

Merklein, H., ''Die Auferweckung Jesu und die Anfänge der Christologie,'' *ZNW* 72 (1981) 1-26.

Meyer, M.W., *Who Do People Say That I Am? The Interpretation of Jesus in the New Testament Gospels* (Grand Rapids 1983).

Moloney, J., *The Word Made Flesh*, (Cork 1977). See *NTA* 27, p. 96.

Mondin, B., *Le cristologie moderne; un panorama* (Rome 1973). The author outlined this Italian book in ''New Trends in Christology,'' *BTB* 4 (1974) 33-74. See Booknote 62.

Mooney, C.F., *Teilhard de Chardin and the Mystery of Christ* (New York 1966).

Moule, C.F.D., *The Origin of Christology* (Cambridge 1977).

Mowinckel, S., *He That Cometh: the Messiah Concept in the Old Testament and Later Judaism* (Oxford 1956).

Müller, P.G., *Christos Archègos. Der religionsgeschichtliche und theologische Hintergrund einer neutestamentlichen Christusprädikation* (Bern 1973). See *NTA* 19, p. 120.

Neill, S., *Jesus Through Many Eyes. Introduction to the Theology of the New Testament* (Philadelphia 1976).

Nolan, B.M., *The Royal Son of God. The Christology of Matthew 1-2 in the Setting of the Gospel* (Fribourg 1979).

Norris, R.A., ed., *The Christological Controversy* (Philadelphia 1980).

North, R., *In Search of the Human Jesus* (London 1970).

O'Collins, G.,, *Interpreting Jesus* (London 1983).

O'Donnell, R.E., "The Servant Christology in the New Testament," *The Dunwoodie Review* 10 (1970) 177-95.

O'Grady, J.F., *Models of Jesus* (New York 1981). See *RSB* 1983, pp. 115f.

Pannenberg, W., *Jesus—God and Man* (London 1973).

Parker, T.H.L., ed., *Essays in Christology, for Karl Barth* (London 1956).

Parrinder, G., *Jesus in the Qur'an* (London 1976).

Pawlikowski, J., *Christ in the Light of the Christian-Jewish Dialogue* (New York 1982).

Pelikan, J., ed., *Twentieth Century Theology in the Making*, vol. 2, *The Theological Dialogue: Issues and Resources* (London 1970). Section 2 is on Christology.

Perrin, N., *A Modern Pilgrimage in New Testament Christology* (Philadelphia 1974).

Pfeffer, W., "Christus-Omega. Neutestamentlichexegetische Untersuchungen zur Christologie von Pierre Teilhard de Chardin," in *Europäische Hochschulschriften*, XXIII, 117, 1-2 (Frankfurt 1979) 307-475.

Pinto, E., "Jesus as the Son of God in the Gospels," *BTB* 4 (1974) 75-93.

Pittenger, N., *Christology Reconsidered* (London 1970).

Polag, A., *Die Christologie der Logienquelle* (Neukirchen 1977).

Pollard, T.E., *Johannine Christology and the Early Church* (Cambridge 1970).

Pregeant, R., *Christology Beyond Dogma: Matthew's Christ in Process Hermeneutic* (Philadelphia and Missoula 1978). See *CBQ* 1979, pp. 165-7.

Rahner, K., "Christology Within an Evolutionary View of the World," *Theological Investigations*, vol. 5, pp. 157-192, from German 1962; "The Two Basic Types of Christology," *Theological Investigations* vol. 17, pp. 213-23, from German 1971; "Christology Today," *ibid.*, pp. 24-38, from German 1973: "What Does It Mean Today to Believe in Jesus?" *ibid.*, pp. 143-56, from German 1976; K. Rahner and W. Thüsing, *A New Christology* (London 1980). E.T. of a 1972 book in German.

Rawlinson, A.E., *The New Testament Doctrine of the Christ* (3rd ed., London/New York 1949).

Renwart, L., "Jésus-Christ, Fils de Dieu," *NRT* 105 (1983) 88-117. Reviews several books on Christology.

Richard, L.J., *A Kenotic Christology. In the Humanity of Jesus the Christ, the Compassion of Our God* (Washington 1982). See *NTA* 26, pp. 335f.

Riesenfeld, H., "The Mythological Background of New Testament Christology," in W.D. Davies and D. Daube, *The Background of the New Testament and its Eschatology, for C.H. Dodd* (Cambridge 1964) 81-95.

Rihbany, A.M., *The Five Interpretations of Jesus* (Boston 1940).

Robinson, J.A.T., *The Human Face of God* (London 1973). Also "The Use of the Fourth Gospel for Christology Today," in B. Lindars . . . 61-78.

Rowdon, H.H., ed., *Christ the Lord: Studies in Christology. Presented to Donald Guthrie* (Leicester 1982).

Rupp, G., *Christologies and Cultures. Toward a Typology of Religious Worldviews* (The Hague 1974).

Sabourin, L., *The Gospel According to St. Matthew*, vols. 1 and 2 (St. Paul Publications, Bombay 1982 and 1983), especially vol. 1, pp. 125-56; *The Bible and Christ. The Unity of the Two Testaments* (Alba House, New York 1980), esp. 129-36, "The Prefiguration of Christ." Also *The Gospel According to Luke* (Bombay 1984). See the Introduction.

Sabugal, S., *Christos. Investigación exegetica sobre la cristologia joannea* (Barcelona 1972). See *NTA* 17, p. 410.

Saebo, M., "Messianism in Chronicles? Some Remarks to the Old Testament Background of the New Testament Christology," *Horizons in Biblical Theology* 2 (1980) 85-109. See *NTA* 26, p. 162.

Saliba, I.A., "The Bishop of Antioch and the Heretics: a Study of a Primitive Christology," *Evangelical Quarterly* 54 (1982) 65-76. See *NTA* 27, p. 81.

Sanday, E., *Christologies Ancient and Modern* (Oxford 1910).

Sanders, J.T., *The New Testament Christological Hymns. Their Historical Religious Background* (Cambridge 1971).

Schierse, F.J., *Christologie* (Düsseldorf 1979).

Schillebeeckx, E., *Jesus, an Experiment in Christology* (London 1979); *Christ. The Christian Experience in the Modern World* (London 1980); *Interim Report on the Books Jesus & Christ* (London/New York 1980). See also Booknote 63.

Schilson, A. and Kasper, W., *Christologie im Präsens* (3rd ed., Freiburg 1974).

Schmaus, M., *God and His Christ* (New York 1971).

Schmid, J., *The Gospel According to Mark* (New York 1968).

Schnackenburg, R., "The Gnostic Myth of the Redeemer and the Johannine Christology," in *The Gospel According to St. John*, vol. 1 (New York 1968) 543-57; " 'The Son' as Jesus' Self-Designation in the Gospel of John," *ibid.*, vol. 2 (1980) 172-86.

Schnider, F., *Jesus der Prophet* (Freiburg, Sch. 1973).

Schoonenberg, P., *The Christ* (London 1972).

Schwanz, P., *Imago Dei, als christologisch/anthropologisches Problem in der Geschichte der Alten Kirche von Paulus bis Clemens von Alexandrien* (Halle 1970).

Schweizer, E., "Towards a Christology of Mark?" in J. Jervell & W.A. Meeks, eds, *God's Christ and His People, Studies in Honour of N.A. Dahl* (Oslo 1977) 29-42; *The Good News According to Mark* (Philadelphia 1970).

Sevenster, G., "Christologie der Urchristentums," in *Die Religion in Geschichte und Gegenwart*, vol. 1 (Tübingen, 3rd ed. 1957) 1745-62.

Simonson, C., *The Christology of the Faith and Order Movement* (Leiden 1972). Has to do with the World Council of Churches.

Smith, D.W., *Wisdom Christology in the Synoptic Gospels* (Rome 1970).

Smulders, P., *The Fathers on Christology* (De Pere, WI 1968).

Sobrino, J., *Christology at the Crossroads. A Latin American Approach* (London 1978).

Starcky, J., "Logos," *Supplément au Dictionnaire de la Bible* 5 (1952) 486-96.

Suggs, J., *Wisdom, Christology, and Law in Matthew's Gospel* (Cambridge 1970).

Sykes, S.W. and Clayton, J.B., eds, *Christ, Faith and History. Cambridge Studies in Christology* (Cambridge 1972).

Tapia, R.J., *The Theology of Christ: Commentary. Readings in Christology* (New York 1971).

Taylor, V., *The Names of Jesus* (London 1953); *The Person of Christ in the New Testament Teaching* (London 1958).

Thom, G., "A New Road to Chalcedon?" *JTSA* 30 (1982) 23-32. See *NTA* 27, pp. 55f.

Thompson, W.M., *Jesus, Lord and Savior. A Theopathic Christology and Soteriology* (New York 1980).

Tödt, H.E., *The Son of Man in the Synoptic Tradition* (London 1965). See on this controversial study *Matthew* 144f.

Tracy, D., *Blessed Rage for Order. The New Pluralism in Theology* (New York 1975), esp. 206-223.

Tuckett, C., "Christology and the New Testament," *ScotJT* 33 (1980) 401-16.

Turner, H.E.W., *Jesus the Christ* (Oxford 1976), pp. 60-85 "Christologies from the side of God," 86-107 "Christologies from the side of man."

Van Beeck, J., *Christ Proclaimed. Christology as Rhetoric* (Ramsey, NJ 1979).

Van Buren, P.M., *The Secular Meaning of the Gospel, Based on an Analysis of its Language* (London 1963). The third part is on Christology.

Van Iersel, B.M.F., *"Der Sohn" in der synoptischen Jesusworten* (Leiden 1961). Also " 'Son of God' in the New Testament," *Concilium* 153 (1982) 37-48. See *NTA* 26, pp. 280f.

Vawter, B., *This Man Jesus: an Essay Toward a New Testament Christology* (London 1975). See *Gregorianum* 1978, pp. 610f.

Vermes, G., *Jesus the Jew, a Historian's Reading of the Gospels* (London 1973); " 'The Son of Man' Debate," *JSNT* 1 (1978) 19-32.

Vielhauer, P., "Ein Weg zur neutestamentlichen Christologie? Prüfung der These F. Hahns," *Evangelische Theologie* 25 (1965) 24-72.

Walker, W.O., "The Son of Man Question and the Synoptic Problem," in W.R. Farmer, ed., *New Synoptic Studies* (Macon 1983) 261-301.

Weissbach, J., *Christologie und Ethik bei Dietrich Bonhoeffer* (Munich 1966).

Wikenhauser, A., *Pauline Mysticism: Christ in the Mystical Teaching of St. Paul* (London 1960).

Williamson, R., "Philo and New Testament Christology," *Expository Times* 90 (1978f) 361-65.

Yerkes, J., *The Christology of Hegel* (Missoula 1978).

Youngblut, J.R., *Rediscovering the Christ* (New York 1974). A Quaker teacher discusses "the Christ myth."

Zamoyta, V., ed., *The Theology of Christ: Sources* (Milwaukee 1967).

<h1 style="text-align:center">Scripture Index</h1>

Subject Index